Writers of Wales

Christopher Meredith

Writers of Wales

Christopher Meredith

Diana Wallace

University of Wales Press

2018

www.uwp.co.uk

British Library Cataloguing-in-Publication Data
A catalogue record for this book is available from the British Library.

ISBN 978-1-78683-114-9
e-ISBN 978-1-78683-115-6

Typeset in Wales by Eira Fenn Gaunt, Cardiff
Printed by CPI Antony Rowe, Melksham

Contents

Preface

A novelist, poet, critic and translator, Christopher Meredith is a major writer who writes primarily in English about Wales. The author of four richly complex novels, one of them an acknowledged classic in Wales, and four substantial collections of poetry he is, despite a growing international reputation, barely known in the rest of the UK. This in itself tells us something about the geographies of literary reception and the domination of a London-focused literary scene.

This book is a study of his writing which aims to draw attention to the breadth and quality of his work. As a bilingual Welsh writer who learned his second language as an adult, Meredith's work very clearly comes out of a specific place, time and community. His early poetry in particular is often engaged in a search for his 'place' – linguistically, geographically, historically, socially and in terms of form and literary tradition. As an aspect of this quest, he often writes about his parents, the places where he grew up, and the occupations he has undertaken. This study therefore begins with an introduction which situates him as a writer within that geographical, historical, social and familial context.

Meredith is best known for his first novel, *Shifts* (1988), rightly recognized as the classic literary statement of post-industrialization in Wales. He is, however, unusual in being equally a novelist *and* a poet and it is perhaps partly because his poetry and prose have tended to be read separately that the breadth of his achievement has not always been apparent. In this book, therefore, I aim to read across the two genres, pairing poetry and fiction in each chapter in order to listen to the echoes between them. This strategy foregrounds the concern with language, form and representation which runs through his work and connects it to his interest in the historical and geographical specificity of human experience. Despite the formal experimentation of his writing, there are important continuities in his work which mean that we can read it as a history of a place and a people, primarily the Anglicized Welsh of south-east Wales, and in its very specificities recognize it also as an exploration of the human condition.

I am indebted to many people for help and support in writing this book. My primary thanks go to Christopher Meredith who has been generous with his time throughout while remaining tactfully aware that his role was, as he wryly put it, to be the 'body in the library'. It was Jane Aaron who convinced me that I could write this book and she has, as always, been an inspirational support. Gavin Edwards and Jeni Williams read chapters in progress and the book is a far better one than it would have been without their expertise. Jeremy Hooker has been one of Meredith's most astute critics and I am indebted to him and Mieke for their hospitality and several useful conversations. University of Wales Press's anonymous reader provided constructive comments which were very helpful.

I would like to thank Christopher Meredith for permission to quote from his work and to reproduce the photographs from his family papers within the volume. I am grateful to Seren for granting permission to reproduce quotations from the works of Christopher Meredith which they have published.

My thanks also go to the following for various kinds of help: Andy Croll, Chris Evans, Jane Finucane, Claire Flay-Petty, Lesley Hargreaves, Cyril Jones, Phil Kelly, Barrie Llewelyn, Amanda Radford and Michael, Rhiannon Sargent, Marion Shaw, Dawn Percival, Ceri Thomas, Rhidian Thomas, Nigel Wallace, Esyllt Williams; Jean Kember and the Bruton Place book group, Judith Barker, Katherine MacDonald, Pat Adams, Rachel Davies, Victoria

Evangelinou. Thanks especially to Llion Wigley at the University of Wales Press for his kindness and patience.

This book is for Seán (who helped with the research), and for Jarlath.

Illustrations

Abbreviations

AF   Christopher Meredith, *The Story of the Afanc King and the Sons of Teyrnon* (Newtown: Gwasg Gregynog, 2006).

AH   Christopher Meredith, *Air Histories* (Bridgend: Seren, 2013).

BI   Christopher Meredith, *The Book of Idiots* (Bridgend: Seren, 2012).

BM   *Black Mountains: Poems and Images from the Bog~Mawnog Project*, Poems by Christopher Meredith, Images by Elizabeth Adeline, Lin Charlston, Kirsty Claxton, Deborah Aguirre Jones and Pip Woolf (Cardiff: Mulfran, 2011).

CC   Christopher Meredith, *The Carved Chair: A play for radio*, *Planet*, 65 (October/November 1987), 68–92.

CG   Christopher Meredith, *Cefn Golau: Shooting a Novelist*, Places: Y Man a'r Lle, 4 (Newtown: Gwasg Gregynog, 1997).

G   Christopher Meredith, *Griffri* (1991; rev. edn Bridgend: Seren, 1994).

I   Christopher Meredith, interviewed by Diana Wallace, 23 June 2016.

M   Mihangel Morgan, *Melog*, trans. Christopher Meredith with Afterword (Bridgend: Seren, 2005).

MF   Christopher Meredith, *The Meaning of Flight* (Bridgend: Seren, 2005).

S   Christopher Meredith, *Shifts* (1988; repr. with an Afterword by Richard Poole, Bridgend: Seren, 1997).

SA Christopher Meredith, *Still Air*, images by Sara Philpott (n.p.: Singing Nettle Press, 2016).

SH Christopher Meredith, *Snaring Heaven* (Bridgend: Seren, 1990).

ST Christopher Meredith, *Sidereal Time* (Bridgend: Seren, 1998).

T Christopher Meredith, *This*, Poetry Wales Poets Series: 1 (Bridgend: Poetry Wales Press, 1984).

Christopher Meredith by the east gate of the former steelworks
at Ebbw Vale, August 2016. Photograph: Diana Wallace.

Introduction: A writer in his place

Born at St James's Hospital, Tredegar on 15 December 1954, Christopher Laurence Meredith was the second son of Emrys Henry Meredith, a steel worker and former collier, and Joyce Meredith, née Roberts, formerly a domestic servant.[1] There was snow on the ground as his mother carried him into the open air and up Market Street for the first time. 'I know because my parents told me so', he asserts in 'Birth myth' (*AH*, 24–5), a poem which celebrates and ironizes the stories we construct about our origins, patched together from the half made-up memories of our parents. Opening with one of the most famous Welsh birth myths, Owen Glendower's assertion in *Henry IV* that 'At my nativity / The front of heaven was full of fiery shapes', Meredith immediately undercuts this with an ironic, 'Well, snow. Full of snow'.[2] 'But don't we hunger for the birth myth', he admits, enumerating the oversize signs which accompanied other marvellous births – Madam Patti, Greek godlets, Hercules, even – '(dare I?)' – Christ. In contrast to the '*signs [which] have marked [Glendower] extraordinary*',[3] as the Shakespearian epigraph has it, the snow in Market Street, Tredegar 'marks [Meredith] ordinary'. For Meredith, it is partly that ordinariness, the quotidian which is rarely celebrated, which is important.

Yet, as the poem suggests, Tredegar has its own mythic topography, less celebrated but equally as shaped and shaping as the landscapes of Greek myth: 'the name [Market Street]'s an Ithaca, Persepolis' (AH, 25). The snowfall is historically evidenced – 'I've sort of checked' – by photographs of miners at Tŷ Trist Pit in that winter. Sunk in 1834, Tŷ Trist was one of a series of pits opened by the Tredegar Iron Company, established by Samuel Homfrey in 1800 and renamed the Tredegar Iron and Coal Company in 1837. Aneurin Bevan, born in Tredegar in 1897, began work there at the age of 14 before going on to become Labour MP for Ebbw Vale from 1929 to 1960 and the architect of the National Health Service.[4] Meredith's grandfather, uncles and father were all colliers at Tŷ Trist. It closed in 1959 so that 'this was a tide that had gone out by [Meredith's] early childhood', although he played in the ruins of the pit.[5] The landscape Meredith invokes in the poem encompasses the miners in their 'daicaps' silhouetted against the black girder work of the colliery and the geography of Market Street stretching from the Town Clock up to 'Saron Chapel where Ieuan Gwynedd / had preached against Blue Books' (AH, 24–50).[6] These are the pre-industrial, industrial and post-industrial landscapes of south Wales with their layerings of literary, public and private histories – the leader of the last Welsh rebellion, the daicapped miners, the independent minister, and 'A woman with a baby in a whitened street / . . . walking towards eternity from the clock / uphill, in the cold' (AH, 25) – which become the (mythic) territory of Meredith's writing.

A strong sense of place within historical time underpins all Meredith's writing. As he writes in *Cefn Golau: Shooting a Novelist* (1997): 'I believe in the locatedness of experience, its historical specificity' (*CG*, n.p.). For Meredith as a Welsh writer this is a political assertion. 'If we choose to be Welsh,' he wrote in an early review of Tony Curtis's poetry, 'it haunts what we write.'[7] The specificity of Meredith's own imaginative work, both poetry and prose, has its roots firmly in his *milltir sgwâr*, the square mile or patch of land which so often defines a Welsh writer's childhood.[8] For Meredith this centres on Tredegar, particularly around the Cefn Golau council estate where he grew up. The estate bore the same name as the mountain it backed on to and the cholera grave-yard just above it. An area which is 'charged with history and grief', it entered deep into his consciousness (*CG*, n.p.). As he writes:

When I dream of places I usually dream of spots within a few miles of this centre, of the places where these dead lived. Even when the dreamplace is unrecognizable my dreamself knows precisely which part of the Tredegar area it is . . . I've driven at huge speeds through vertiginous perspectives of avenued skyscrapers out of American myth and known immediately that this was Commercial Street, Tredegar. (*CG*, n.p.)

While this sense of place expands in his later writing to include Breconshire, where Meredith has lived since 1978, the Brecon Beacons and the Black Mountains, it centres around what the poet and critic Jeremy Hooker has called (borrowing the term from Meredith's 'The slurry pond' (*AH*, 26)) Meredith's 'heartland' in the Tredegar area.[9]

This 'heartland' is not the empty picturesque landscape of the Romantic or even the neo-Romantic writer: 'My heartland', Meredith asserts, 'was a place of edges / though I scarcely knew it' (*AH*, 26). Dominated for 200 years by heavy industry, and now scarred by post-industrial decline and social deprivation, the Tredegar area nevertheless includes spaces of semi-wilderness. In 'The slurry pond', Meredith writes back to Wordsworth's 'Ode: Intimations of Immortality from Recollections of Early Childhood' (1807) with its assertion that 'Heaven lies about us in our infancy!'[10] At the same time he rewrites the clichés of the post-industrial south Wales valleys as irredeemably bleak. Here where 'coal surfac[es], becoming air', geological and economic history have shaped a very specific post-industrial landscape:

> A ruined city lay around *us*
> in our infancy
> the pumping station, railless sidings,
> workings of an age
> we didn't realise was not quite dead. (*AH*, 26)

Wordsworth's 'Ode' asserts the importance of the natural world to the child's development in part as a counter to the industrialization which was transforming Britain at that time but his poem is class and gender-blind. In contrast, Meredith's italicizing of '*us*' politicizes the specificity of a shared childhood playing among the discarded 'rubbish' of that not-quite-dead industry.

Despite the prosaic title, Meredith's poem acknowledges the formative and transcendent nature of childhood experience of landscape. He and his playmates see 'no edge / between the natural and made': 'Quarries and cliffs, moor and shaletip / all were the garden of our / innocence'. The children are aware of the dangers in 'that other edge', represented by the opencast mine, the old mine shafts and the 'hardened pus' around the slurry pond. Meredith's 'heartland' is, then, paradoxically always a 'place of edges'. 'Edges are where meanings happen', he suggests in 'Borderland' (*AH*, 8), a central poem in *Air Histories* (2013). Even the form of 'The slurry pond', a sonnet in iambic heptameter, incorporates an 'edge' as the lines fracture in the middle.

This distinctive geographical terrain with its fractured history is the underpinning for Meredith's concern with the complex relationships between language, place, memory, identity and historical process. In one sense the geographical specificity of Meredith's work situates him in the Welsh-language tradition of 'canu bro' (poetry of place). Like Ruth Bidgood, with whom Hooker has productively compared him, Meredith is (to borrow Matthew Jarvis's apt description of Bidgood) *'a poet of a community in its place'*.[11] His landscapes – whether pre-industrial, industrial or post-industrial – are deeply inscribed with the evidence of their shaping by human history and labour. They are peopled by individuals who are in turn shaped by their environment. His own family's history connects to these landscapes, as his writing demonstrates, in complex and sometimes unexpected ways.

Meredith's father, Emrys Meredith, was born on 31 October 1920, one of the twelve children – seven sons and five daughters – of Tom Meredith, a collier from Tredegar, and Emily (always known as Daisy) Holloway, from Merthyr Vale. Emrys was the sixth son. The oldest son Charles was always known as Charl, pronounced with a rolled 'r' like the Welsh Siarl. A younger brother, Ronald, died at the age of 12 in 1933, an event Emrys Meredith remembered on 'his own last bed' (*AH*, 48).The Meredith family

Figure 1. Joyce Meredith (née Roberts) and Emrys
Meredith, 1943. Reproduced by kind permission of
Christopher Meredith.

lived in 64 Walter Street, Tredegar, a terraced street in an area of
the valley bottom known as 'The Tip' because it was built on a
waste dump. The street had chapels at either end: the Bethania
Congregational Chapel at one end and the James Street Primitive
Methodist chapel at the other. Tom Meredith went down the pit
at the age of 11 in 1891. He worked at Tŷ Trist for most if not all

of his working life until he retired at the age of 68. A lay preacher with the Primitive Methodists (the radical end of the Methodists), Tom Meredith was also a keen cricketer and snooker player. He died when Christopher Meredith was around four and a half.

A profoundly politicized man who valued reading and education, Emrys Meredith resented the fact that he was forced to leave school in 1934 or 5 at the age of 14 to work. After working in a butcher's shop for a few weeks, slaughtering pigs and making deliveries by bicycle, he started work at Tŷ Trist, the same pit as his father and some of his brothers, earning just 14s. a week, later moving to Oakdale. As a collier he was in a reserved occupation when the war broke out in 1939 but wanted to join up to fight fascism. The family was split over the issue: his brother Haydn was a conscientious objector and Christopher Meredith believes that his grandfather was also anti-war (he still has his grandfather's copy of Robert Blatchfield's socialist classic *Merrie England* (1893)). Emrys Meredith went to a tribunal and argued his way out of the colliery on a technicality. He joined the Royal Marines, serving in No. 44 (Royal Marine) Commando which took part in the Burma campaign. He served overseas for over two years, from late November 1943 to mid-1946, an experience which deeply impressed him and had a profound effect on his son's thinking about the connections between personal experience and historical process.

In an essay on Alun Lewis, the anglophone Welsh writer who died on active service (probably by his own hand) in Burma in 1944, Meredith draws an interesting distinction between Lewis and his father. Lewis, he suggests, was caught between contrary identities, 'between Welshness and Englishness, between officers and men, between social classes . . . and he had no clear map of commitments to guide him'.[12] He lacked, Meredith writes, 'the powerful political motive of fighting fascism – which moved my own father to get out of his reserved occupation in the pit a few valleys from Lewis's home and end up himself in Burma'.[13] Here Meredith pays tribute to his father's political commitment but also uses this history to tease out the elements that made Lewis's best writing 'genuinely exploratory'.[14]

Figure 2. Emrys Meredith (on right) in uniform, 44 (Royal Marine) Commando. Inscribed as a Christmas card from Kowloon, South China, December 1945. Reproduced by kind permission of Christopher Meredith.

From 1944 to 1945 Emrys Meredith was in Burma for fourteen months as part of the offensive to retake the area from the Japanese. He took part in Operation Screwdriver in March 1944, which involved a landing under heavy fire and ensuing battles on the Western coast of Burma. 44 Commando then withdrew to India and Ceylon briefly. In January 1945 he took part in two amphibious beach landings at the Myebon peninsula which were part of a whole brigade assault, Operation Lightening. During the Battle of Hill 170 at Kangaw he was involved in heavy fighting on a hill codenamed Pinner where 44 Commando held off a ferocious assault and 'suffered heavy casualties' (I). Following Kangaw, 44 Commando was preparing for a third landing (Operation Zipper) which was only averted when the US dropped the atomic bomb on Hiroshima.

Once the war had ended, he was involved in the clean-up operation in the Far East, burying corpses on the islands. He went to Singapore and then Hong Kong and was a guard on the fence at a Japanese prisoner of war camp. The Japanese prisoners were, he recalled, treated very badly. Meredith's poem, 'The ones with the white hats' uses some of his father's memories, though it is not, he has said, in his father's voice:[15]

> After it was over
> it started.
> We stopped fighting and got in ships.
> We stopped off at islands
>   to bury rotting people. (*AH*, 23)

In the aftermath of war, as the title suggests, the roles of 'good guy' and 'bad guy', soldier and prisoner, are reversed. '[W]e restored order', the speaker asserts, before detailing the shooting of looters and escapees, and finally recording that the prisoners were taken to an island, run 'not quite naked' down the gangplank and made to watch while their kit was burned. Such retold memories resonate through Meredith's writing, suggesting the way war shaped his own generation as well as his father's.

A direct use of his father's experience comes in the powerful story, 'Averted Vision' (1990), about two soldiers, the English Lovat and the Welsh Edwards, on a prison ship. Lovat accidentally drops a tommy gun on the face of a prisoner in the hold and, afraid of the consequences, tips the injured man overboard.[16] It was, Meredith has said, a 'windfall story':

> In its details it's pretty much as my father told it, along with details I heard from him in bits and pieces, down to the seasickness, the fact that it was an old coal ship, the young soldier dozing and dropping his tommy gun, the business with the torch and going down the ladder, the fact that the murderer hadn't seen active service, the phrase about not counting the prisoners, though I've given that line to the murderer if I remember rightly. There is some invention in it and of course the whole interior life of the two men is invented or re-invented. But unusually in my prose, its form and essential details were a dark gift.[17]

The story was chosen for broadcast on BBC radio in 1994, suggesting the power of its structure.

The title metaphor draws attention to the question of point of view: 'averted vision' is a technique used by astronomers, utilizing the way in which the retina works in the dark and the fact that faint objects can be seen more clearly if they are viewed out of the corner of the eye. The point of view in the story alternates between Edwards, who has seen active service, and Lovat, who joined too late to 'do [his] bit'.[18] Although Lovat is the son of a barber, he represents the colonizing race. To him, the Japanese prisoners are 'inscrutable heathens', but he also refers to Edwards belittlingly as 'taff':[19]

> [Edwards] glanced at the injured face in the pool of torchlight and looked round the hold once more. The smell of vomit and coal.
> 'Well done, Lovat.'
> 'He's only a jap.'
> He's a jap, I'm a taff. Who the fuck are you? [20]

Both the Japanese and the Welsh are equally 'othered'. Lovat justifies his murder of the Japanese prisoner by asking 'who would count them at the other end? Who counted?'[21] Who decides who counts is the question the story asks.

Lovat uses the technique of averted vision to look at the stars from the ship but when he pushes the prisoner into the sea, he stares 'straight into the man's face': 'Lovat snapped the torch off. He continued staring but the face had disappeared.'[22] Edwards practises his own form of averted vision in that he anticipates what Lovat will do, but is unwillingly complicit with it:

> Edwards knew how it would be. Lovat would come back. Edwards would say, that was quick. Lovat would be quiet a moment and then say. Edwards would say nothing. Lovat would say why. Try to. And that would be all. And a thousand thousand.[23]

Edwards's battle-trauma is evoked through the repetition of an incomplete quotation from 'The Rime of the Ancient Mariner':

'The many men so beautiful and they all dead did lie and a thousand thousand slimy things.'[24] The final words of this stanza, which Edwards repeatedly elides, 'Lived on; and so did I', suggest that, like the Ancient Mariner, Edwards is weighed down by his complicity in what he has witnessed but cannot articulate it.[25] The question of vision, of who sees what from where, is one that Meredith returns to repeatedly in his writing. As he puts it, 'The project of fiction is to imagine different points of view – it's a human thing' (I). In his fiction he frequently alternates or manipulates points of view to ask questions about guilt and complicity.

For Emrys Meredith, the war was a 'definitive watershed' in his life: 'he went out as a Christian socialist,' Meredith says, 'and came back close to a Communist and an atheist' (I). He saw Nagasaki after the bomb had been dropped but his only direct comment about what he saw was: 'All gone' (I). It was, Christopher Meredith notes, a bigger bomb than Hiroshima but killed fewer people 'because of the shape of the land' (I). The ways in which the 'shape of the land' determines people's lives, or deaths, is another theme that runs through Meredith's writing, as is the effect of trauma, individual and national. Nightmares were a lifelong legacy of the war for his father: 'He was very traumatized I suspect' (I).

A scene that recurs in Meredith's work is the image of his father returning from work and giving him either a tube of sweets or a toy gun. In an early poem 'Opening My Palms I Saw', the father is a menacing figure.[26] Washing in carbolic soap after a shift at the steel mill brings back the memory of 'a frightened boy at home / before the grey pillar who, unbuckling the burberry, / looking down extends a gift of sweets'. The poem ends with the image of 'useless stigmata' on the poet's hands, 'insanity shaped like a myth / and my father's face', suggesting the shaping power of family. In 'Opening Time' the emphasis is on the boy's indifference: 'The man . . . put a hand into his pocket and brought out a tube of sugared sweets. The boy took them saying thanks and went on reading . . .' (*SH*, 79). In 'Homecoming', it is a gun the father gives him and the weight of historical trauma is hinted at. It is a *'Thompson's Sub'*, his father tells him, 'Bar size and weight, / the detail's right, exactly

Figure 3. Joyce Meredith, sent to Emrys Meredith,
August 1945. Reproduced by kind permission of
Christopher Meredith.

like the one / I had' (*MF*, 40). But when the delighted boy 'spray[s]
the room' with pretend gunfire, his father 'turned aside and waved
a hand before his face. / *No. No. Don't point that thing / at me.*' Trauma,
guilt and complicity are all interwoven here.

After the war, Emrys Meredith worked in Bulmer's cider factory
in Hereford, catching a bus there daily from Tredegar, and then as

a railway guard. This was 'his favourite job', although it was badly paid (I). Meredith's ironically titled short story 'Progress' is a loosely fictionalized version of his father's decision not to go down the pit again, a job he hated.[27] He then went into the steel works in Ebbw Vale where he worked in the hot mill, but left because of issues to do with his involvement in the union. After a stint in the Glas Coed munitions factory, he returned to the steel mill and worked there till he retired. 'As I remember him, he was a steel worker right through', Meredith has said, noting that his father idolized Bevan, but only met him once, when Bevan came to open St James's Hospital (formerly Ty-Bryn workhouse): 'I think he shook hands with him.'[28]

Meredith's mother, Joyce Roberts, was born on 23 April 1925, the daughter of Liz Roberts and Will Roberts (who died before Meredith was born). The Roberts family lived in Troedrhiwgwair, to the south of Tredegar in the Sirhowy valley. Built in the mid-1800s to house workers at the Tredegar Iron and Steel Company, this consisted of a couple of rows of houses on the steep-sided mountain. (The Roberts family probably lived at number 15, now demolished (I).) Although small, the village had a school, an old farm which had been a pub, The Fountain, a library, post office, church and chapel. Across the Sirhowy river to the south was Bedwellty Pits where Aneurin Bevan had worked as a check-weighman. A place Meredith associated with summer (I), Troed-rhiwgwair was an important part of his emotional and literary landscape. This had been a rural area with the remains of farms still evident but the mountain behind the village had been mined and quarried and was full of water with abandoned adits and other industrial remains. Will Roberts had probably been a collier but didn't work towards the end of his life. Meredith recalls that:

> One man who'd lived in Troed told me they used to call him Rob the Gipsy, but my mother hadn't heard that and didn't much like it when I mentioned it to her. He certainly made clothes pegs and rabbit nets and kept ferrets. My father told me he went ferreting with him a few times.[29]

Joyce Roberts had one sister, Betty, and a brother, Billy, who had TB and rheumatoid arthritis and became an invalid who never left his bed.

After the disaster at Aberfan in October 1966 when a tip of slag and slurry collapsed, engulfing Pantglas Junior School and killing 144 people (116 of them children), there was widespread anxiety about the possibility of more such incidents. Colliery spoil heaps across south Wales were investigated for safety. In 1973 the local authority commissioned a survey of Troedrhiwgwair which raised concerns that the mountain behind the village was unstable. As a result the school was closed and the majority of the residents were encouraged to move to new houses.[30] Despite protests, the village was effectively closed although some people refused to leave. Of the ninety-three families, only fourteen remained and many of the houses were left derelict. 'It was a clearance', is how Meredith remembers it (I). In the 1980s the remains of the village were used to film the television programme *District Nurse* (produced by BBC Wales and shown between 1984 and 1987, featuring Nerys Hughes) set in the late 1920s. Meredith remembers that the old school was burned down for one episode (I). In 1986 the council set up an enquiry to decide whether to clear the village altogether or to rebuild. Their decision was to issue compulsory purchase orders and clear the village. The remaining villagers protested vigorously and in 1988 a second public enquiry found in their favour.

Meredith's memories of childhood visits to the village where his grandmother still lived with his invalid uncle Billy are revisited in 'Six Poems for Troedrhiwgwair' in Meredith's debut collection *This* (1984) and republished in *Snaring Heaven* (1990). The poems trace his connections to the place from his mother's memories of playing 'under the one gaslamp in the lane' (*T*, 13) through his own visits to his grandmother's house to his return as an adult bringing his mother to visit the now almost derelict village. Troedrhiwgwair is the 'not-town':

> two sunned terraces under the hill,
> the road's end and a path through the trees,
> fountain farm and a green lane to the stream. (*T*, 13)

Within this 'unknowably old' countryside, the evidence of industrialization is visible in the 'rusted gaspipe / uncoiling like an adder from the earth'. This is nevertheless a place of freedom, a 'wimberry world' where children can 'unlearn / Our books' (*T*, 14).

In 'Wasps', the 8-year-old child visiting the Roberts house, 'my mother's home but / Not quite mine', finds that the 'Dark / Of a kitchen always dark' chafes against the politeness required of him (*T*, 15). His arthritis-racked 'Grammer' is 'like a mountain / In a black pinny, her face not a face, / A hardening of darkness'. (In a later poem, 'Colour', his grandmother is 'simplified in monochrome' in a photograph which is 'a lie', its shadows 'masking pale blue eyes' (*MF*, 18).) Escaping to the hillside, the child is struck by a horror 'like the whiteness of a root / Drawn too easily from a yielding earth' (*T*, 16). It's a moment which resembles the sudden fear felt by the child Seamus Heaney in 'Death of a Naturalist' where he runs away from the angry frogs invading the flax-dam where he has played all summer.[31] The fear Meredith records seems caused by something older than the dangers posed by the supposedly unstable mountain:

> It was
> No premonition of the riddled hill's
> Slipping frightened me, though the place grew frailer:
> . . .
> Only panic on the treacherous hill
> Forced me back into the yard, sent me home. (*T*, 16)

The 'panic' which inexplicably causes terror in rural places was attributed by the Greeks to the sudden appearance of Pan.[32] These more primitive fears underlie the dangers of the 'riddled hill', suggesting a landscape which is a palimpsest of successive layers of history.

The layers of history are evident again in the sixth poem in the sequence, 'Taking My Mother to Troed' where the adult Meredith and his mother stroll along the abandoned terraces:

> And at each door she names a ghost,
> The family history and how
> They died, or moved, or why they stayed.
> Rob Roberts her father, Auntie Ada,
> Pen Roberts, George Wimlet . . . (T, 18)

Her 'naming' of people and places 'fixes' them in memory but the very landscape seems unstable as she looks up at the 'breaking hill': '"Oh good god, o'course it've moved."' Unlike many of the villagers who fought to retain their community, she voices no desire to remain in the village: 'She wonders at the few who've stayed, / Says she would not go back to this.' Although the official council monitoring found no slippage in the hill, the poem suggests that human history has undermined the landscape, now returning slowly to nature.[33] Thus in the final poem, 'Larks', the evidence of human habitation is shrugged off the hills: 'Like winddriven midges / We came, clung a moment, went' (T, 19). Human history leaves its traces, but the area is being recolonized by wildlife: the larks 'nail light with hammered air'. This childhood experience of Troed seems to have sparked Meredith's interest in the palimpsestic nature of the Welsh landscape with its visual traces of the rise and fall of stages of civilizations, a motif to which Meredith will return in later poems.

As so many young women of her class did in the inter-war period, Joyce Roberts went into domestic service at the end of the 1930s when she was fourteen. She worked as a maid in the house of Dyson Perrins, owner of the Lea & Perrins Worcestershire sauce factory (I). She then worked at Madresfield Court near Malvern, a mid-fifteenth-century moated manor house which is the ancestral home of the Lygon family. A frequent guest, Evelyn Waugh is said to have based the eponymous house in *Brideshead Revisited* (1945) on Madresfield and the Marchmains on members of the

Lygon family. Sebastian Flyte was allegedly modelled on Hugh Lygon.[34]

Meredith's poem 'My mother missed the beautiful and doomed' about his mother's experience as a domestic servant offers a powerful revisioning of Waugh's novels and other texts of that period. The poem offers history from below, from the perspective of a kneeling maid:

> Where Waugh, hot for some pious ormolu,
> dreamed Brideshead
> she swept carpets, cleaned grates. (*MF*, 38–9)

Fifty years later, looking at a postcard of 'the House' while she smokes a cigarette, Meredith's mother evokes that bygone era through the glamour of films like *Rebecca*: 'Her Ladyship 'ould doll up to the nines / come dinner, like a filmstar'. Past and present are layered together to explore the individual's complicity with world historical process. The glowing cigarette figures the effort of memory, 'drag[ging] air' back through the past to 'brighten memory's fuse', but also class difference and complicity. The 'tobacco galleries' in the cigarette evoke both the galleries of Madresfield Court and the 'maze of galleries where / her people cut the coal'. As Hooker notes, the processes of history and of smoking are equally destructive: her smoking is 'like an internalisation of the history in which the House is implicated: coal mining, armament production, the Spanish Civil War'.[35]

The poem unpicks the mechanisms maintaining class structures within historical process. Through half-open doors she sees the foreign secretary, 'his collar of vermiculated astrakhan / flawed with sparkling rain'.[36] While she kneels by the scuttle, 'an egg of coal in either hand', his chauffeur ruffles her hair and calls her 'Little Cinderella'. There is an ambiguity in his gesture and in the words which 'half flattered her / and kept her down'. This is paralleled with the wider political history invoked by the chauffeur's 'tight black boot' which echoes the 'bentarmed cross' of Nazism. The poem lays bare the parallels in the power structures: the chauffeur's hand 'rained a blow or a flirtation' as the bombs 'rain' on 'undefended children' in Spain. The final lines return to the cigarette as an image of internalization:

> Unwilled complicity can hurt so much.
> She clutches at the deaths of millions.
>
> 'A skivvy all my life' she says
> and strikes another match.

Here, as in 'Averted Vision' and 'The ones with the white hats', Meredith uses his parents' experiences to explore difficult questions around the individual's complicity within historical process.

The poem which precedes 'My mother missed the beautiful and doomed' in *The Meaning of Flight*, and is implicitly paired with it, is 'The solitary reaper', Meredith's bitingly witty riposte to Wordsworth's poem of the same name (*MF*, 36–7). Both 'My mother . . .' and 'The solitary reaper' privilege a female working-class point of view but the reaper voices the anger that is internalized in 'My mother . . .'. In Wordsworth's poem, the poet watches a 'solitary Highland Lass' singing while she reaps the grain and speculates: 'Will no one tell me what she sings?'[37] He does not, however, ask the girl herself who has no *speaking* voice within the poem. Like the nightingale to which she is compared, she is an objectified symbol of a natural beauty which requires the poet to transform it into comprehensible linguistic art.

The flipping of point of view to politicize assumptions we take for granted is an important technique in Meredith's work. Here Meredith gives the reaper a voice to turn Wordsworth's 'sentimental anthropology' back on him:

> See him trekking up the hill,
> Yon solitary English gent.
> He stood a moment as I worked,
> Heard me sing a while, and went.

> I saw him scribble in a book
> Pausing now and then to look
> While I cut and bound the crop,
> And though I saw, I didn't stop. (*MF*, 36)

This opening stanza uses a version of Wordsworth's ballad stanza (an octave rhyming ababccdd) but the following three stanzas break out of this form. The reaper remarks that such gentlemen 'think the world has two languages – / English and the barking of dogs. / They translate themselves by shouting.' Given that Wordsworth's reaper was probably singing in Gaelic, this comment from a Welsh-speaking writer with a keen interest in translation is doubly barbed.

The poem traces a historical continuum from the nineteenth-century gentlemen with their notebooks and fortunes built on slavery, to the be-jeaned twentieth-century second home-owner making 'the fourwheeled drive / to the cottage they restored'. The 'bucktoothed' poet's assertion that 'See. I also sing / so I'm a native too' is contrasted with the reaper's vision of the Highland clearances to come:

> I saw my thirteen unborn children dead
> and my dugs like satchels in my lap,
> the croft stove in and leaking smoke,
> the black masts pointing towards Canada. (*MF* 37)

In contrast with Wordsworth's romantic appropriation of the 'Highland lass' to enable his poetry, Meredith puts the reaper back into a specific history of the oppression of working-class people in Britain and gives her a voice which articulates her situation.

In the context of this poem, Meredith's comments about the compulsory purchase and closure of his mother's native Troed-rhiwgwair in 1973 – 'It was a clearance' (I) – take on an added resonance. The forced eviction of tenants from entire areas of the Scottish Highlands in the eighteenth and nineteenth centuries was allegedly in the interests of 'improved' agricultural practices to make room for more profitable methods such as sheep farming. Many families were forced to emigrate and the process devastated the Gaelic culture and language. As Marx writes in *Capital* (1887), the ruling classes 'conquered the field for capitalistic agriculture, made the soil part and parcel of capital, and created for the town industries the necessary supply of a "free" and outlawed proletariat'.[38] In rewriting Wordsworth, Meredith's poem makes connections across history and geography that are grounded in part in his own family experience.

Emrys Meredith and Joyce Roberts were married in 1943. Their son, Philip Gary, was born on 29 December 1947, followed by the loss of two babies, one stillborn and the other living only a few hours (I). Christopher was born in 1954, and Andrew two years later. The family were living in a rented house on Whitworth Terrace (probably 21), when Christopher Meredith was born. When he was two or three they moved to 33 Walter Conway Avenue on the Cefn Golau council estate above Tredegar. Newly built in the mid-1950s on then modern lines, the estate backed on to open moorland on Cefn Golau mountain which separates Tredegar and Rhymney, a formative landscape for Meredith. Overall, he remembers having 'quite a happy childhood' (I). Although he identified with Billy Bunter in that he was always worrying about things, he maintains that he was 'totally unaware of class as a kid' and that, despite the politics around him, his awareness of its implications was slow dawning (I). Although there was a mixture of families on the estate, including some dysfunctional ones, council estates at that point had not become the kinds of places they became after 1979. 'All my friends came from other parts of town,' he remembers, 'it was not an issue that I came off the estate' (I). During his childhood sheep and ponies used to come down from the hills on to the estate and Meredith remembers the shepherd coming to collect the sheep. First cattle grids and then a concrete stockade were put up to keep them out. In the 1970s, Emrys Meredith bought number 33 Walter Conway Avenue. After 1979, however, Meredith says, 'the massive acceleration of de-industrialization and the selling-off of assets sucked money and jobs out [of the estates] and

Figure 4. Christopher Meredith (on right) with his brother Gary, in the living room at 33 Walter Conway Avenue, Tredegar, 1950s. Reproduced by kind permission of Christopher Meredith.

sucked in a drug economy. Council estates became sinks for single mothers' (I).

Meredith's childhood experience of this landscape was clearly formative. In an essay for *Planet*, 'Up the Mountain' (1994), he described its distinctive topography:

[T]hat mountain was the wilderness I got lost in. Literally. From our side, in Tredegar, Cefn Golau was a treeless, featureless keel of moorland which came down to meet the back gardens of the top street on the estate. Below us, a ten minute walk away, was the Park, with a bandstand and a bowling green like the baize on a card table, and at our backs was the raised eye-brow of wilderness, the Mountain up which we regularly went. Somewhere between that tame and that wild I had to find my space.[39]

Figure 5. Christopher Meredith (on left) with his brothers Gary and Andrew, at 33 Walter Conway Avenue, Tredegar, 1950s. Reproduced by kind permission of Christopher Meredith.

Figure 6. Christopher Meredith (on right) with his brother Andrew, at the Mile Field near Fields Road, Tredegar, c.1959. Reproduced by kind permission of Christopher Meredith.

In one sense all Meredith's writing has been about 'finding his space' or 'place'. The paradoxical combination of the industrial and the rural in the south Wales valleys was, Raymond Williams suggested, a distinctive element of the landscape from which the Welsh industrial novel emerged. It was the 'characteristic place' which formed the life and communities that such writing represents:

> at any time in any Welsh mining village, there is the profoundly different yet immediately accessible landscape of open hills and the sky above them ... The pastoral life which had been Welsh history, is still another Welsh present, and in its visible presence – not as an ideal contrast but as the slope, the skyline, to be seen immediately from the streets and from the pit-tops – it is a shape which manifests not only a consciousness of history but a consciousness of alternatives ...[40]

That landscape-inspired 'consciousness of history' is everywhere in Meredith's writing. It has its roots deep in his childhood experience of a 'heartland' which also 'was a place of edges' between tame and wild, rural and industrial, Welsh and English.

On the fringes of the mountain Meredith and his friends played in a world that was halfway between rural and industrial, sometimes attempting to ride the wild ponies or 'dismember[ing] the capsized hulks of dumped Ford Populars'.[41] Meredith was about seven when, with two friends Dai Edwards and Boozer Bosley (he was called Boozer not because he drank but 'for the sake of what I later learned to call cynghanedd'[42]), he got lost on the mountain. They had gone on an expedition over Cefn Golau to Rhymney, 'a foreign city whose inhabitants and customs we were eager to study'.[43] Once in Rhymney, Boozer disappeared to visit an aunt and Meredith and Dai realized that they had no idea how to get home. Put on a bus by a kindly woman they arrived home to discover that their parents had called the police.

This expedition was Meredith's first experience of the uplands proper where there were 'rushes and cotton grass and frogspit and the small glossy leaves of wimberry bushes'.[44] He recalls being 'astounded' by the marshy patches: 'How did the water stay on top of the mountain?'[45] He had to reassess his understanding of the world. Instead of believing that the tame areas were 'like islands' in the wilderness, he realized that 'wildernesses did have edges . . . *They* were the islands.'[46] 'But,' he concludes, 'it was a theory I kept having to change. I never got it right – still haven't – or found my place.'[47] That attempt to map the edges, to divine the relationship between wild and tame in this geologically and historically distinctive locality, in order to 'find his place' is at the heart of Meredith's early writing.

Not far from Cefn Golau estate is the small cholera cemetery of the same name opened during the 1832 cholera epidemic. Cholera victims were buried there to try to prevent the disease spreading. Unfenced and with no trees, road or path to it, this was another 'place of edges' that was formative for the child who became Meredith the writer. It is the place he chose to write about in the series of limited edition pamphlets entitled 'Places: Y Man a'r Lle', commissioned for Gwasg Gregynog. Meredith's short essay, *Cefn Golau: Shooting a Novelist* (1997), is accompanied by an evocative black and white illustration by the artist Sara Philpott. It is a meditation on the defining nature of place but also, in its discussion of George Orwell's essay 'Shooting an Elephant' (1936), on those issues of complicity to which Meredith returns repeatedly in his work.

As a child from the Cefn Golau estate, Meredith writes of his 'fellow feeling for these dead': 'The town seemed to want to marginalise us as, a century or so before, they'd exiled their dead out of fear' (*CG*, n.p.). Like Troedrhiwgwair, Cefn Golau cemetery was a liminal space, 'a sort of half-place, not quite wilderness', where the borders between life and death, Welsh and English, were made visible:[48]

> [T]his was our country on the borders between wild and tame. We played by the pond, skimming pebbles, and walked the mountain, and sometimes we approached the stark angled teeth of the headstones . . . Putting my hand on the stone and feeling it had grown cold when the sun had gone I realised there first of all that the dead stay underground forever, even when you go home for tea. (*CG*, n.p.)

Figure 7. Cefn Golau cholera cemetery, above Tredegar,
in 2016. Photograph: Diana Wallace.

Meredith's family were English-speaking so the tombstone of 'John
Williams o'r lle hwn [of this place] who died in agony at nineteen'
was 'in a language [Meredith] couldn't understand yet' (*CG*, n.p.).
Nevertheless it taught Meredith about the 'locatedness of experience' and the notion of belonging: 'The fact of mortality which
confronted me so powerfully wasn't so much a universal as a
pointer to all the specificities' (*CG*, n.p.). The tombstones which
connoted both strangeness and familiarity, he writes, 'bore witness
to the richness of things': 'For me no place could have affirmed life
more' (*CG*, n.p.).

In terms of formal education, Meredith benefitted from the
introduction of comprehensive schools in the 1960s. In 1966 he
went to Tredegar Comprehensive School, the first comprehensive
school in Gwent, which had been newly formed in 1965 by the
amalgamation of the four prior schools (two secondary moderns,
a technical and a grammar school). The school Meredith attended
was on the east side of the valley but a new purpose-built school

was later built on the site of Tŷ Trist Colliery. His elder brother, Gary, went on to drama school in London at this point, training at Rose Bruford College (1966–9), and became a professional actor and director, with strong roots in his local area.[49] When Gary left home their mother gave him a lump of coal wrapped in paper to put in his pocket, and she did the same when Christopher left. 'My mother was superstitious', Meredith says (I), but there is a symbolic weight to this gesture that suggests a recognition of the need to remember the place (geographic, geological and social) from which one comes.

Meredith's younger brother, Andrew, followed him to the school and remained in Tredegar after leaving, working first in the steelworks as a crane driver in the Scrap Bay and then, after the steelworks closed, in a factory.[50]

As with many writers, it seems to have been the private and sometimes illicit pleasure of reading, rather than formal schooling, that was the most intense part of Meredith's education as a writer. In an essay entitled 'Secret Rooms' (1995) Meredith recalls how as a child he would raid his own money box for the coins to buy books from W. H. Smiths. He would take the cheap hardback copies of Biggles books up to the tip behind Queen Victoria Street to read them sitting on a tump of grass:

> That night I'd carry on reading under the blankets with a torch. It was better than masturbation . . .
>
> I loved the smells and textures of books, but more than that I loved the intense privacy and involvement of reading.[51]

While he was fascinated by punctuation ('Oh, those lovely, commas'), the strange vocabulary ('Books had words you didn't find anywhere else like *mirthless* and *indignantly*'), and the complexities of shifting points of view, there was a disjunction between the world these books depicted and his own experience: 'books reflected no social or cultural reality I knew'.[52] Set in a pre-war era they featured characters who wore short trousers and school caps and said things like 'Golly' and 'do let's'.

A family tradition of reading helped him to grasp the implications of this disjunction. His father's family had been 'bookish',
his father was 'a great reader' and his uncle Charl had 'a house
full of books'.[53] It was when Meredith discovered a couple of
suitcases of books in the attic of their council house, brought from
Walter Street by his father, that he began to 'find . . . how books
touched real history':

> I climbed into the lift with a torch and folded back the flimsy lids and
> played the blade of light across the waiting spines of Lawrence and
> Wells, Odhams reprints of 'classics', *Penguin New Writings*, Marxist
> tracts and Left Book Club editions. There was Hermin Levy's *A Philosophy
> for a Modern Man* and Orwell's *The Road to Wigan Pier* . . .[54]

This selection represents a comprehensive education in early
twentieth-century radical and leftist thinking.

It was George Orwell's *The Road to Wigan Pier* (1937) which
provided Meredith with '*Contact*' with 'real history'.[55] The classic
statement from the Left about the disenfranchised and impover-
ished, *The Road to Wigan Pier* was written by a writer who himself
came from the privileged world of what he called the 'lower-
upper-middle class'.[56] Born in British India, Eric Arthur Blair (who
adopted the nom de plume George Orwell) was educated at
Wellington and Eton before joining the Imperial Police. *The Road
to Wigan Pier* documents the time Orwell spent investigating
conditions among the working classes in the industrial north of
England during the Depression. In analysing the class prejudice
which underlies the rejection of socialism, Orwell uses details of
his own autobiography as being typical of his own 'lower-upper-
middle' class.

The copy of *The Road to Wigan Pier* included a photo from the
pithead of a stay-down strike at Nine Mile Point Colliery in Cwm-
felinfach in the south Wales valleys in 1935. As a teenage collier,
Meredith's father had gone on strike in sympathy with Nine Mile
Point men who were protesting over the use of scab labour.[57] This
was the point of '*Contact*' for Meredith:

Here was Orwell, a humanized representative of fat owls and golly boys with caps, on an expedition to meet people something like me. I can see myself now as a kind of cut-price Achebe, who, aghast, recognised himself among the threatening faces on the riverbank in *Heart of Darkness*. Insofar as I had any representatives in the kind of books I read as a kid, they were the men with blue chins who frequented pubs and led Coker of the Fifth astray, or bit-part maids in William stories, or the characters who dropped their aitches, got barked at by the dog and were regarded as shifty by the Famous Five.[58]

As a 'cut-price Achebe', the young Meredith recognizes the critical importance of point of view: colonial history looks very different if you are standing on the riverbank not the boat.[59] While Orwell has been a hero of Meredith's 'on and off', because he is 'wonderfully subversive' and 'fantastically readable'; he was also a member of the ruling class making a 'heroic' effort to see things from the other side (I). There are the beginnings of both a Marxist and postcolonial analysis here in Meredith's early understanding of these dynamics, and both theories offer useful ways of reading his *oeuvre*.

From Tredegar Comprehensive, Meredith went on to the University of Wales, Aberystwyth where he studied English and philosophy, graduating in 1976. One figure who made an important impression on him was Jeremy Hooker, then a lecturer at Aberystwyth. Meredith recalls a formative moment:

In the early 1970s, as an undistinguished undergraduate sitting through Eng lit lectures at Aberystwyth, I was struck by the teaching of one youngish lecturer in particular. What was striking had nothing to do with the lecturer's delivery. His style was without pyrotechnics ... But I recall coming out of a lecture on Joyce's *Dubliners* feeling that vertiginous depths of possibility had opened in a text I had thought I was already familiar with, and thinking that there was a bit more to this reading malarkey than I'd supposed. It's barely an exaggeration to say that this was when I started to learn to read.[60]

Hooker was to play a founding role in the development of the teaching and criticism of what was then called 'Anglo-Welsh literature'. More recently, his continued interest in place and landscape has made him an informed critic of Meredith's work.

Reading James Joyce as a student was another formative moment for Meredith as a writer. In his teens Meredith had written poetry as well as songs but not much fiction. He saw the poetry and songs 'as being pretty separate from one another'.[61] He now concluded 'Poetry's dead' and began to write short stories (I). These were 'nearly good' in that they 'were doing what I do now: making imagery cohere across a long piece' (I). A second influence on these mostly unfinished stories was the American writer James Leo Herlihy. 'What I noticed about their short stories,' Meredith has said, 'is how *worked* they are – without being pat, how complete they are – and that's what I wanted to do in the fiction that I started to write.'[62]

As a writer Joyce offered a useful model for Meredith both in his choice of his native area as his subject, and in his use of modernist techniques. In *Dubliners* (1914) Joyce set out to offer a portrayal of his native city, then in the economic doldrums following a period of earlier prosperity, which was both realist and highly crafted. His intention was 'to write a chapter of the moral history of my country and I chose Dublin for the scene because that city seemed to me the centre of paralysis'.[63] Similarly, Meredith is interested in a kind of 'paralysis', or complicity, in people within a culture that has been traumatized by colonial and economic exploitation. Joyce, along with Virginia Woolf and Katherine Mansfield, was one of the earliest writers to use free indirect discourse with the point of view shifting between narrator and characters. He also used symbol, myth and imagery to structure fiction. Likewise, Meredith is a writer who appears to be a realist yet, as noted above, gives his work the coherence which comes with an underpinning framework of imagery or symbol.

Equally crucial to Meredith's development as a writer was the fact that he learned to speak Welsh while at Aberystwyth. 'Learning Welsh,' Meredith has said, 'is one of the most important things I've ever done.'[64] As a child in an English-speaking Welsh family in Tredegar, he almost never heard any Welsh. The first language

Figure 8. Christopher Meredith (second from left) with friends
outside Pantycelyn hall of residence, Aberystwyth, *c*.1975.
Photograph: V. A. Meredith.

other than English he remembers hearing was Italian, spoken by
a bus conductor (I). Welsh was not taught officially at his school
in Tredegar although he learned a little Welsh history. He knew
one girl who spoke Welsh. 'As a child, Welsh seemed something
marvellous that I could aspire to', he says (I). He remembers going
over to Rhymney because he had seen some Welsh books in a shop
there and buying a 1920s book of stories for children and a copy
of *Teach Yourself Welsh* but he did not get very far with this. In the
sixth form the French teacher ran a few Welsh lessons from which
he picked up a couple of phrases.

In Aberystwyth, he lived in a Welsh-speakers hall of residence
and found himself in 'the privileged position of being able to listen
a lot' (I). By the end of his third year he felt he was beginning to
get somewhere. During that summer while he was working in the
library he rented digs with a Welsh-speaking student who spoke

only Welsh to him, a generously inclusive gesture which Meredith still remembers with appreciation. Meredith also read avidly, ploughing through Ivor Owen's *Four Stories for Welsh Learners / Pedair Stori i Ddysgwyr Cymraeg* (1964) with the aid of a dictionary.

Now a fluent Welsh speaker, Meredith made the decision to speak Welsh to his two sons although his wife, Valerie, an English-woman from Preston, is not a Welsh speaker. This consciously maintained bilingualism is a testament to how seriously Meredith takes the need to preserve Welsh as a living language. 'I think in Welsh most of the time,' he says, 'though I wish I wrote more in Welsh' (I). While Meredith values the Welsh language for the 'contact it brings with my country/history/culture', he also believes that being bilingual brings 'linguistic-cultural insights':

> Welsh is syntactically very different from English, and in terms of power and influence the two are nearly at opposite ends of the scale. To have a detailed grasp of this is very enriching . . . Two languages alongside each other are like two mirrors in parallel. They reflect off into infinity.[65]

While Meredith writes primarily in English there is considerable 'interplay' between his two languages, particularly a 'seepage' from Welsh to English in his work.[66] What Pierre Bourdieu would call the 'cultural capital' carried by the Welsh language has traditionally been far less than that of many other languages.[67] Meredith notes the irony of the fact that 'people laugh at the use of English loan words in Welsh' while 'some people still think it's smart to borrow bits of French and German in their English'.[68] This 'interplay' in his work has increased over the years to the extent that *Air Histories* includes facing-page versions of poems in English and Welsh.

After graduating from Aberystwyth in 1976, Meredith spent a year as a shiftworker at the British Steel Corporation's Ebbw Vale steelworks where his father worked. This was another formative experience, out of which came his groundbreaking first novel, *Shifts* (1988), which won the Arts Council of Wales Fiction Prize. In 1977–8 he completed a Postgraduate Certificate of Education at the University of Wales Swansea. He then took up a post teaching English at Brecon High School (a mixed comprehensive which opened in 1971) in 1978 where he remained until 1993. In August 1981 he married Valerie Anne Smythe (born in 1954) from Preston in Lancashire who taught art at Gwernyfed High School in Three Cocks (Aberllynfi), Powys, from 1980 until 2013. They have two sons, Rhodri Frank Meredith, born in 1983 and Steffan Gwyn Laurence Meredith, born in 1987.

During his time as a teacher, Meredith wrote and published his first short collection of poetry, *This* (1984). The poems were a selection from a manuscript collection which won an Eric Gregory Award and some had already been published in *Poetry Wales* and *Anglo-Welsh Review*. *This* also won an Arts Council of Wales Young Writer Prize in 1985. *Snaring Heaven*, his first full-length collection, was published in 1990 and included some poems from *This*, along with new poems and some free translations from the Welsh. His historical novel, *Griffri*, was published in 1991 and shortlisted for the Arts Council of Wales Book of the Year Award. During this period he was also a regular book reviewer and contributed a column to *Planet*. In 1993 Meredith took up the position of senior lecturer in creative writing at Glamorgan University (now the University of South Wales). He was promoted to professor in 2007 and remained at the university until he retired in 2013. During his period at the university he published a further two novels – *Sidereal Time* (1998) and *The Book of Idiots* (2012) – and two more collections of poetry – *The Meaning of Flight* (2005), which was longlisted for Welsh Book of the Year, and *Air Histories* (2013).

* * *

Meredith's four novels can be read as a sustained meditation on the history and geography of south-east Wales which looks back to the medieval period in *Griffri*, and then forward through the industrial and post-industrial twentieth-century in *Shifts* to the affectless twenty-first-century of contentless-jobs in *The Book of Idiots*. Perhaps not surprisingly in this context and given his own experiences, Meredith's work engages very directly with the ways in which identity is shaped by place and history. 'We' not 'they', or even 'I', is perhaps the key pronoun of his work. The italicizing of *'us'* in 'The slurry pond' (*AH*, 26) which I have already noted, is a marker of his self-reflexive care with pronouns. Jeremy Hooker links the use of 'us' and 'our' in this poem to Glyn Jones's characterization of the Welsh poet writing in English as 'Not a man apart, a freak, but rather an accepted part of the social fabric with an important function to perform.'[69] While this is useful, it is, as Hooker notes, potentially problematic in leading to 'the sort of belonging that can result in nostalgia and complacency'.[70] Hooker points to the way in which the final image of the poem, the 'mud heart' of the slurry pond which 'sucked you down' (*AH*, 26), symbolizes the dangers of this place and undercuts any easy nostalgia. Meredith's use of 'we' is a necessary political stance which does not underestimate the necessity of detachment.

The politics of such pronouns were explored in Meredith's otherwise sympathetic review of the 1992 reprint of Ned Thomas's *The Welsh Extremist* (1971). He spotlights Thomas's description of his ideal reader, the person that is, he is trying to convert: English, left-leaning, a reader of Leavis, Lawrence, Forster and (of course) Orwell. 'On the whole,' Meredith remarks, '*they* still haven't really grasped that *we* exist.'[71] He goes on to pinpoint Thomas's tendency to talk about Welsh and non-Welsh speakers as separate groups and his 'uneasy incomprehension' of the industrial south: '"How far do *they* feel themselves to be Welsh at all?" [Thomas] says.'[72] The use of the third person, Meredith points out, implies that to Thomas '*we're* English people with funny accents'.[73] 'All this hints', Meredith concludes, 'that Ned Thomas didn't see who his most important audience was. *They* were, are, the Anglicised Welsh. *They?* I mean *we*.'[74] With that 'we' Meredith claims his own constituency, the people he speaks from, if not precisely for.

This identification is necessarily a political one, rooted in a particular history. In 'Up the Mountain', written in 1994, Meredith's use of the pronoun 'us' further aligns him with the anger of the dispossessed and the victims of what amounted to another kind of 'clearance', the aftermath of the miners' strike. The trigger for his recalling of the time he got lost on Cefn Golau is that, thirty odd years later and following the privatization of the coal industry in 1994, the mountain is being 'ripped open for strip mining': 'The whole western flank of the hill is being flensed and gutted like a dead whale.'[75] He notes that the coalfield which was supposedly so uneconomic that the nationally owned collieries were closed in the 1980s has now become 'hot economic property', fought over by fourteen large private mining companies. The miners' strike of 1984–5, led by the National Union of Miners under Arthur Scargill, was a defining moment in British industrial relations. The defeat of the strike significantly weakened the power of the unions and strengthened the position of the prime minister, Margaret Thatcher, allowing her to pursue her radically pro-market economic policies. Meredith comments:

> The cynicism and duplicity of the manoeuvre of provoking a cata-strophic strike so as to denationalise all this lucre would have been staggering if it hadn't come to seem so familiar over the last fifteen years. The aim of the company who gets *us* will be to rip out as much coal as cheaply as possible.[76]

He returns once again to the question of complicity and its relation to the 'compliant consumerism that's the result of an industrialised society', acknowledging that 'In our natures we're all accomplices in the conspiracy of tame against wild.'[77] But in 'these particular acts of despoliation,' he asserts, 'I feel no complicity of guilt at all. Only anger.'[78] That anger is one of the elements which fuels Meredith's writing and its engagement with place, language and history.

The following chapters trace the chronological development of Meredith's work as well as its roots in the specificity of a particular time and place. His writing returns repeatedly to the question of work – whether as steelworker, schoolteacher or poet – and how this both defines and destroys. In relation to Meredith's concerns with identity, belonging and historical process, the themes of betrayal and complicity, both personal and national, are also recurring motifs. While the novels trace a chronological historical trajectory, there are clear thematic links between Meredith's fiction and poetry which the structure of this book aims to make visible. His work in both genres is equally characterized by an intense interest in language, form and representation.

2

Working and writing in post-industrial Wales: *This* (1984) and *Shifts* (1988)

'Most people don't write about work,' Christopher Meredith has pointed out, 'and yet it's such a big part of people's lives' (I). His comments suggest that not much has changed since Raymond Williams made a similar point in 1979:

> Before Hardy the work of the majority of people never got into fiction as an important experience at all. Of course, the work of the bourgeois world is sometimes rendered as in Balzac's fiction, but not of that of the labourer, the industrial worker. Their experience still offers the possibility, with all sorts of difficulties, of seeing whether the realist form is capable of extension and transformation.[1]

A concern with work, with the 'paradox . . . that your job is both what you are and what destroys you', is one of the most important strands in Meredith's work.[2] It is closely intertwined with his concerns with language, place, history and time: the jobs we do often depend upon where and when we live or, conversely, on whether we are prepared to move. The history of industrialization in the south Wales valleys demonstrates this in particularly stark relief. Meredith's 'extension and transformation' of literary forms to enable the exploration of the subject, however, involves poetry and drama as well as the novel.

In retrospect, the poems in Meredith's first collection, *This* (1984), signal, sometimes obliquely, some of the key themes which were to preoccupy him over the next few decades. During this time he was also writing, over a period of some years, what became his groundbreaking novel about post-industrial Wales, *Shifts* (1988).

Although formally very different, two texts are linked by a concern with the subjects of work and place which has its roots in his own experience and that of his family and community.

Meredith's own working life began with a paper round when he was a child. When he was in sixth form he got a summer job in a factory near Abergavenny which made car filters. Workers for the assembly line, mainly women, came in by bus from the Heads of the Valleys. It was, he remembers, 'Absolutely bloody awful and I learnt a lot about alienation and work there' (I). Workers got half an hour for lunch and a ten-minute break in the afternoon twice a week. On one occasion, he remembered, the foreman came in and gave the workers on the assembly line swivel chairs. Half an hour later they were photographed in the chairs and then the foreman removed the chairs again. 'It made me interested in work and how destructive it is,' Meredith says. 'It was the most destructive job I've had. School teaching was the hardest but that was the most destructive. Work simultaneously defines and destroys you. A job becomes part of a person even if they hate it' (I).

Before he went to university Meredith worked for three months for the British Steel Corporation in the Ebbw Vale steelworks where his father worked. He worked in the open hearth, the furnace that melts steel and recycles scrap, and at this point enjoyed the experience, finding it 'anarchic' (I). Although it was dangerous and dirty he felt then that 'I can do this, I can work properly' (I). After graduating in 1976 with what he felt was not a vocational degree (a BA in English and philosophy) he had no interest in a career which he saw as 'a quaint idea invented by the middle classes' (I). There was not a lot of work around and, he says, 'I was so green!' (I). So he returned to the Ebbw Vale steelworks. This time the experience was very different. First, the steelworks was in the process of running down – steelmaking ceased at Ebbw Vale in 1977 – so all the jobs were on contracts. Secondly, as he put it, the job 'doesn't seem the same when you realize this is the rest of your life' (I). His father had worked in the coke ovens for many years, becoming foreman there, so he oversaw the closing of the coke ovens, after which he became tinplate inspector. Meredith himself worked in

Figure 9. Christopher Meredith on the mountain above
Defynnog, *c.*1980. Photograph: V. A. Meredith.

the hot mill and left a few weeks before that closed to train as a
teacher.

Taking up his teaching post at Brecon High School in 1978
entailed not just a new job but a move to a very different geographical area. From 1979 to 1981 Meredith lived in Defynnog,
about ten miles west of Brecon, in 7 Church Row, part of a row of
former almshouses backing directly onto the ancient churchyard
around the church of St Cynog. Parts of the church are reputed to

37

date from the eleventh century and a Romano-Celtic stone bearing a Latin inscription and vestiges of ogham script, found built into the church tower, is now in the church porch.[3] With no back gardens, the almshouse windows look directly onto the graveyard. Meredith recalled that: 'Three Gwenllians were buried just outside my kitchen window, and beyond them was a stupendous, funereal yew.'[4] According to some estimates the Defynnog yew may be anything between 2,000 and 5,000 years old.[5] After Meredith's marriage to Valerie Smythe, the couple moved to Crud-y-Rhos in Bronllys, a house with views of Mynydd Troed and the Black Mountains. In February 1987 they moved to Brecon itself.

These new places kick-started Meredith's writing but also sent it in new directions. It was while working as a teacher and living in the 'freezing, tiny house' in Defynnog during a couple of very hard winters that Meredith found himself turning back to the poetry he had dismissed as a student:

> To my surprise I discovered that the death of poetry had been a temporary business. The discipline of having to read poems I mightn't otherwise have looked at in order to teach them and to play advocate for them to teenagers had something to do with this, as well as the place where I was living.[6]

His work as a teacher was 'grindingly hard' and the house had no central heating so 'I'd get back home dog-tired to a dark cold house and have to clean out the ashes from the single grate . . . and light a fresh wood-and-coal fire.'[7] On the other hand, this was the most rural place Meredith had ever lived, and that experience, of hearing apples drop to the ground or watching logs burning on his hearth, fed directly into the poems which became his debut collection.

Finding a place: This *(1984)*

Living in Breconshire seems to have given Meredith the distance he needed to look back at his earlier experience and transform it into art. Throughout *This* there is a strong sense of a poet actively seeking his 'place' – both in the sense of his *bro* (land, region or vale), and in the sense of his subject matter, his voice and his forms: 'And this, perhaps, is where I find my place / In all that web of routes and possibilities', he writes in 'By Bronllys Castle' (*T*, 35). In the first poem in *This*, 'Breaking Wood', Meredith uses the work of chopping firewood to explore the play of closeness and alienation between himself and his father:

> Swotting for exams I'd stop at noon
> and recreate myself in the yard
> with axe and splitting stick for firewood.
> The axe was too big, and blunt
> from squaring pitprops a hundred years ago
> my father said.   (*T*, 7)

The move from mental to manual labour is both 'recreation' (in the sense of refreshing entertainment) and 're-creation' of self. The axe reconnects the educated poet to his father's manual job, especially the tradition of coalmining. 'Recreat[ing]' himself through manual work earns his father's approval but so does learning:

> . . . My father called this good.
> In his book it was right, in working men's eyes,
> to learn and labour and try to rise.

The poem explores possible identities formed through work through different kinds of wood: the split firewood; the axe handle 'dead like a fern on coal'; the 'wood become dead page' on which the poet writes; and finally the firewood that the adult poet takes back to his parents in the boot of his car. In the distance between father and son, which is also the difference between someone who has been a manual labourer and one who has 'risen' but feels that he must 'apolog[ize] for what I am', there is an ambivalence about what 'work' might mean and how it is valued.

In a review of *This*, John Barnie praised its 'attention to sensuous detail reminiscent of [Seamus] Heaney' and suggested that a number of the poems in the collection 'are concerned with the adult poet's sense of alienation despite himself from the working class familial bonds which he felt so strongly as a child'.[8] In sociological terms, Barnie sees these poems as testimony to the spread of post-war higher education which, he argues, 'creamed off the talented among working class boys', separating them from their community and leaving them 'caught between a reverence and a need for the past and a recognition that education has separated them in profound ways from it'.[9] The result is 'a yearning to be accepted by the community as one of its own, and a compensating emphasis on memory of childhood days before the crisis was precipitated'.[10] This theme, he argues, is 'so common among South Wales poets as to be a distinguishing feature of Anglo-Welsh verse' although he also notes that it is important in the work of Heaney, as in 'Digging' or 'Follower'.[11]

The comparison with Heaney is a useful one, not only in terms of Meredith's treatment of sensuous detail and childhood memory but also his handling of poetic form and language. In both 'Digging' and 'Follower', Heaney uses the metaphor of a physical activity – digging potato drills in the former and ploughing in the latter – to explore the relationship between father and son and to affirm the latter's commitment to poetry.[12] 'Between my finger and my thumb / The squat pen rests. / I'll dig with it' he concludes in 'Digging'.[13] Heaney's poetic treatment of Irish rural experience, including manual labour, seems to have provided a liberating (and non-English) model for Meredith. An informed familiarity with Heaney's work is evident in several poems in *This*, most explicitly 'The Early Purge' (*T*, 29–30) which rewrites Heaney's 'The Early Purges'.[14] Moreover, the second poem of *This*, 'After rain in Galway' (*T*, 9), seems to invite a comparison with Irish poets and suggest that Meredith should not be confined within the 'Anglo-Welsh' context Barnie invokes.

The theme of work runs through several poems in *This*. Reading the tombstones 'In Ebenezer Churchyard, Sirhowy', the poet notes the grave of 'Jane Pryce diweddar o Swydd Feironydd / dead with her baby and others respectable' identified by 'their trades in

English' inscribed on the eroding headstones (*T*, 20–1). This is a return to Meredith's early *milltir sgwâr* and the graveyard of the Ebenezer Independent Chapel in Tredegar which includes the graves of those 'who walked from the west. / Twelve shillings a week instead of eight.' The need for work forces a change of place (as it has done for Meredith himself), and thus a change of identity. In 'The Vegetable Patch' (*T*, 32), it is the manual work of digging over the vegetable bed each year which provokes a meditation on the evidence of the past. The poem perhaps obliquely glances back at Heaney's 'Digging' but here it is the poet who wields the spade. The broken shards of pottery that are turned up offer fragments of potential contact with previous inhabitants. Like chopping firewood, the mundane work of digging connects the poet to history.

The labour of teaching is connected more closely to the question of language and of writing as work, another theme which runs through Meredith's writing. 'The Early Purge' (*T*, 29–30), as noted, reworks Heaney's 'The Early Purges', which deals with the drowning of unwanted kittens witnessed when the poet was six: 'But on well-run farms pests have to be kept down' concludes the adult Heaney.[15] In contrast, Meredith depicts a teacher watching a boy struggling to write:

> While others wrote I sneaked up.
> 'No work?'
> He huddled on his book
> but I pulled him back.
> Two broken lines of writhing words
> faulted like seams deep down in troubled earth,
> buckled, smashed.

Like Heaney's kittens, this boy will be 'purged'. He is labelled – '"Lower ability" we wrote on reports, thought: / pity. Thick.' – and 'shifted' to another class. His inability to produce appropriate written 'work' condemns him to manual labour, possibly mining coal. In another poem, 'Jets' (*T*, 31), the teacher-poet attempts to assuage doubts about his own 'work', by comparing himself to the pilots of the fighter jets training overhead: 'At least I'm not out there learning to kill' he thinks. But both poems acknowledge his own complicity in the system which uses his labour: 'I *work for* who in office / Shuts books to put more octane in the tank' (*T*, 31; emphasis added).

The move to Bronllys gave Meredith yet another landscape where history was written as if on a palimpsest. Exploring the picturesque area round his 'new home' in 'By Bronllys Castle' he is tentatively looking for his 'place' (*T*, 35–6). Instead he finds a 'man-soaked countryside' saturated with a history of violence and oppression. The castle is a place of Gothic foreboding where it is easy to imagine 'The predatory eye of some cool thug / Asserting lordship from his dead tower'. A Norman motte and bailey, Bronllys Castle was probably built by Richard FitzPons in the eleventh century on land he had seized during the Norman incursion into Wales. It is a very material representation of the history of Anglo-Norman oppression which would become the subject of Meredith's second novel, *Griffri*. The poem ends with the poet failing to find the path, sliding through mud and weeds into a fence and startled by an owl, another 'cool predator' – this is not yet his 'place'. In comparison with 'Six Poems for Troedrhiwgwair', what is missing in this still unfamiliar rural landscape is the layering of family and community history which gives meaning to the places of his child-hood.

The work of these years shows Meredith finding his way through experimentation to the subjects, styles and voice that he would make his own. His accommodation with the Welsh language he had learned as an adult is a crucial part of this and he also ex-periments with Welsh poetic forms. The use of alliteration and assonance in 'Come Blade', which opens 'Loose with work I slack walk' (*T*, 23), for instance, produces a style Barnie sees as 'com-pounded of Hughes, Dylan Thomas and Hopkins, with behind it the potential in English rhythm and sound exploited by Middle and Old English poets'.[16] Except for the echoes of cynghanedd it is not obviously Welsh. Only two poems in *This* include any Welsh language other than place-names. The title poem, 'This' (*T*, 22) refers to 'some pwca'r trwyn' (the fairy or goblin said to haunt Trwyn Farm in Mynyddislwyn).[17] 'In Ebenezer Churchyard, Sirhowy' includes the words inscribed on the tombstone already quoted above (*T*, 20–1). Otherwise, while the places and names may be Welsh, the rest of the language often appears resolutely English. Indeed, 'This', which opens 'There's not a puddle by a mountain track / but has some inundation myth / no nook without some gelert dead', rejects the romanticism of Welsh legend which saturates the landscape to the point of cliché. Instead, it posits a 'lover on his own / a dowdy shrunk atlantis'. The poet here, as in 'By Bronllys Castle', appears as a lone individual separated from family, community and beloved.

There was at this point a wider debate going on around the use of the term 'Anglo-Welsh' and the question of whether the new generation of new poets (among them Tony Curtis, Duncan Bush, Robert Minhinnick and Mike Jenkins) were less closely connected to the Welsh language than earlier poets such as R. S. Thomas or Idris Davies had been. In a contribution to a roundtable on the Welsh language and Anglo-Welsh poets in *Poetry Wales* in 1984 entitled 'Saying it in Saesneg' Meredith addressed his own relationship with Welsh, making its increasing importance to his writing clear. He analysed an imitation Shakespearean sonnet he had written five years earlier which opened in what appears to be an archaic Shakespearan register: 'When I do see my visage in the glass.'[18] Meredith points out that the first line is, in fact, a translation of the opening line of a poem by the nineteenth-century Welsh poet Islwyn (William Thomas): 'Wrth edrych ar fy agwedd yn yr drych.'[19] One lesson that Meredith draws from his *soi-disant* 'smug little imitation' is 'the danger of working too much from literature and not enough from experience'.[20] The second point he makes is that the poem illustrates the 'interplay' between the two languages, the ways in which 'associations of sound, image, and theme' can occur.[21]

The crucial point for Meredith, however, is 'that the Welsh language is a major element of the context in which I write'.[22] While he eschews the slightly forced modes that can come with experimentation with Welsh alliteration in English ('Come Blade' is perhaps an example of this), he notes that there was one piece where he felt that he had to use some Welsh:

> I did this reluctantly, after many drafts over a long period – I'm always irritated by foreign tags in poems – but the words insisted on being there. It says something about the difficulty of being Welsh and having to write in English.[23]

Having learned Welsh meant that he was now in a position to understand his own history and literature. The 'fractured, discontinuous historical sense of most Welsh people', he argues, has led to various responses: absurd posturing patriotism, 'doomy sentimentalism', and 'English-like incomprehension and dismissive contempt'.[24] Within this context, the dismissal of romantic Welsh legend in 'This' is a conscious refusal to indulge in either self-deceiving patriotism or sentimentalism.

The two poems which close *This* – 'Christening Pot Boiler' (*T*, 39–40) and 'Still Life' (*T*, 41) – celebrate the arrival of the poet's son and suggest a new beginning poetically as well as personally. Drawing on the Welsh tradition of the praise poem, 'Christening Pot Boiler' is an energetically inventive list of synonyms or metaphors for an unborn/newborn child which ends in a flurry of feminine rhymes:

> home breaker
> mess maker
> distraught squaller
> future crawler,
> welcome (*T*, 39–40)

This experiment with the traditional technique of *dyfalu* (a 'cadenza-like sequence of swift metaphors and lightening comparisons'[25]) demonstrates the importance of Meredith's engagement with traditional Welsh poetry in both the original and translation. The device is associated with Dafydd ap Gwilym, especially in poems such as 'Y Seren' (The Star) or 'Yr Wylan' (The Seagull).[26] It has been sympathetically rendered in the translations of his work by Glyn Jones, a writer Meredith admires, as in 'The Fog', for instance: 'Call you clumsy canvas, big / Rain-spiller, blanket-baggy, / Black web-work, mountain-masker.'[27]

After *This* was published, Meredith found that he was writing very little poetry (although he was contributing reviews and articles to magazines such as *Planet*), partly because of the 'particularly nasty' political conditions in the early 1980s: 'There was an atmosphere of political fear, with great erosions of civil liberties, the miners' strike, the Cardiff conspiracy trials.'[28] The steel strike of 1980, now mostly forgotten but a kind of dry run for Thatcher's determination to break the unions during the miners' strike, is another important context.[29] This was one of the biggest strikes of post-war history when 100,000 workers employed by the nationally owned British Steel Corporation downed tools for thirteen weeks, partly for a wage increase but also to protect jobs that were threatened by BSC's plans to cut around a third of its workforce. Ian Jack who visited Port Talbot during the strike felt that this was the beginning of a 'new age' in terms of class divisions.[30] Another context which affected many Welsh writers in the early 1980s was the aftermath of the 1979 referendum in which 20.26 per cent voted for and 79.74 per cent against devolution for Wales. For many of the 'second flowering' of Anglo-Welsh writers, such as Harri Webb, this was so devastating that some stopped writing altogether.

While Meredith tried to address some of these political issues directly in poems, he found it difficult and turned back to the novel he had started three years earlier. This writing was 'a fairly secretive process': 'I wasn't even entirely sure if it was a novel at first', he has said, suggesting the lack of models then available.[31] As he records in 'Telling and the Time' (2000), he finally decided to make himself work on the novel every day until it was finished.[32] Writing *Shifts* took seven years but it was a matter of 'routines', of setting aside one hour a day and making himself write.[33]

During this period he also wrote a play for radio, *The Carved Chair* (1987), which was performed at the Sherman Theatre in Cardiff by Made in Wales Stage Company in May 1986. A two-hander, *The Carved Chair* is what might be called a 'butty play'. (In an interview with the Rhondda novelist Richard John Evans in 2001, Meredith suggested that they had between them invented a new form – the 'butty novel'.[34]) Its characters are two middle-aged men, Mal and Ben, 58-year-old redundant steelworkers. Mal is a failed artist: the picture of the steelworks which he had hoped would 'get to the centre of things . . . just turned out a mess' (*CC*, 73). The themes and motifs of the play anticipate those which Meredith was exploring in greater depth in *Shifts*. The action (or non-action) of *The Carved Chair* is the conversation between the two men while they are killing time in a museum or art gallery waiting for Ben's wife, who is looking at a painting by Renoir. As unlikely a pair of tragi-comic philosophers as any in a Samuel Beckett play, Ben and Mal's seemingly rambling and very funny conversation begins to set out a kind of manifesto for the art that Meredith was creating himself.

The play stages a contrast between different concepts of art. The painting of an over-dressed woman Ben's wife is admiring sounds very much like Renoir's 'The Parisian Girl' (La Parisienne) (1874), probably the best-known painting in the National Museum in Cardiff. This Impressionist painting of a young woman in an elaborately flounced blue dress connotes both high art and an appropriate artistic subject matter. Tellingly, Ben prefers the 'ones with the dots' (*CC*, 69) – the technique known as 'Pointilism' (*CC*, 92) as Mal tells him. Lugging plastic bags full of tinned food, Mal and Ben find a carved chair standing on its own in a gallery. Unable to decide whether or not this is an exhibit (Mal cites the example of Duchamp's urinal – 'Piss artist was he?' is Ben's response (*CC*, 70)), they eventually sit on it. The chair features caryatids on the front legs and a green man – 'a man's face in a tree. With his mouth open' (*CC*, 70) – on the backrest. In contrast to the Renoir, it represents a native Welsh tradition which is as much about craftsmanship (and wood) as art.

At the heart of the play is an image that is reworked in *Shifts*: showing a new safety officer around the cellars under the steelworks, Mal finds a large room not on the plans:

MAL: . . . The torches could just about reach right across to the far wall
. . . And right in the middle (*hesitates*)

BEN: Aye?

MAL: Right in the middle there was a – a wheelbarrow.

(CC, 75)

The bathos of this is enhanced by the fact that the wheelbarrow is full of 'dust. Dirt. Lumps of mortar. That's all' (*CC*, 76). This seems an anti-climax, a dead-end. And yet the wheelbarrow in this underground industrial chamber, like the carved chair or Duchamp's urinal, is recognized by Mal as sculpture: 'Ready-made art they call it' (*CC*, 79). In a key passage he articulates a theory of art which echoes this image:

MAL: . . . When I felt like I was getting somewhere with it, I used to think the painting was like a maze, only more complicated. It would be in the dark and the brushes would be like lamps that lit it all up so you could see where you were going. Gradually you'd work towards the one place, the centre where it all grew out from. It wouldn't be literally in the centre of the picture, but I mean like a focus.

(CC, 87–8)

The 'risk' of art (*CC*, 89), he notes, is that you don't know if you will ever get to where you want to be. The almost banal following exchange suggests a different possibility:

MAL: . . . It's having that focus, that's what's important for me.

BEN: You've found it haven't you?

MAL: There never was one.

BEN: This could be it.

MAL: What?

BEN: That wheelbarrow. This room. This could be where everything leads.

MAL: There's nothing here.

BEN: Except us.

(CC, 90)

'There's nothing here.' *'Except us.'* It is perhaps too literal to read this play as Meredith's own discovery of his own subject matter – the wheelbarrow as 'found art' representing the ordinary experience of working life (what was missing in Meredith's imitation Shakespearean sonnet) and the two tragi-comic middle-aged and redundant working-class 'm[e]n of steel' (*CC*, 80) who are not the usual stuff of high art. Yet, like an outline sketch map, this play points the way to the new kind of art which Meredith was developing in *Shifts*.

Shifts *(1988) and 'shifts': work, history and language*

'The simplest descriptive novel about working-class life,' Raymond Williams argued in 1982, 'is already, by being written, a significant and positive cultural intervention. For it is not, even yet, what a novel is supposed to be.'[35] Within this context it is not surprising that as he was writing *Shifts* Meredith was not 'even entirely sure if it was a novel at first'.[36] Published just six years after Williams's comments, *Shifts* is far more than a simple description of working-class life. Indeed, it goes a considerable way towards effecting the kind of extension and transformation of the realist novel Williams argued was necessary. *Shifts* combines a sharply observed realism with modernist-informed experimentalism. Written from Meredith's own experience of industrial work, the novel also uses a wide range of intertexts – from Shakespeare, Dylan Thomas's *Under Milk Wood* (1954) and Hardy's *The Return of the Native* (1878) to Dick Whittington, Superman comics (the 'man of steel') and Beatles' lyrics – in order to question their value to *post*-industrial working-class Welsh lives.

For at the same time as it describes in detail the experience of working in heavy industry in south Wales, *Shifts* is documenting the end of that tradition. The novel is, as Stephen Knight has said, 'the classic statement about [the post-industrial] situation, both social and personal'.[37] As such it is both within and reworking the tradition that Williams identified in 'The Welsh Industrial Novel'

(1979). He saw this form as emerging after 1917 and evidencing what he calls a 'specifically Welsh structure of feeling, but . . . still facing quite radical problems of form'.[38] What distinguishes the industrial novel, Williams argues, is the fact that industrial work and its characteristic place and communities are not just a background or setting but 'pressing and formative, and the most general social relations are directly experienced within the most personal'.[39] This tradition encompasses, for instance, the work of Jack Jones, Gwyn Jones, Gwyn Thomas and Lewis Jones. Its most famous text is probably Richard Llewellyn's romanticized *How Green Was My Valley* (1939), made into a popular Hollywood film starring Roddy McDowell by John Ford in 1941. Llewellyn's novel is, Williams remarks acerbically, 'widely and properly seen as the export version of the Welsh industrial experience'.[40] In contrast, *Shifts* examines what happens to that 'specifically Welsh structure of feeling' when the forms of industrial work which shaped it disappear.

Set in 1977 during the nine months before the closing down of the steel-making parts of a steelworks in a declining south Wales valleys town, *Shifts* interweaves the stories of four characters in their late twenties: Jack Priday has just returned to his home area after several years in Lancashire and is in search of work and somewhere to live; his former school friend Keith Watkins works at the steel plant and, in the face of its imminent closure, turns to local history in search of some kind of meaning; Judith, Keith's wife, is bored by their marriage but seems unable to commit to either a job or getting pregnant; finally, 'O' or Rob (nicknamed 'Snobs' in school), also a steelworker, is routinely bullied by his fellow-workers and finds structure through routines such as keeping a tally of his re-using of a Sunblest plastic bag for his sandwiches or the rats he kills. Finding work at the steelworks but thrown out by his landlady, Jack moves in with Keith and Judith and starts an affair with Judith. Eventually O tells Keith about the affair, Jack leaves the area again and with the closure of the steelworks the other characters look for other jobs. Through these interwoven stories Meredith explores how human beings find meaning for their lives through work and what Jack refers to as the 'fucking biological imperative' (*S*, 75).

As the title suggests, the novel is concerned with the several types of time and how these structure human lives. The first is the monotonous routines of industrial shift work. The opening associates this mechanized clock time with O:

> O clocked off at exactly half past three. He had stood with his card in the timeclock, his palm poised above the punchlever, and waited till the second hand jerked up to the twelve . . .
> O stood, as usual, near the litter basket with Sully, Wayne and a few others waiting for their bus outside the gate. He looked across at the bank of colourless grass and its few blackened unidentifiable trees. They looked dead but were only January dead. (*S*, 7)

The unsettling visual rhyme between 'O clocked' and 'o'clock' immediately destabilizes what might appear to be a realist novel. O's name, 'signifying nothing' as Jack notes (*S*, 26), suggests the ways in which the mechanical clock time of industrial work destroys individual identity, reducing human beings to 'zero'. Rob's given name suggests that he has been 'robbed' of the identity that should be his birthright. Later Jack speculates that O, like Nogood Boyo in *Under Milkwood*, dreams of 'Nothing' (*S*, 188). As Richard Poole suggests in his 'Afterword' to *Shifts*, 'Macbeth's curt dismissal of existence as "a tale / Told by an idiot, full of sound and fury, / Signifying nothing" is nihilism pure and simple, the testament of a man who has irrevocably cut himself off from humanity' (*S*, 220). But a further question here is, who is the 'idiot', and who is telling the tale?

The 'only January dead' trees signal a different kind of time: the annual cycle of natural or biological seasonal change disrupted by the exigencies of industrialization. Working nightshifts has altered Keith's biological sense of time: 'Put his bodyclock wrong (*S*, 33). Jack's attempt to construct himself as part of a natural cycle – '"return[ing] to the breeding grounds . . . The old salmon leaping up the river . . . The fucking biological imperative"' (*S*, 75) – rings hollow when it is revealed at the end of the novel that the girl he left in Accrington was pregnant (*S*, 209–10). Biological time contrasts with the images of clocks which run through the novel: the stopped clock in the Cefn Club; the black plastic clock Jack gives to Keith and Judith; the market clock looking 'indifferently' over the town square (*S*, 51). Jack reflects on the 'time wasted when you sit in buses or wait in a queue. All your life nearly' (*S*, 168). This is time, as Jack's subsequent comment 'Let me go at two to my devotions' (*S*, 169) suggests, which is without the meaning bestowed on it by the structures of either religious belief or meaningful work. While this emptiness at the heart of human existence might be existential in Sartrean terms, the overriding suggestion in the novel is that in this time and place it has a particular historical and social specificity.

The second major 'shift' indicated by the title is the process of de-industrialization in Britain, particularly in south Wales, as a moment of radical historical and social change. As the steelworks runs down, the neat certainties of shift work begin to loosen and the men are employed on short-term contracts. However uncongenial shift work is, its loss leaves a vacuum which exposes how male identity is defined by work. Jack's father worked at the steelworks until he retired: 'Every shift leaving the house with his sandwiches in the old oxo tin' (*S*, 10). The 'oxo' tin, implying 'zero times zero', indicates the hollowness of these 'shifts'. He was 'The old hardworking *good timekeeping* type who didn't know that in the end that makes no difference' (*S*, 10; emphasis added). In contrast, Jack is given a contract for thirty-six weeks and told paternalistically: 'If the plant is still working in your department you'll be laid off and if you've been a good boy we'll take you on for another contract' (*S*, 12). Reminded of the 'old days' another steelworker, Ben, expostulates:

> 'They'm on'y fucking rolling one shift mind, days regular five days a bastard week. Three shifts a day it used to be. Three shifts a fucking day seven days a week . . . Twenty four hours a day. Six till two, two till ten, ten till bollocking six. Continuous rolling. End of a shift you 'ouldn' know whether you was coming or bastard going.' (*S*, 106)

Ben's anger expresses resentment at these imposed structures *and* frustration at their reduction and the subsequent loss of work, income and status. This is the problem that Meredith identifies when he states of the novel: 'the psychology of the thing's complex, built on a paradox – that your job is both what you are and what destroys you' (*S*, 231).

The imminent closure of the steelworks leaves the characters in a kind of limbo similar to the 'paralysis' Joyce depicted in *Dubliners*. Even marriage is only another kind of palliative, like sex, alcohol or drugs: Jack dismisses Keith and Judith's marriage as 'the anaesthesia to which they are accustomed' (*S*, 90). Jack is an unreliable witness but the novel makes it clear that these characters have to find new ways to give meaning to their lives. When Sully, another steelworker about to be laid off, proposes to his girlfriend because 'There's fuck all else to do' (*S*, 130), Jack reflects that: 'Sully, like everybody else, was just looking for a bearable way of living' (*S*, 130). Although Sully is fond of his girlfriend, however, Jack seems unable to love.

Meredith's depiction of the process of de-industrialization resonates closely with Raymond Williams's account of Welsh history as a series of 'radical shifts'. As Williams argued in 'Wales and England' (1983):

> if there is one thing to insist on in analysing Welsh culture it is the complex of forced and acquired discontinuities: a broken series of *radical shifts*, within which we have to mark not only certain social and linguistic continuities but many acts of self-definition by negation, by alternation and by contrast.[41]

Shifts explores the effects of those 'radical shifts' forced on characters by a historical process over which they have no control and which they barely understand. The languages and narratives which structured lives in this place in the past – the Welsh language, rural work, industrial work, religious belief, civic engagement, class unity and unionization – no longer have currency. This is a society and a culture that is 'broken' by the force of repeated historical changes but within which the traces of social and linguistic continuities are just discernible and signal potential alternatives.

Jack, Keith, Judith, O and the other characters have to negotiate the process of redefining or 're-creating' themselves but their options, weighted down by history, are limited. Their unconscious attempts to redefine themselves are often revealed through dreams or nightmares: Judith dreams of swimming in a lake surrounded by mountains, an image of freedom (*S*, 31); Jack of going 'home' to the house he grew up in which has been knocked down, a half-nightmare which he attempts to replace by an image of an ice cave, a different kind of 'home' (*S*, 158, 175); O, perhaps, dreams of 'nothing'. Keith takes refuge in history itself which Jack sees as another dead-end: 'You like history because it's safe' (*S*, 208) he tells him. Part of the structural irony of the text is that history is far from safe.

'History is the reality to which we are trying to awake', Meredith wrote in a 1986 review of Gwyn Thomas's historical novel about the 1831 Merthyr Rising, *All Things Betray Thee* (1949).[42] Meredith's formula revises Stephen Dedalus's famous pronouncement in *Ulysses* (1922) – 'History . . . is a nightmare from which I am trying to awake.'[43] Both resonate with Marx's Gothic image of the constraints of history: 'The tradition of all the dead generations weighs like a nightmare on the brain of the living.'[44] While *Shifts* is a novel about history rather than a historical novel, it shares with *All Things Betray Thee* a concern with moments of radical change. Thomas's novel depicts the beginnings of industrialization as an 'engine of change' while *Shifts* depicts its end.[45] While Meredith criticizes Thomas for a falsification of historical specificity – *All Things Betray Thee* makes no reference to the Welsh language and places and characters are given English-sounding names – he praises the novel as 'a valiant and energetic attempt to show dawning political self-awareness from the inside and so to recover a piece of our history *pertinent to these times*'.[46] Like *All Things Betray Thee*, *Shifts* portrays a 'community in turmoil' but it provides exactly the vivid 'social detail and multi-cultural mix' which for Meredith was missing from Thomas's novel.[47] What *Shifts* also does, however, is point to the loss of the possibility of a communal political solution (however violent) which animates Thomas's account of the Merthyr Rising. In this sense *Shifts* reverses the trajectory of *How Green Was My Valley* where Llewellyn suggests that what finally destroyed the homogenous and pastoral Welsh community was the class action of unionization.[48] Despite their entanglement, Jack, Keith, Judith and O are isolated individuals, not part of a coherent stable community.

Reviewers initially tended to praise *Shifts*'s 'gritty realism' in a way that appears to locate it in the tradition of realist industrial fiction. While Meredith found this gratifying – he had 'never come across any convincing fiction about my own part of the world and that was something I wanted to achieve' – he also found the tag 'irritating' and 'limiting'.[49] 'Perhaps "grittily realistic" is just genteel code for working class' is his acerbic conclusion.[50] What a focus on the social realism of the text can obscure is how technically sophisticated and 'worked' the novel is in its deployment of four alternating points of view and its patterning of imagery, language and style. As Poole puts it: 'Under the text's seemingly plain skin beats an ambitious symbolist heart, and the more one probes it, the more one uncovers the complex patterning of a poetic novel of ideas' (*S*, 215).

Shifts is a 'butty novel' which complicates the triangle of *The Carved Chair*. At the steelworks the returned Jack bumps into Keith in the showers in a scene which suggests their symbolic function as doubles:

> As he turned to face out, someone in the opposite cubicle did the same. It was like turning to face a mirror.
>
> . . .
>
> My old butty my old mate straight out of prehistory and not fossilized not mummified but alive, like myself in a mirror.
>
> Jack stepped forward.
>
> 'Excuse me' he said. 'Are you Keith Watkins, mild-mannered reporter of the Daily Planet, or are you a Man of Steel?' (*S*, 68)

In *Shifts* Meredith utilizes the 'polyphony of shifting view points and times' which had fascinated him in fiction as a child.[51] The novel shifts between four different points of view using character focalization which often moves into stream-of-consciousness techniques to render interiority. While a scene is sometimes repeated from another point of view (as when we see Jack and Keith's different responses to the figure of Britannia on the iron table leg), we never see two different points of view within a single scene until the end.

Meredith was conscious that the shape of the book echoed its themes: 'The book came to be about the fact that we are marooned individuals yet we live in communities. This is the paradox of Thatcher's "There is no such thing as society"' (I). The novel's focus on individual interiority foregrounds the characters' failure to connect. As Judith tells Jack at the end: 'Neither you or him [Keith] have got anything to do with me' (*S*, 201). While this can be read as an existential condition it is also the result of very specific historical and social circumstances. Jack remembers his father's analysis of the effects of capitalism: 'They got all the coal and ore so they go and rip up the rails . . . maroon us' (*S*, 204). What Raymond Williams calls the 'discontinuities: [the] broken series of radical shifts' which mark Welsh culture and identity are echoed in the discontinuities of the narrative structure of the novel itself.

Similarly, the landscapes of the novel depict the characteristically paradoxical juxtaposition of the industrial and the rural which Williams sees as 'manifest[ing] a consciousness of history'.[52] As a 'returned native' (*S*, 79) who has stopped 'two valleys short' (*S*, 43) of his birthplace, Jack provides a participant-observer's view of the place:

> Below him, to the north east, his home town lay. A cushion of trees where the park was. A tumble of grey slated oblongs where the shopping streets followed the hill. The terraces opposite contouring the valley side. Gaps of demolition and the ageing-new estates. Far to the north where the valley disappeared into the moorland were the factories. At the southern end, a tip, startlingly black in the hard light, in the process of being reclaimed . . . Above the terraces and a few posher houses on

the eastern side of the valley were the pine plantations . . . beyond the mountain the two miles tangle of steelworks.

To the west slightly, saddled in a curve of the mountain he stood on was the Grib pond . . . Grib pronounced grebe, like the bird . . .

Near the pond were the cemeteries. There was some reason for having the cemeteries on the mountain . . . Keith would know. (*S*, 69–70)

While it's not named, such detailed descriptions place the action in Meredith's home patch: Cefn Golau, Tredegar, Ebbw Vale. The name 'Gwedog Valley' (*S*, 83), which Meredith adopts for his fiction, is borrowed from the name of an ancient farmhouse in the Tredegar area 'Llyswedog' or 'Llys Gwedog' (Gwedog's Court).[53]

This is a landscape which offers a palimpsest of history, although Jack does not know this history and Keith is only just starting to understand it. The cemeteries are on 'the tops', as Keith later tells Jack, because after the cholera epidemics in the 1840s, 'They thought it was safer to bury them away from the town' (*S*, 91). Professor Prys-Thomas offers another version of Williams's contrasts when he argues that the steel town is 'on many frontiers . . . the frontier of rural and industrial; the frontier of farmland and desert; the frontier of moorland and dense forest' (*S*, 155). What Keith, Jack and the others are witnessing is the end of one era of that history as the steelworks which has dominated the area for over a century runs down and history 'shifts' into another gear.

Meredith's depiction of the steelworks is both realistic and symbolic. Initially, we see it through Jack's eyes as a 'big, dark and dirty' place (*S*, 22) which is difficult to comprehend:

'These are the reheating furnaces' Willy said. Jack looked up at their varicose web of green and red painted cooling pipes . . . 'Slabs in the slabyard next door are pushed in the other side and heated up to be rolled into coil. Them doors do open up with them chains and the slabs do drop out. These rolls where they do drop out is called the delivery table, just like in the maternity ward.'

Jack remembered his father using the term 'tapping off' when a neighbour's wife was about to give birth. But that was a metaphor taken from the open hearth furnaces. (*S*, 23)

The steelworks has its own language – 'tapping off', 'roughing mills', the 'slabbing mill', 'finishing', 'a bag' (hose), 'bars' (slabs of red-hot-metal) – and generates its own metaphors. Later, Jack comes to see it as a kind of city with its own coherence:

> hard sunlight displayed all the details of the works. It was spread below them on the other side of the railings . . . Jack swept his eyes along it . . . the converter shop, the blast furnaces, the open hearth, the scrap bay, the coke ovens, all recently shut and decaying, then the parts still working; the hot mill, slabyard, galv, pickler, cold mill . . . He had begun to understand how the place worked, or had worked, so that it no longer seemed, as it had at first with its ruddled stacks and rusting cathedrals, like the nightmare version of an utopian city, though a kind of city it was. (*S*, 181–2)

Contrasted with the steel mill are the 'steep and unpeopled mountain-side' (*S*, 182), which represents the rural past, and the marshmallow factory which is about to open on the industrial estate (*S*, 182), which represents the future and women's employment.

Meredith's sophisticated use of an exceptional range of linguistic registers is one of the great pleasures of this novel. A kind of writer manqué, Jack is obsessed with parody, narrative and puns. (Asked 'Are you Jack?' Meredith's inevitable answer is: 'Yes, and Judith, and O and Keith.' (I)) Returning to his home town is a return to a language Jack has consciously to re-adopt: '"Call me Jack. Everybody does." He practised saying it. Slipping fully back into the patois it was "everybody do" . . .' (*S*, 43). For Jack this re-adopted language – 'Hiya butt. How be? A'right butty. Owzigoin? No' bâd mun' (*S*, 46) – is part of fitting in. He also practises jokes and anecdotes: 'Sort of place where you watch the dartboard and throw darts at the telly. File that one away' (*S*, 51–2). Much of the wit in *Shifts* comes from Jack's play with language, including a bravura parody of *How Green Was My Valley:*

> 'Up comes Donald Crisp and Dai Bando on a tandem . . . "Look you boy bach" says blind Dai. "There's been an explosion up at the pit. Hurry you along now begorrah." Roddy leaps on the crossbar. They

pedal and reach the scene. Young women in shawls wring their hands
. . . Robert Donat bandages Paul Robeson's arm. "Ianto Full-pelt it is"
cries lovely Blodwen wringing her shawl. "Stuck he is in the big hole
he is look you . . .".' (*S*, 165)

This neatly skewers the fraudulent nostalgia of John Ford's film
but it also exposes Jack's lack of authenticity: he has 'been building
up this act for a few weeks' (*S*, 165). Moreover, the motivation for
his performance is Keith's return from a trip to the cholera graves
which Jack calls 'morbid' (*S*, 165) and equates with the kind of
manufactured nostalgia in Ford's film.

Raymond Williams speculated that one of the major stumbling-
blocks which made Welsh working-class life inaccessible to the
new kind of industrial realist novel in the nineteenth century was
'the problems of the two languages'.[54] Meredith's solution to this
is to make a strength of the Welsh-English dialect of the south
Wales valleys, or Wenglish,[55] with its distinctive grammatical con-
structions such as the use of 'do' ('everybody do'), or 'en' for 'isn't'
or 'am not' ('I en trying to shift you'(*S*, 186)), and the use of 'bastard'
or 'fucking' as modifying adjectives. Jack is conscious that this is
Welsh English: '"Last Chance Saloon this used to be." This used to
be. *There's Welsh you speak*' (*S*, 71; emphasis added). In Meredith's
hands this dialect is rhythmic, flexible and expressive – poetic even.
But it is also a marker of the 'radical shifts' which have taken place
in this area. Jack is aware of Welsh lexical borrowings as a residue
of the original language of south Wales. His own unstable identity
is related to this. While his father called him John, 'Jack' is the name
he has chosen for himself (a name with multiple associations – 'Jack
the lad', I'm all right Jack', and so on). His mother, however, called
him 'Shwn or Shwna after the local fashion, or rather old fashion'
(*S*, 43). Similarly, his landlady Connie's name turns out to be
short for Ceinwen (*S*, 53) not, as he originally assumes, Constance.
The names of people and places and dialect words with Welsh
origins such as 'mwtshing' (*S*, 72) or 'cwtshed' (*S*, 158) evidence
what Williams calls the 'linguistic continuities' which mark the
valleys.

The character who comes closest to an understanding of the wider historical processes within which they are situated is Keith. His interest in local history allows him to place himself in relation to time and place. The Ebbw Vale steelworks where Meredith and his father worked had its origins in 1789 when Jeremiah Homfrey (brother of Samuel Homfrey, founder of Tredegar Iron Company), with Walter Watkins, found iron ore in the steep-sided wooded Ebbw Valley and established an iron works on Pen y Cae farm.[56] In 1829 the Ebbw Vale ironworks started producing railway tracks. The Ebbw Vale Iron and Steel Works opened in 1862, with a Bessemer converter and the most powerful blowing machine in the world. By the beginning of the twentieth century Ebbw Vale was the 'largest single surviving site of the late eighteenth-century iron industry'.[57] The steelworks closed in 1929 due to the Depression but re-opened in 1938 with the building of the first European hot strip mill which revolutionized the industry. The 1950s were the 'zenith' of the steel industry in this area, both economically and socially.[58] In 1967 the steelworks were nationalized to become part of the British Steel Corporation along with Llanwern and Port Talbot steelworks. By the 1970s, however, problems of scale and location were such that BSC decided to close down the operation. The coke ovens closed in 1972, the blast furnaces in 1975 and the hot strip mill, as portrayed in *Shifts*, in September 1977. The final cast was made in the open hearth in 1978 and steelmaking then ceased at Ebbw Vale. *Shifts* traces the final nine months from January to September of this closure in 1977 but through Keith's interest in local history it situates this within a much longer time span.

In an early scene, Keith walks the area, trying to piece together the beginnings of its history from place-names and the different ages and styles of the buildings. He is trying to re-imagine what the place would have looked like in 1800 just before the first furnaces were built by Samuel Moonlow:

> Naturally, there would be trees everywhere, even here. Old deciduous forest. Just a patch cleared around the furnace for the smelting . . . He tried to picture the trees, and everything changed. (*S*, 17)

As an Englishman, Moonlow symbolizes the industrial colonization of Wales. His name was chosen, Meredith says, to connote English-ness in its evocation of names like Brownlow in Dickens's *Oliver Twist* (I) but it also serendipitously echoes 'Moonlea' the name given to Gwyn Thomas's fictionalized version of Merthyr, domin-ated by the ironmaster Richard Penbury, in *All Things Betray Thee*. The transformation of the rural valley is emblematic of processes which happened throughout the area.

Keith's quest is blocked by the fact that he doesn't understand the language in which much of this history of place is recorded. As Kirsti Bohata points out, 'the pre- and early industrial history of the area, which still manifests itself in old Welsh place-names is inaccessible to the non-Welsh-speaking inhabitants of the area'.[59] Thus Keith speculates on the function of an old house, not realizing that the clue is in its name: 'Old. Farm perhaps. He could see its name on the gate at the side of the Lion. Henfelin [old mill]' (*S*, 16). This example of '"political" code-switching' (that is the refusal to translate a Welsh word for potential English readers) is important, Bohata argues, because it privileges Welsh speakers and makes a forceful point about the 'historical fracture' brought about by the loss of the Welsh language.[60] Later Keith goes up to the cholera cemetery where he attempts to translate the words on a tombstone: 'ER COF AM / John Williams / O'r lle hwn . . .' (*S*, 161). This is the tombstone that Meredith discusses in his essay, *Cefn Golau: Shooting a Novelist*.

A further problem for Keith is how to write this research up for his talk to the local history society. Should he start with the weather, the workers, Samuel Moonlow, the way the site looks today? These are key questions about the structuring of historical narrative to which Meredith would return in later books. Research-ing Moonlow's life, reading copies of a letter and an account book, makes this history both more vivid and more complicated: 'There was such an ocean to chart, even in one day in one man's life, that Keith was amazed that historians would try to grasp and explain whole civilisations' (*S*, 63). A truck shop coin, a token penny minted by Moonlow, seems to offer some kind of answer as Keith tries to explain to Jack:

'This Moonlow bloke came from nowhere, he –' Keith thought of all the processes of extracting, organising, building, making 'he – all this –' waving a hand at the photographs and the papers '– he got it all moving and in the end he, well, him and a couple of blokes, made a town, and he made his own money. Literally.' (*S*, 118)

The huge historical shifts represented by Moonlow are 'too great for the mind to hold' (*S*, 127). In fact, Moonlow is another version of Jack, as Keith dimly recognizes: 'How Jack went to seek his fortune. Keith remembered the fairy tale. How Moonlow went' (*S*, 87). Jack likens himself to 'those farmers. Zulu was it? You stay till a patch of land is exhausted then find another patch. Except that people don't recover like land' (*S*, 66). Both Moonlow and Jack are nomadic capitalists who exploit a place and a people and then move on.[61] At the end of the novel Jack, having failed to find love with Judith (though she may be pregnant), 'move[s] off the exhausted earth' (*S*, 204) and, like the fairy-tale Jack, seeks his fortune elsewhere.

The real breakthrough for Keith is when he finds an election handbill in a condemned house. On the reverse are handwritten notes for a lay-sermon or discussion in 'a language that was his own, but that he could not understand' (*S*, 127). In this smashed building he feels 'the presence of the dead people who had moved through it . . . *This could be something like contact*' (*S*, 127; emphasis added). This echoes Meredith's own experience of connecting with a photograph of the Nine Mile Point strike in *The Road to Wigan Pier*: '*Contact*'.[62] Keith's research elicits a tacit respect from the professional historian when he shows the notes to Professor Prys-Thomas. He translates them – '*Dinistr y Deml* – the Destruction of the Temple; *Dinistr Jerusalem* – the Destruction of Jerusalem; and here, *Diwedd y Byd* – the End of the World. Powerful stuff' (*S*, 155) – making their symbolic significance available to Keith.

It is Keith with his painfully won knowledge of the past who comes closest to understanding historical process in the present. He now has a language in which to interpret these 'shifts'. Watching the last slab passing through the rolls of the roughing stands and into the coiler, he recognizes this as 'Dinistr y deml, though not, of course, diwedd y byd' (*S*, 211):

> The last slab. It was a non-event . . . Yet it seemed to Keith that the changes were very big . . . Odourless, invisible history would blow them all apart and they would hurtle away from each other through space and never really understand what had *shifted* them. Except blowing apart was the wrong idea because it was a continuing process, evolving and breaking slowly and then occasionally twitching like this. And it included everything. (*S*, 211)

A better metaphor, he decides, is an image of a human jaw chewing food:

> History was like that. It transformed things without their understanding it and the brain, which seemed in control – Moonlows and managers and governments – it, they, were trapped too. Except history seemed now too thin a word for this. (*S*, 212)

These ideas about history and time are developed by Meredith in subsequent novels, particularly *Griffri* and *Sidereal Time*.

At the end of the novel, Jack's exit, hitch-hiking with his things in a blue rucksack which echoes the 'little blue cloth that [Mam] used to tie her hair in' (*S*, 205), parodies the opening of *How Green Was My Valley*. It suggests that he, like Llewellyn's Huw Morgan, is in bad faith. Keith, in contrast, has found his place and is learning Welsh. Reading the motto on the wall in the steel mill, 'ARWEINWYR YN Y MAES' (leaders in the field), he recognizes the last three words but not the first: 'Taking the piece of blank paper and pencil from his boilersuit pocket he copied the motto. He would look it up' (*S*, 212–13). Of the other characters, Emlyn has a heart attack; Sully is engaged; Wayne has joined the army and is off to Ulster 'to shoot Sully's in-laws' – an important reminder of the Troubles in Northern Ireland (*S*, 210). Maudie has killed herself to speed up her husband's inevitable death.

Judith's future is more uncertain and this suggests the beginnings of historical shifts in gender roles brought about by de-industrialization. Initially associated with imagery of reproduction, she rejects

Keith in favour of Jack as a potential father for a child: 'This was no good. She wanted the Eggman' (*S*, 34), a reference to the Beatles song 'I am the Walrus' (*S*, 225). By the end of the novel she has rejected both Jack and Keith: 'Neither you or him have got anything to do with me' (*S*, 201). Both she and Keith are trying for jobs in the new factories which employed women on the assembly lines (*S*, 209). Wayne predicts that, 'Some of us will live off our wives' (*S*, 182). Another 'shift' is the advent of feminism. Meredith is looking back to the 1970s from the mid-1980s which saw the emergence of women as a political force in events such as the walk from Cardiff to Greenham Common which established the Peace Camp there in 1981.[63] This political context is hinted at in the novel by Jack, ironically through a comparison between Liz (the woman he has abandoned) and Judith: 'That's history, or her story' (*S*, 153). The word 'herstory' to denote a woman-centred history may have been first used in 1970 (though it seems unlikely that Jack would be familiar with it), but it was certainly in circulation by 1988.[64] This hints at another possible history. At the end of the novel Judith seems to have become a more androgynous 'Jude' (*S*, 212), possibly recalling another Beatles song, 'Hey Jude', which counsels that 'The movement you need is on your shoulder.' If we can trace a line from Jack and Keith through *Griffri* to Wil Daniel in *The Book of Idiots*, there is also a clear line from Judith to Sarah Bowen in *Sidereal Time*.

The novel ends, as it started, with the figure of O: 'On the last day, O clocked off at exactly half past three' (*S*, 213). He has had a 'satisfying week' (*S*, 213): he has placed his last dead rat in the day gang's cabin and as he leaves, he puts his used Sunblest bag in the litter bin (*S*, 214). The penultimate paragraph brings the novel full circle:

> O looked at the straggly, nearly dead trees on the bank. The slab mill had gone and the pulpit and the rest now. A nice, solving blank space. Perhaps there would be more leaves. (*S*, 214)

Both the steelworks and the 'pulpit' (industry and religion) have gone, echoing Keith's 'Dinistr y deml', a destruction of those shaping institutions. The 'nice, solving blank space', however, is not 'Diwedd y Byd' since there may be 'new leaves'.

Poole has interestingly read O as a figure for the author himself:

> I'm tempted to see O – sexually neutral, symbol of death, nothingness and eternity, the being who straddles the novel and clocks it off – as the novelist's projection of himself as creative destructive enigma into his text. (*S*, 231)

The novelist's task now is 'to imagine more print-filled leaves – to reinvent himself for the next opus' (*S*, 231). This ending does indeed bring together images from the novel in a way which suggests the possibility of a new art. The patterning of imagery in the novel connects O's *solving* blank space' to the 'solving crystal' (*S*, 203) in an ancient chamber in Jack's dream:

> On another limb of the galaxy in a small solar system on a cold planet in a remote cave in an ancient chamber is the mystical prism that makes and explains the coherence of everything. (*S*, 169)

In a similar chamber under the steelworks, Jack, Sully, Wayne and O encounter an image which recalls that in *The Carved Chair*: 'In the centre . . . stood the wheelbarrow, dramatically lit from straight above like some devotional object' (*S*, 190). In this 'derelict cave under a doomed city', however, there is 'no crystal to solve everything. Only a skipful of rubbish in the shaft of light in place of an altar' (*S*, 191). This is the scene for O's showdown with Jack when he reveals that he has told Keith that he saw Jack 'with your hand up Keith's wife's mwt' (*S*, 192). Neither work (the wheelbarrow) nor the biological imperative offer a meaning which can sustain Jack and keep him in the valley. The ice cave he dreams of as 'home' becomes an image of his own frozen possibility. Unlike Mal and Ben, he cannot see the potential in the wheelbarrow or the redemptive possibilities of his friendship with Keith.

The possibility of art as a transformative act of 'making' is suggested by another more ambiguous image, a Tate and Lyle syrup tin, which Meredith has suggested connects to that of the 'solving crystal' (I). In the day gang cabin is a leaking radiator built by the men out of two-inch pipes: 'An empty Tate and Lyle syrup tin was shoved under the leak. Jack noticed how startlingly pure the dripping water seemed inside the silvered can' (S, 29). Although it isn't noted in the text, Tate and Lyle syrup tins carry a biblical quotation, 'Out of the strong came forth sweetness', which connotes transformation. As an image of 'making', of craftsmanship, the radiator resembles the sculptures the welders make from scrap (one a crucifixion) which Norman shows Jack, telling him; 'You got to make something of wherever you do find yourself' (S, 203). For Jack, this recalls again the labyrinth beneath the doomed city with 'the still point, the solving crystal' (S, 203). Yet Jack realizes, in an image which rewords his casting himself as a salmon:

> when you crawl all the way back against all the solar winds that push you from the source because the river only runs one way, when you get there, naturally you drop your spacesuit and shit on the altar. (S, 203–4)

Unlike the welders or Keith, Jack has failed to 'make something of wherever you do find yourself' (S, 203). Moreover, he has '[shat] on the altar' in the sense that he has betrayed his friendship with Keith through the affair with Judith.

This complex of imagery – the ice cave, the solving crystal, the blank space, the Tate and Lyle tin – offers an example of the intricate patterning Meredith achieves in this technically accomplished first novel. It also connects to *This* which includes several poems – 'Cold' (T, 24–5), 'Ice Progress' (T, 26) and 'An End to Singing' (T, 27) – which use the imagery of winter to think about creativity. In his contribution to 'Scintilla Poets in Conversation', Meredith has written about how his need to make warmth and light during the winter in Defynnog 'became blended in my apprehension with the need to make poems and stories': winter thus becomes, paradoxically, a 'time of fruitfulness'.[65] In 'Ice Progress', images of cold and steelmaking combine to personify the ice as a kind of muse:

'Ice has spoken to me / Licked her roughened tongue / Along my bones' awakening the poet and Opening [his] numb blind eyes' (*T*, 26). A little of that feeling about winter seeps into *Shifts* in the imagery associated with Jack, with the caveat that he fails to make it fruitful by transforming his quick wit and obsession with narrative and language into art.

A complex, sophisticated and linguistically innovative novel, *Shifts* broke new ground in its depiction of working-class life and the post-industrial predicament. It has, quite rightly, become an iconic text, 'an automatic choice on most courses on Welsh literature in English' in Stephen Knight's words.[66] It was nominated by Dylan Moore as a contender to the title of 'Greatest Welsh Novel' in a poll run by Wales Arts Review, being pipped to number one only by Caradog Prichard's *Un Nos Ola Leuad / One Moonlit Night* (1961).[67] What is surprising, however, is that it has tended to be seen as a stand-alone text, a one-off, and not connected to the rest of Meredith's work which goes on to build on this initial achievement in surprising and innovative ways.

3

'Onlooker and participant': *Snaring Heaven* (1990) and *Griffri* (1991)

Despite its ostensible retreat from the contemporary world, Christopher Meredith's second novel, *Griffri* (1991), a historical fiction set in twelfth-century Gwent, develops themes that are already evident in *Shifts* and *This*. Like most fictions of the past, *Griffri* says as much, if not more, about the time in which it was written as it does about the time in which it is set. A novel about the role of the artist within times of traumatic historical upheaval, it comes out of Meredith's feelings about the political climate of the 1980s. It also develops his earlier concern with the work of making art from language, a theme that is also central to *Snaring Heaven* (1990). Both texts bear witness to Meredith's deep engagement with Welsh history and literature. An important inspiration while Meredith was learning Welsh had been Gwyn Williams's *The Burning Tree* (1956) (I), a collection of Welsh poems from the sixth century to 1600 with facing-page English translations.[1] Both novel and poetry demonstrate its influence in the development of his writing.

Given a period of fifteen months away from teaching thanks to a Welsh Arts Council bursary, Meredith was able to write full-time and alternated work on poetry and the novel. Writing was no longer a secretive process: this time Meredith 'actually had a desk to sit at rather than a corner of the kitchen table or the living-room floor'.[2] As he recalled:

> What I did was at first to work on poems in the morning . . ., then have
> a break and do the background work for the novel in the afternoons

> ... As the collection got more finished, so that I was tweaking, rewriting, organising, etc, and I got to the point where I was ready for the serious writing on *Griffri*, I swapped the pattern and worked on the novel in the mornings and ... on the poems in the afternoon.[3]

The last third of *Griffri* was written and the whole redrafted after Meredith had gone back to full-time teaching, 'tough circumstances' in which to achieve this.[4]

The continuity of themes between *Griffri* and *Snaring Heaven* produced by this intensive method of working is evident not only in the fact that the novel's protagonist, Griffri, is a poet but also by the fact that *Snaring Heaven* includes one of the poems from *Griffri*. Presented as Griffri's elegy for Gwrgant in the novel (*G*, 149) and given the title 'Intricate May' in *Snaring Heaven* (*SH*, 61), this is a translation of a medieval Welsh poem, 'Cyntefin Ceinaf Amser', from the Black Book of Carmarthen, translated as 'Sadness in Springtime' by Tony Conran.[5] Meredith 'made a point of not looking at [Conran's version]' when he did his own 'free translation'.[6] Furthermore, some lines from *Griffri*, reworked into poetry, appeared as 'Meilyr's song' in *The Meaning of Flight* in 2005 (*MF*, 46, 71). Another embedded text in *Griffri*, 'The Story of the Afanc King and the Sons of Teyrnon' (*G*, 180–5), was republished as a fine edition with linocut illustrations by Sara Philpott by Gwasg Gregynog in 2006. As Meredith notes in the 'Afterword', the story fuses a Native American Algonquin myth with a style based on the First Branch of the Mabinogi (*AF*, n.p.). The rich interplay between these texts is a testament to the close relationship between Meredith's poetry and prose. Writing about a poet in *Griffri* becomes a way of writing about poetry in a time of historical upheaval. Griffri's comments about writing and his distinction between the public and private purposes of poetry offer a way of thinking about Meredith's own practice.

As Jill Farringdon noted, *Snaring Heaven* displayed 'the same nexus of concerns' as appeared in *Shifts*, 'the sensibilities evident in the novel distilled into fine, resonant poems'.[7] This contrasts with a very different review by Wayne Burrows: 'There is no cohesive

Figure 10. Christopher Meredith in Brecon, 1991, around
the publication of *Griffri*. Photograph: V. A. Meredith.

voice here, neither a fixed body of subject matter nor straight
authorial presence.'[8] In the context of the two novels, this alleged
lack of a 'cohesive voice' looks more like an interest in the plurality
and contingency of voice/s within history: 'to know is to become
/ In time' as Meredith puts it in 'Snapshot' (*SH*, 28). Rather than
a 'fixed body of subject matter', there is a distrust of any easy notion
of coherence which comes from an understanding that all being,
knowing and representation is mediated by language within history. *Shifts*, *Griffri* and *Snaring Heaven* are all concerned with the
possibilities and politics of art as representation. If Jack in *Shifts* is
a writer manqué while Keith looks to history to achieve a coherent

sense of identity, Griffri is a professional poet whose lived experience teaches him the impossibility of constructing a coherent linear historical narrative out of the violent chaos of the 'now'.

Snaring Heaven *(1990)*: *'to know is to become / In time'*

Snaring Heaven included twenty-eight new poems, as well as nine poems and the sequence 'Six Poems for Troedrhiwgwair' from *This*, and a piece of prose-poetry, 'Opening Time' (previously published in *Anglo-Welsh Review*).[9] The collection is far more carefully orchestrated than Burrows's comments suggest. Meredith has said that both *This* and *Snaring Heaven* were 'sequenced like a piece of music so they echo'.[10] *Snaring Heaven* opens with a poem, 'Desk', which revisits the themes of 'Breaking wood' (now placed second) but from the perspective of a poet who 'actually [has] a desk to sit at'.[11] Poems are paired or tripled, sometimes by title ('On Hay Bridge' (*SH*, 25–6), 'Another go at Hay Bridge' (*SH*, 27)), sometime by subject ('The vegetable patch' (*SH*, 30), 'Snaring heaven' (*SH*, 31–2), both on gardening), and sometimes, less obviously, by a theme ('Intricate May' (*SH*, 61), 'Prisoners' (*SH*, 62–8)) which is foregrounded by their juxtaposition. The collection moves towards poems which engage directly with the fraught politics of the 1980s, using allusion and quotation to create parallels between past and present. This sequencing produces illuminating echoes, often between very different poems, which circle back to key themes: identity, place, history. They return repeatedly to the purpose of art, of 'snaring heaven' (*SH*, 31–2), in the face of existential alienation and the chaos of historical experience.

The opening poem, 'Desk', recounts how the poet rescues an old school desk 'scummed . . . dark / With ink, dead skin, the rain of dust, the grease / Of knees and cuffs and fingertips, *with work'* (*SH*, 7: emphasis added) and lovingly but rather inexpertly restores it. The quatrain form, with its true and off-rhymes (dark/work, true/glue, planed/learned, staff/graft, guilt/rebuilt, bars/scarred) and its handling of enjambment and caesura, resembles that used in Seamus Heaney's 'Follower'.[12] Both poems depict a physical act of labour – ploughing in 'Follower', carpentry in 'Desk' – which is contrasted with and becomes a metaphor for poetry. In 'Desk', the poet's act of 're-creation' (echoing 'Breaking wood'), is also a form of resurrection, making the desk 'a place / For another sort of work' where the teacher is re-created as a poet. Like Heaney's 'Digging' (similarly the opening poem of his first major collection[13]), Meredith's 'Desk' is the confident assertion of a writer who has found his place and his proper 'work':

> . . . We're both scarred

> But the worm in each of us is dead.
> I'm not paid much, but neither am I bored
> Nor hurt by work's attrition as we go
> To real work. This page, the silence, these words.

Writing, this poem asserts, is 'real work', as much a form of 'making' as a craft skill such as carpentry or stone masonry. In 'Miller's Answer: Making, Saying, and the Impulse to Write' (2011), his professorial inaugural lecture many years later, Meredith returned to the difficult paradox of writing as *'making'*.[14] 'I believe', he asserts, 'that *all* writing (though not all speaking) above the level of a shopping list is "made" through skill which we acquire by learning and practice as surely as we have to learn how to play the violin or to tile a roof'.[15] His interest in these questions is evident from 'Breaking wood' which, placed after 'Desk' in *Snaring Heaven*, preserves those earlier uncertainties about what 'work' might be. It reminds us of the complex history, of family and place (as with Heaney's 'Digging'), which underlies the poet's chosen role and the ways in which it entails a break with the past.

This doubled opening leads into a series of poems, old and new, which engage with the poet's natal landscape: Cefn Golau, Tredegar, the Sirhowy valley and Troedrhiwgwair. 'View from the hill' (*SH*, 11) layers together images of place, the solar system and the bodily nature of the act of perception. From the hill, the poet sees the valley of his birth patterned by 'fretted lines of streets' within 'a landscape pleated like a brain', over which is stretched 'the night sky . . . punched through / with stars like nerves'. The images connect poet and landscape to the maternal body:

> Below is everything you are,
> animal, machine and child
> re-entering along the nerves
> through yielding womb walls.

The image of 'the planet turning from the sun' (*SH*, 11), a key representation of diurnal repetition which recurs in Meredith's poetry, places him in relation to place and time, the Sirhowy valley and the solar system. This poem and another, 'Cefn Golau in snow' (*SH*, 12), lead into the sequence about Meredith's mother's home area (visible across the valley from Cefn Golau), 'Six Poems for Troedrhiwgwair', from *This*.

As a collection, *Snaring Heaven* is grounded in these poems about Meredith's *bro*, his natal landscape with its contrasts of rural and post-industrial and its connections to paternal and maternal history. This is the landscape that has shaped and represents 'everything [he is]'. But as the title 'View from the hill' suggests, the emphasis is on the act of looking which requires a play of distance and connectedness. As a later poem in the collection puts it, the poet is both 'onlooker and participant' (*SH*, 64, 65), intimately rooted in this landscape and separate from it, aware of himself as 'eye' and 'I'. What Heaney describes as the 'penalty of consciousness' means that the poet can only describe his community if he is an observer as well as a participant.[16] The price of perception is separation.

Images of looking run through *Snaring Heaven*, most explicitly in two poems about photographs – 'Snapshot' (*SH*, 28) and 'On his photograph outdoors' (*SH*, 29) – which are also poems about the making of art. The act of perception links together poem, place and poet. The 'View from the hill' is of both the local (the Sirhowy valley) and the universe ('the night sky'). Beginning with the local, the collection looks outwards, from Cefn Golau to the solar system in poems like 'Planet' (*SH*, 36), 'Moon through binoculars' (*SH*, 37) and 'Jupiter' (*SH*, 38–9). The Shakespearean sonnet 'Planet' looks back at the earth from space, seeing it 'Ice white and ice blue' while 'The camera clicks us clicks us so we know / How pale we are as we spin from or to / The night' (*SH*, 36). To know ourselves involves placing ourselves in relation to the local, the global and the universal, as well as the body.

The cover image of the 'Vela Supanova Remnant' (*SH*, 4), the structure which results from the explosion of a star, should focus our attention on the web of imagery in the collection concerned with planets, stars, time and space. The picture also resembles light microscopy images of nerve cells or neurons in the brain, thus 'View from the hill' conflates the two: 'the night sky . . . punched through / with stars like nerves'. As the title of the collection suggests, the poet's job is to 'snar[e] heaven', that is 'to capture . . . creation through artistic perception'.[17] The cover image points to the double meaning of 'Heaven', encompassing both the vault of the sky with the sun, moon and stars, and the abode of the divine. In the title poem, the project of 'Snaring heaven' is explored through the metaphor of gardening: 'Gardens are mantras / contrived to trap / tranquillity' (*SH*, 31). The poem itself is a kind of mantra, or sacred utterance, which meditates on the common notion of paradise as a garden, or the garden as an image of heaven, to explore the act of creation. The making of a garden involves the contrivance of order and pattern: the natural growth of plants is held within the 'airspace of neat beds / and borders' / contemplative / geometries'. Similarly, the making of art is a way of imposing order, pattern and meaning on the chaos of experience, a theme which *Griffri* explores in more pessimistic detail.

Three different kinds of time are important in *Snaring Heaven*. Between the poet observing his locality in the present moment and the unimaginable immensity of time-space symbolized by the supernova remnant is a third term: human history. In 'On Hay Bridge' and 'Another go at Hay Bridge', Meredith returns to the history of the border area which he had explored in 'By Bronllys Castle' (*T*, 35–6). In 'On Hay Bridge' (*SH*, 25–6), he watches a salmon

– 'a yard long, dark slate / blotched with sour milk' – swimming upstream in springtime. The salmon becomes an image of historical continuity: 'Gerallt saw her eight hundred journeys back'. 'Gerallt', Gerald of Wales or Giraldus Cambrensis, was the twelfth-century Norman-Welsh author of *A Journey Through Wales* and *The Description of Wales*, key sources for *Griffri*.[18] The history evoked here is one of violent conquest as the Normans burn homesteads and build stone towers:

> Castles studded conquerors' intent,
> stitched the sleeve with rock.
> Lords dead in Gwent. A headless corpse in Cwm Hir.

The headless body of Llywelyn ap Gruffudd (*c*.1225–82), the last independent prince of Wales, buried at Cwm Hir after his defeat by the English, signifies the end of an attempt to establish a united and independent Wales. Welsh history here is a narrative of defeat; as Raymond Williams put it, 'To the extent that we are a people, we have been defeated, colonised, penetrated, incorporated. Never finally, of course.'[19]

Within such a history of conquest and defeat, Meredith's poem considers the role of the poet. Recalling Bedo Brwynllys, the fifteenth-century Breconshire poet, who 'sang sweet and politic of loving girls', he rejects such complicit quietude: 'Namesake, let me not be you.'[20] But the romanticization of defeat persists to the present:

> Eight hundred years and still we say
> you lose less by retreat.
> Some martyred hero and a moving song
> will do to warm an evening perhaps.

As Hooker remarks in his reading of this poem, Meredith is 'emphatically a political poet: a Welsh poet concerned with betrayal or complicity, and with questions of how to act and how to be'.[21] Such a history makes for homelessness but it is through identification with the salmon – which recalls both the salmon of Llyn

Llyw, the oldest of all creatures in the Mabinogi, and what Jack in *Shifts* calls 'the fucking biological imperative' (*S*, 75) – that the poet finds an image of strength: 'Give me that pied yard of muscle / to inch against what pushes me from home.' The following poem, 'Another go at Hay Bridge' (*SH*, 27), returns to the same place in autumn. Rather than looking to history, the poet locates himself in space-time: 'with my head in the skydome / by constant discs of mars and jupiter'. The onset of winter, as 'the tilting earth shaves away daylight', will bring frost 'but too, the pleiades', a consolatory image. The dark river below is echoed by the milky way: 'Somewhere above the other river runs.' Human time is mirrored, and put into perspective by, the time of the planets, a theme to which Meredith will return in *Sidereal Time*.

Homelessness and disconnection from place are related to the art of making poetry in several poems concerned with photographs. 'Snapshot' (*SH*, 28) contrasts the poet's attempt to 'learn with aching care' the place he has come to call home with the easy snapshots taken by visitors who admire the view; he has learnt that 'to know is to become / In time.' The question of home is reframed in terms of consumer society in 'She plans a purchase' (*SH*, 33), another poem that engages with Heaney. Shown photographs of a woman's 'Dream home', complete with a well in the garden, the poet bites off a 'showy' literary allusion: 'Heaney's got a poem about wells.' The pictures, he recognizes, are a substitute which 'try to fill an aching space': the well is 'A hole sunk to the lifesource of a place [which] helps her get by.' Using the allusion to Heaney's 'Personal Helicon', even as he recognizes its pretention, Meredith's poem becomes a meditation on 'how place gives way to rhyme'. Heaney's poem reflects on his childhood fascination with wells to figure the roots of his own poetic inspiration (Helicon was the mountain home of the nine muses in Greek myth). As an adult, poetry becomes Heaney's way of understanding his place within the world: 'I rhyme,' 'Personal Helicon' concludes, 'to see myself, to set the darkness echoing.'[22] For Meredith, poetry similarly marks and fills the absence left by the loss of connection to home and place. Lacking poetry, the woman needs other consolations:

'These rhymeless ones need places more than I' (*SH*, 33). Meredith's poetry emphasizes the same nexus of concerns as Heaney's – the poet's sense of connection and disconnection from the world of his childhood – but with a more self-conscious irony, and an up-dated sense of the alienation wrought by capitalism.

The consolations of art are revisited in the face of ageing and existential ennui in 'A Waiting-room' (*SH*, 47). If 'Today will just be more of the same' then what is the function of art? In the face of such alienation, the artist's attempt at creation can seem futile: 'All making taints itself with this: / The fear of only being.' The final lines of the poem suggest, somewhat pessimistically, that 'making' – whether art, craft or children – is all we can hold against what Dylan Thomas called 'the dying of the light':

> The song, the carpentry, the seed,
> After the end of true delight
> Are habits that affirm or ease
> The rolling by of day and night.

Similarly, 'What's Certain' (*SH*, 49–51) considers the consolations of religion, history, place and art in the face of the poet's father's illness. They talk of 'What literature can't do to save the world':

> But in our heads were random echoes
> Making harmonies of rain and light,
> The facts of meat and pain and nothing else.

The random 'harmonies' of the natural world, exemplified by the internal rhyme (rain/pain), suggests a consolatory art set against the facts of our life as suffering, mortal bodies.

The penultimate group of poems is linked by a sharper focus on the political landscape of the 1980s and its connections to Welsh history. The fragmentary 'Notes for a novel, perhaps' (*SH*, 53–60) engages with the recent history of Wales through the lives of Meredith's father and grandfather. Images of light and dark reflect the contrasts in these lives, epitomized in the paradoxical image of the miner, 'Reach[ing] into the dark to fetch what makes / our civilisation tick.' The child remembers his father reading in chapel with the dirt of the pit grained into his unwashed back under his suit: 'The man talking ... his face all light, about rising. That one day a week and the rest the dark working on the spine.' Running through the poem as a refrain are lines from the final verse of Thomas Campbell's elegy for the soldiers killed in the eponymous 1800 battle 'Hohenlinden':

> *Few, few shall part where many meet*
> *The snow shall be their winding-sheet*
> *And every turf beneath their feet*
> *Shall be* [a soldier's sepulchre]. (*SH*, 58)[23]

These words are 'A rhyming art to salve the eyes / With visions of heroic worlds.' Having joined up with the laudable intention of 'Fight[ing] fascism', the young solider finds that language serves a more brutal function: the words he is taught to chant, 'We will kill / without fear / without remorse / without dread', throw into question the values of the patriotic sacrifice lauded by Campbell. The final section of the poem contrasts the solder in khaki standing in a crowd in which 'I was the enemy' while a 'thin man in a sheet and spectacles' speaks to them in Hindi, words which the soldier does not 'understand'. Language and art are complicit in the violent oppression of other cultures.

Placed immediately after this poem, 'Intricate May' (the translation of a medieval Welsh fragment which appears in *Griffri*) frames the most political poems in the collection – 'Prisoners' (*SH*, 62–8) and '1985' (*SH*, 69) – and allows us to hear the echoes between past and present oppressions. 'Everyone has forgotten how awful the 1980s were,' Meredith has said, 'They were a dark time. But a time to be optimistic about being Welsh.'[24] *Griffri*, 'Prisoners' and '1985' all consider the role of the poet within a context of political violence and oppression, both contemporaneous and historical, and raise the question of complicity through inaction. As 'Prisoners' reiterates in a tripled line, the poet is 'onlooker and participant'

(*SH*, 64, 65, 67), politicizing Meredith's earlier concern with the play of connectedness and disconnection.

Both 'Prisoners' and '1985' are concerned with the fate of a 'friend' who was held in prison for over a year accused of conspiring to cause an explosion (*SH*, 68). In 1982 nine people were arrested for conspiracy to bomb thirteen targets across Wales and England, allegedly part of a campaign by WAWR (Workers Army of the Welsh Republic).[25] Most of them were members of the Welsh Socialist Republican Movement, formed in 1980, and some spent up to seventeen months in jail before bail. Of those who finally became defendants in what became known as the Cardiff conspiracy or Cardiff explosives trial, September to November 1983, five (Adrian Stone, Nicholas Hodges, David Burns, Robert Griffiths and Brian Rees) were acquitted of conspiracy, while Dafydd Ladd pleaded guilty to possessing explosives and Jenny Smith was released. The jury accepted 'the claims of planted evidence, false statements and maltreatment during interrogation' and an investigation into police conspiracy followed.[26]

Meredith makes this context explicit in a note to 'Prisoners' (*SH*, 68) which also gives translations of the two epigraphs in Welsh which situate the poem in the longer history of Welsh oppression. The first, '*Nyt oes le y kyrcher rac carchar braw*', is from the thirteenth-century 'Marwnad Llywelyn ap Gruffudd' by Gruffudd ab yr Ynad Coch, an elegy to the last ruler of an independent Wales already invoked in 'On Hay Bridge'.[27] Meredith translates this as 'There is nowhere to go from the prison of fear.' This provides the title image of the poem which layers together the friend's imprisonment and interrogation for conspiracy with the poet's experience of his wife's pregnancy. The second epigraph is two lines from Gerallt Lloyd Owen's ode 'Cilmeri' (named after the place where Llywelyn ap Gruffudd was killed), which won the chair at the eisteddfod in Swansea in 1982. Translated as 'The morning sky estuaries of blood in the split of mountains', these lines provide the second central image of the poem, which figures both the death of Llywelyn and the birth of the baby. Meredith's engagement with Welsh poetry, both medieval and contemporary, is crucial here.

These epigraphs provide the powerful opening imagery which frames the consideration of the contemporary poet's place and role in 'Prisoners' (*SH*, 62–8):

> Don't you see the oaktree flailing
> Like a pulse against a pattern
> Of disintegrating clouds
> And dawns in the cleft of mountains
> Making estuaries of blood?

This reworks the form and imagery of the *marwnad*, used to express national mourning for Llywelyn ap Gruffudd and the loss of the Welsh cause:

> See you not the way of the wind and the rain?
> See you not the way the oaks beat together?
> See you not the sea stinging the land?[28]

Meredith's image of the oak tree flailing against a blood-red sky, repeated at the end of the poem, also recalls the tree from the Mabinogi which provides the title of Williams's collection: 'A tall tree on the river's bank, one half of it burning from root to top, the other half in green leaf.'[29] For Williams this image suggested 'an outstanding mood of the Welsh poet': 'the awareness at the same time of contrary seasons and passions'.[30] For Meredith, the oak tree is a political image but his poem is similarly concerned with oppositions: onlooker/participant, action/inaction, darkness/light, birth/death, personal/political.

In contrast with the frenetic opening imagery, the poet himself, waiting for the birth of his child, seems imprisoned by a Thoreauvian '*quiet desperation*'. He is 'Onlooker and participant' in relation to both the political prisoner and his wife's pregnancy. His domestic and existential ennui is broken by the news of his old friend imprisoned and interrogated. Now it is the hissing of the word '*Conspiracy*' which 'Wraps to the pattern of the thoughts / We'll soon be too afraid to say.' This is the 'prison of fear', the threat of an

Orwellian *'thoughtcrime'*. The epigraph from 'Cilmeri', however, also provides an image for the birth of the poet's child: 'Blood and offal flood a delta, / A dawn in the cleft of mountains.' The poet is again both 'Onlooker and participant' – 'I find a place and egg them on' – and it is the newborn child who offers him a place and a purpose:

> Slabbed on the mother's belly he
> Almost unsays inquisitors.
> All things are cause for waking
> To ourselves.

While the poem is shadowed by the poet's sense of fear 'Closing on me like a prison', it staunchly asserts the importance of the local against those who deny the significance of what happens in a small country: 'Friend, it would be parochial / To pretend the action's elsewhere.'

In '1985' (*SH*, 69), a much shorter poem, Meredith brings the Cardiff conspiracy trial together with the 1984–5 miners' strike. Structured as a ballad-like dialogue between the poet and two unnamed friends, one imprisoned during the strike and the other for alleged possession of a bomb, the poem economically interrogates the word 'Friend'. Within this context, quietude is a form of complicity: '*And friend, since you call me friend, / where were you?*' ask those who were imprisoned. These are questions to which *Griffri* returns. Like *This*, *Snaring Heaven* ends with poems – including 'Christening pot boiler' (*SH*, 70–1) from *This* – that celebrate the poet's children and offer a kind of redemptive purpose and place. Placed after these political poems, however, they gain power and significance.

The final prose-poem, 'Opening Time' (*SH*, 75–80), is a kind of verbal version of a Stanley Spencer resurrection painting in which a man rises from the grave and returns to his childhood home on an estate closely resembling Cefn Golau. There he sees his mother, and watches his father give his younger self a tube of sweets (a scenario Meredith revisits in several poems). Bookending *Snaring*

Heaven with 'Desk', this returns us to the themes of resurrection implicit in that opening poem but with the darker understanding that 'whatever was at the end of my walk, it could not be paradise' (*SH*, 80).

Griffri *(1991)*: *'Song can tell us what we are'*

'History', Meredith had written in his 1986 review of *All Things Betray Thee*, 'is the reality to which we are trying to awake'.[31] *Griffri* is an exploration of the nightmare of history and a demand that we awake to its implications, both past and present. By the late 1980s, historical fiction was an unfashionable genre, mainly because of an association with women writers and popular romance. The awarding of the Booker Prize to A. S. Byatt's *Possession* in 1990 marked a renaissance of the form. Critical work on the genre had focused primarily on what Avrom Fleishman called the 'English historical novel', beginning with Walter Scott's *Waverley* (1814).[32] Georg Lukács in his pioneering Marxist study of the genre, *The Historical Novel* (1936/7), had lauded Scott as the progenitor of the 'classical historical novel'.[33] This focus on an Anglo-Scottish model meant that, despite texts like Thomas's *All Things Betray Thee* or the historical fictions of nineteenth-century Welsh women writers, discussions of historical fiction had effectively ignored Anglo-Welsh examples. Indeed, this is still the case at the time of writing and this helps to explain the neglect of Meredith's work outside Wales.

Rather late in his career Raymond Williams began to think about the potential of the historical novel. In 1982, he argued that: 'We have many period novels. We have a few historical novels. We have only the beginnings of a historical materialist novel, *yet it ought to be one of our three major forms*.'[34] For a socialist writer, he hypothesized, the 'necessary inclusion of interpretation of defeats and failures, and the relations between these and subsequent adaptations' might only be possible in the historical novel.[35] The two examples he gave were Jack Jones's *Black Parade* (1935) and

Thomas's *All Things Betray Thee*. In his 1986 introduction to the latter, Williams noted that though the novel's setting was 1835, 'the connection is beyond it: to 1986 if we can hear it'.[36] He also pointed out that the underlying movement of the story, told by the travelling harpist Alan Hugh Leigh, was the shift from 'observer to participant'.[37] The first two parts of Williams's own unfinished historical epic, *People of the Black Mountains: Vol. 1: The Beginnings* (1989) and *People of the Black Mountains: Vol. 2: The Eggs of the Eagle* (1990), were published posthumously and hailed as 'the great historical novel Wales has long deserved'.[38] Within a barely nascent tradition of anglophone Welsh historical fiction, Meredith was ahead of the curve in re-shaping the genre in *Griffri* to reflect a concern with historiography as a subjective and fragmentary representation of the past in a specifically Welsh context.

Set during the Anglo-Norman incursions into the border area of Gwent, *Griffri* works across what Beverley Southgate (following John Demos) has called the 'borderland' between history and fiction.[39] Meredith went back to the historical sources, rather than fictional models, and the novel has its genesis in a cryptic passage in *Brut y Tywysogyon, The Chronicle of the Princes*:

> [1156–1158] The following year Morgan ab Owain Wan was slain through treachery by the men of Ifor ap Meurig; and along with him was killed the best poet, and he was called Gwrgant ap Rhys. And then Iorwerth ab Owain, Morgan's brother, ruled the land of Caerleon and all the territory of Owain.[40]

It is from what is *not* said here that Meredith weaves a novel about treachery between brothers, the instability of historical narrative, the role of the poet in a time of political turmoil, and the dangers of 'unwilled complicity' (*MF*, 39). As a form of historiography, the chronicle is an official account of events but, as Meredith says, 'Chronicles are strange things, a mixture of bits and pieces. They don't explain how one event connects with another. That to me makes them more interesting, as a novelist, than historians who actually shape the narrative.'[41] In contrast to the 'tidied-up' narratives of official history, Meredith's interest is what he has called

Figure 11. Christopher Meredith, 1991, around the
publication of *Griffri*. Photograph: V. A. Meredith.

'the unknowability of history',[42] and its plurality – '"histories",
you know, not history'.[43]

A *künstlerroman*, *Griffri* is narrated in the first person by Griffri
ap Berddig, poet at the court of a minor Welsh prince. Born around
1140 (Meredith was purposely vague about dates since these would
have no relevance to Griffri), he is around fourteen when Stephen
dies and Henri II becomes king (*G*, 72). Griffri is apprenticed to
the *pencerdd*, Gwrgant ap Rhys, in the court of Morgan ab Owain
Wan, prince of Gwynllwg. There Griffri learns his trade as a poet,
the 'keeper of memory, the lister of the dead, and . . . he who affirms
the road you choose' (*G*, 9) – or more brutally, 'a paid arselicker'
(*G*, 9). When Gwrgant is killed with Morgan ab Owain Wan in the
act of treachery recorded in the *Brut*, Griffri steps into his master's
shoes as *pencerdd*, becoming onlooker and participant in events
that he witnesses but does not necessarily understand. At the heart
of this story is the act of fratricide which may be hidden behind

the facts recorded in *Brut y Tywysogyon*. Griffri comes to understand that it was the machinations of Morgan's brother, Iorwerth ab Owain, which led to his murder so that Iorwerth could take Morgan's place as prince of Gwynllwg. This fratricide is repeated in the next generation by Iorwerth's son, Hywel, who is responsible for the death of his older brother, Owain ab Iorwerth, and the castration of his cousin, Owain ap Morgan (Pencarn), the son of Morgan ab Owain. The theme of fratricide is allegorized in the embedded story of the Afanc King and the Sons of Teyrnon (*G*, 180–5), related by Griffri's wife Cristen, which tells of Gwri's murder of his twin brother, Eurin.

A second primary source for *Griffri* is the work of Gerald of Wales whose twelfth-century *Description of Wales* argued that the Welsh societal structures led to 'frequent fratricides'.[44] Despite his sobriquet, Gerald was three-quarters Norman, the son of a Norman knight, William de Barri and Angharad, who was the daughter of Nest and the Norman Gerald of Windsor. His accounts are history written by and for the conqueror, to the extent of giving advice on 'How the Welsh can be conquered'.[45] As Gerald saw it, there were three things that weakened the Welsh: an inheritance system whereby land was divided between all the sons; a system of fostering sons, which weakened ties between brothers; and the fact that the Welsh 'refuse to accept the rule and domination of one king'.[46] Gerald appears in *Griffri* as a social climber, a 'nosy' 'Frenchman' with 'a few mangled words of Welsh', who is 'known among the French as "the Welshman" and treated as a great authority on all matters concerning us' (*G*, 156). If the chronicle lacks a narrative of cause and effect, the problem with Gerald's *Journey* and *Description* as historical sources is that they are shaped by a particular point of view, that of the Norman conqueror.

Griffri is narrated in two sections, or 'hearths', twelve years apart, each related to a Cistercian monk and chronicler, Idnerth. Conscious of his role as *pencerdd*, Griffri tells Idnerth:

How can we put what we are into items on a list? Your chronicle and my recitation of genealogies are so much dust. That's where song of either tongue or instrument can do something real, once in a while anyway. It can tell us what we are. (*G*, 9)

Both chronicle and genealogies are 'tidied-up' forms of history. Only through 'song', Griffri maintains, can we convey 'truth', though in a society where the poet's job is to 'praise the mighty' even poetry is subject to the demands of the 'client' (*G*, 9). But there is a deeper problem here. Griffri recognizes the fallibility of memory and the difficulty of re-constructing a coherent account of the past:

> Remembering can be a constant sorting out, a putting of things into lists, even. Now is a kind of chaos, a brink we teeter on endlessly. So when in remembering we sort things out, we miss the point of what it was actually like. (*G*, 11)

Thus Griffri's narrative is punctuated by his own uncertainty: 'What I remember must surely be reconstructed from what I've learnt since', he tells us, 'so it's not a complete, true memory' (*G*, 50). Moreover, 'Memory and invention must be close neighbours – their stocks are forever mingling' (*G*, 172). History, whether public historiography or private memory, is always a construction, always the imposition of a narrative pattern on the chaos of experience.

Just as Griffri's private memory is fragmented, his understanding of official public history is patchy. Through his eyes we see the history that is recorded in *Brut y Tywysogyon* obliquely, without dates to anchor us. Listening to older men talking about 'the time of the first Henri', Griffri uses a visual-spatial metaphor: 'I never got any clear picture of this. It seemed to me that the men, casting nets into the past, drew up an intricate, threshing confusion, a heaving plait of creatures that lived in struggle' (*G*, 72). The sequence of kings and battles we think we know – William the Conqueror, Henry I, Stephen, Maud, Henry II – is further de-familiarized by Meredith's use of French and/or Welsh names: Henri ap Gwilym Bastart, Estefyn of Blaes (*G*, 47). Language slips and becomes strange, but the 'net' of words is the only way in which humans can understand this confusion. The genealogies and praise songs use narrative to create order from chaos – 'That continuity, that praise, Gwrgant said, was the thing to hold to, to help make the heaving confusion into a pattern' (G, 72) – but at the cost of misrepresenting experience.

In one sense Meredith's novel offers a typically postmodern understanding of the difficulties of writing history: 'These summaries are bound to be a kind of lie,' Griffri tells us, 'but what else is there?' (G, 177). That history is a constructed narrative like fiction (a 'lie') is a commonplace of post-structuralist thinking: in Hayden White's words, historical narratives are 'verbal fictions, the contents of which are as much *invented* as *found*'.[47] As he argues, 'histories gain part of their explanatory effect by their success in making stories out of *mere* chronicles; and stories in turn are made out of chronicles by an operation . . . called "emplotment"'.[48] By 'emplotment', White means 'the encodation of the facts contained in the chronicle as components of specific *kinds* of plot structures, in precisely the way that [Northrop] Frye has suggested is the case with "fictions" in general'.[49] Any set of historical facts can be configured as comedy, tragedy, romance or satire according to the ideological interpretation of the historian.[50] Historical events offer the historian a series of 'elements' which can be

> *made* into a story by the suppression or subordination of certain of them and the highlighting of others, by characterisation, motific repetition, variation of tone and point of view, alternative descriptive strategies . . . no historical event is *intrinsically tragic*; it can only be conceived as such from a particular point of view.[51]

It is the question of point of view in relation to history-making that Meredith interrogates in *Griffri*. The events recorded as 'mere chronicle' in *Brut y Tywysogyon* are shaped into a story from the conqueror's point of view by Gerald of Wales. Shift the point of view and you become aware of plurality: '"histories" not history'.[52] *Griffri* retells these events as a history of defeat, not the romance of a 'moving song' (SH, 25), but the violent tragedy of a people 'defeated, colonised, penetrated, incorporated'.

In *Griffri* Meredith uses a first person narrative which is unreliable, not because the narrator is trying to mislead us but because, embedded in the chaos of 'now', he does not recognize what is happening. First person narrative, Meredith has said, is 'an extremely difficult and demanding mode'.[53] He singles out Glyn Jones's *The Island of Apples* (1965) as 'one of the great unreliable narrator works ... a brilliant one off'.[54] One of the few literary sources Meredith is aware that may have influenced *Griffri* is Dickens's *Great Expectations* (1861): like Pip, Griffri's life is 'predicated on an illusion' exposed in the second half of the novel.[55] Thus *Griffri* destabilizes the conventions of the traditional realist historical novel as well as exposing the constructedness of official historiography. In this sense *Griffri* is what Linda Hutcheon has called 'historiographic metafiction'; that is, a text in which a 'theoretical self-awareness of history and fiction as human constructs (historio*graphic meta*fiction) is made the grounds for its rethinking and reworking of the forms and content of the past'.[56] In *Griffri*, this is not postmodern game playing but recognition of the effects of trauma on national and personal identity. Although he asserts that it is poetry which 'affirms who we are, or who we think we are' (*G*, 154), Griffri comes to doubt his own identity and his place in his community: 'Us. That was force of habit. I'm not sure if I'm *us* any more' (*G*, 154).

Place is a key issue here. Like *Shifts* and *Snaring Heaven*, *Griffri* is embedded in Meredith's natal landscape: the area between Caerllion and Tredegar, centring on the Sirhowy valley around Troedrhiwgwair. This geographical setting foregrounds the way in which Meredith is presenting the transitional moment when twelfth-century Gwent became a contested borderland as what Lukács called the 'prehistory of the present', a history that 'can tell us what we are'.[57] Dafydd Johnston suggests that in *Griffri*, as in *Shifts*, landscape offers 'a rare element of continuity in a region which has suffered a fracture in its history as a result of Anglicisation'.[58] He sees *Griffri* as an attempt on the part of an anglophone Welsh writer to repossess the Welsh past of an Anglicized Gwent and to position it as an integral part of Wales: 'Gwynllwg [is where] the national crisis is taking place.'[59] This, I would argue, underestimates the ways in which the fractured history is inscribed on the landscape itself.

In the early sections the gap between the older narrating Griffri and his experiencing younger self is acute and we see the child struggling to make sense of his world. Griffri grows up in 'an out of the way place' (G, 14) which nevertheless shapes his identity:

> Our house on the treeline I remember best because we lived there in the summer . . . The house was high on the east side of the valley in a southward angled curve of pasture just below the heathery mountain back. The curve sharpened down the mountain into a deep cleft thick with trees that ran south at first and then turned westward as it opened out near the valley floor, where there were a few clearings for oats and meadowland and the house where we spent most of the winter. (G, 11)

Meredith has said that this is based on the area around Troed-rhiwgwair, where his mother grew up.[60] The cleft runs down from Cefn Manmoel past Troedrhiwgwair and into the broad flat bottom of the Sirhowy valley (called the Gwedog in *Griffri*). The *hafod* (summer house) described here is 'Mason's farm', set on the hill above Troed, south-east of what is now Tredegar, while the *hendre* (old farm, or home farm) near the valley floor is Troedrhiwgwair itself.[61] The system of transhumance allowed stock to graze on the hills in summer and return to the lower pastures in the winter. As a child Griffri's world is bounded by this landscape: 'I will never know any other place so well,' he asserts, 'Yet in another sense I didn't know it. I didn't know where or how it was' (G, 12). Twyn yr Hyddod, just across the valley, is 'the edge of the earth' (G, 13) for a child. The intense significance of this childhood landscape for Meredith is evident in the poems from *This* and *Snaring Heaven* already discussed as well as later poems such as 'Twyn yr Hyddod' (*MF*, 43).

Griffri explores various ways of experiencing and understanding the significance of place. Griffri's father offers him one way of locating himself geographically when he takes him up the mountain and shows him 'Cadair Arthur' to the north, and 'Môr Hafren' to the south (G, 12). His mother offers him an alternative understanding through story: the cleft of the hill where they live in summer was made by the 'porridge finger' of a giant, Gogrfran Oer, during a battle with a boar (*G*, 12). When Griffri is taken to Morgan after his father's death and apprenticed to Gwrgant, he has to learn 'the shape of this new world' (*G*, 20) from Gwrgant's house, a short distance from one of Morgan's courts. Built on a 'cliff of split and plated rock' above a rolling meadow and river, the court is a 'modest beili' (*G*, 21) inside a palisade, which Meredith based on a ruin near Machen.[62]

As Griffri gets older, his spatial understanding expands as he travels to Morgan's court at Caerllion, and to the shrine of Dyfrig in Llandâf. As Kirsti Bohata has noted, the description of Caerllion with its Roman remains as a 'cultural palimpsest' offers a fascinating spatial metaphor for the ways in which different meanings may be inscribed upon a landscape.[63] Griffri sees the landscape in terms of the stories from the Mabinogi, the Dream of Macsen Wledig and older myths:

> Gwrgant had shown me the remains of the old city from the age of giants. He said it was older even than the time when Macsen and Cynan from the north had marched on Rome. I saw walls of rock and great cracked slabs. There were modern houses built among the stones. (*G*, 39)

This is contested space, both militarily (Caerllion will be the subject of battles between Welsh and French) and culturally. Gwrgant notes that, 'The French think that Arthur lived here' and Rhys Ddu, storyteller to Ifor of Senghenydd, remarks that he is 'thinking of moving Arthur to Caerllion in future in his stories' (*G*, 39). This is, Bohata notes, a 'cultural theft' with 'dire material and political consequences'.[64]

Questions of ownership, inheritance and patrimony are at the heart of these conflicts and these shape and mis-shape identity through issues of loyalty and complicity. After his apprenticeship to Gwrgant, Griffri has to learn his trade as a poet, as well as his place in this new community alongside Gwrgant's wife, Non, their son Cadi and daughter Mair, and an 'unidentified two year old with a vicious bite' (*G*, 16). The novel is structured by pairs of doubles – the nearly identical Morgan and Iorwerth, and their sons, Owain ap Morgan (later known as Owain Pencarn) and Owain ab Iorweth. These doublings contribute to the confusion of Griffri's narrative but are also an integral part of the novel's symbolic structure. In the child Griffri's memory Morgan is a 'red man' wearing a 'torc of twisted iron' (*G*, 16), while his brother Iorwerth 'looks just like the red man except that his hair is darker' (*G*, 16). Similarly, it is not until later that the 'unidentified' is identified as Hywel ab Iorwerth, fostered by Gwrgant. Officially adopted by Gwrgant, Griffri himself is doubled by Cadi (whom he replaces as Gwrgant's 'son' after Cadi's death), by Gwrgant (the 'father' he succeeds as *pencerdd*), and the madman Meilyr.

The tradition of fostering, originally intended to strengthen friendship ties,[65] exacerbates this confusion of identities and weakens the Welsh system of patrimony. Just as Hywel ab Iorwerth (the 'unidentified') is fostered by Gwrgant, his older brother Owain has been fostered by Morgan, and Morgan's oldest son, also Owain (both boys being named after their grandfather Owain Wan) is fostered by Iorwerth. It is no wonder that Griffri is confused. This is the system that Gerald of Wales criticized as resulting in 'people being murdered, brothers killing each other and even putting each other's eyes out'.[66] After his father has been murdered and Iorwerth has taken his crown and land, Owain Pencarn comments to Griffri: 'To lose a patrimony is hard' (*G*, 159), but adds that 'Iorwerth is my father now . . . All the years of fosterage should have been a good training' (*G*, 159). Both Norman and Welsh systems of inheritance lead to violence:

[Owain] 'The French order these things better. Just one to inherit.'
[Griffri] 'You admire that?'
'It's clear-cut.'
'And look where it leads. Their sons looking outward. Wars and fortresses erupt across the world.'
'You prefer to keep murder cosy and in the family.' (*G*, 160)

In a society where murder is kept 'in the family', Owain's desire to marry seals his fate.

Only at the end of the novel, after a series of revelations, do we understand the chain of events which begins with a scene witnessed by the young Griffri. Having taken a party of soldiers to patrol the border between Gwynllwg and Senghenydd, the domain of Ifor Fychan ap Meurig, Iorwerth returns with the body of one of his soldiers, Eneas, claiming that he was shot by Ifor's men, because 'They thought I was Morgan' (G, 31). 'He was a good man', Gwrgant comments, 'An intelligent soldier' (G, 32). He produces (with difficulty) a *marwnad* to whip up feeling against Ifor. Griffri later learns that it was Iorwerth who shot Eneas to ratchet up hostilities between Morgan and Ifor. Later, Iorwerth stage-manages Ifor's kidnapping of Griffri to engineer the death of Morgan and Gwrgant, allegedly at the hand of Ifor. This probable fratricide is repeated in the next generation when Hywel ab Iorwerth murders, or causes the death of, his older brother, Owain ab Iorwerth, and (like his father) steps into his brother's position. Owain, Griffri tells us, 'was killed, *they say*, by Iarll Bryste's men' (G, 168; emphasis added). But Iorwerth's comment to Hywel – 'What I am afraid of is that you're too much like me.' (G, 174) – suggests the doubling of this fratricidal impulse across the generations. Griffri's response repeats Gwrgant's earlier comment – '"He was a good man" I said. "An intelligent soldier. I'll – I'll make a poem for him"' (G, 168) – suggesting both poets' complicity in these actions.

Meredith is concerned with the psychological effect of violence, trauma and the loss of independence on a national and individual level. 'One of the things [*Griffri*] is about is violence,' he has said, 'two kinds of violence: one passionate and one intentional and cold'.[67] In an interesting analogy, Hayden White compares history-making with psychotherapy: both historian and psychotherapist are engaged in a process of 're-emplotment' of events which have been forgotten 'either through accident, neglect or repression'.[68] As he notes, the 'greatest historians have always dealt with those events in the histories of their cultures which are "traumatic" in nature and the meaning of which is either problematical or overdetermined in the significance that they still have for current life'.[69] While White lists revolutions, civil wars, industrialization and urbanization as examples of 'traumatic' events, he does not mention colonization, which is surely, from the point of view of the colonized, one of the most violent of traumas. 'The memories of the previously colonized and repressed,' Southgate argues, 'may not always accord with the histories in which they see their pasts represented.'[70] While he suggests that the oral memories of partici-pants may prove a 'useful corrective' to accepted narratives,[71] Meredith's novel suggests the unreliability of such memories and explores instead the possibilities of 'song' as a way of negotiating the problems of historiography.

Bohata's important postcolonial reading of *Griffri* argues that the novel represents the violence of cultural exchange within coloniz-ation: the Anglo-Normans appropriate territory, power and myth, while the Welsh adopt the Norman practice of blinding prisoners.[72] The latter provides the most disturbing incidents in the novel. In the first, Griffri witnesses Ifor Fychan ap Meurig blinding a French hostage:

> [Ifor] said, quietly, 'Hold his legs' which two young men did, and, with admirable speed and a kind of bored expertise, he dug out the prisoner's eyes . . .
> 'Turn him round, Ifor?' [Dafi] said. 'Top and tail?'
> 'No no no no no' Ifor said, smiling at him as he got to his feet. 'Minimum force . . . In politics, my boy, restraint is everything.' (*G*, 127)

This is the cold violence of a psychopath – 'a most accomplished thug who happened not to be French' (*G*, 10) as Griffri calls him. By the second half of the novel the Welsh have adopted the practice, with Iorwerth and Hywel blinding hostages in the siege of Caerllion. It is Meilyr, the madman, who sees the significance of the fact that Hywel has adopted a Norman helmet and mailshirt: 'The helmet's set a mark on him' (*G*, 196), he remarks, evoking the mark set on Cain after his murder of his brother Abel (Genesis, 4: 8–15). The historical Hywel's success in assimilation is suggested by the fact that Gerald of Wales mentions him approvingly as '[maintaining his] good faith and credit by observing a strict neutrality between the Welsh and the English'.[73] Meilyr's following comment – 'Now we know ourselves' (*G*, 196) – suggests that Griffri's confusion of identity ('I'm not sure if I'm *us* anymore' (*G*, 154)) is self-deception.

The Norman practice of blinding prisoners and the Welsh tendency towards fratricide come together horrifically in the second of these scenes when Hywel blinds and castrates his cousin and foster-brother, Owain Pencarn. 'For my brother' (*G*, 207), Hywel says as he puts in the blade, spinning this as vengeance for the death of Owain ab Iorwerth but symbolically suggesting his fratricidal relationship with both Owains. Meredith's novel follows the history recorded in *Brut y Tywysogyon* more closely than may at first appear:

[1175–**1175**] In the year after that, unknown to his father, Hywel ap Iorwerth of Caerleon seized Owain Pen-carn, his uncle. And after gouging his eyes out of his head he had him castrated lest he should beget issue who might rule thereafter over Caerleon.[74]

Making Owain Hywel's cousin and foster-brother foregrounds the issue of fratricide. Indeed, instances of fratricide, castration and similar intra-familial violence occur frequently in *Brut y Tywysogyon*, confirming Gerald of Wales's account: in 1152 Owain Gwynedd 'deprived Cunedda ap Cadwallan, his nephew . . . of his eyes and his testicles'; in 1170 Meurig ab Addaf was slain in his sleep by his first cousin, Maredudd Bengoch, and Dafydd ab Owen slew his eldest brother, Hywel ab Owain ; in 1174, Dafydd ab Owain imprisoned his brother Maelgwyn; and in 1175, Dafydd ab Owain imprisoned his bother Rhodri ab Owain 'for seeking from him a portion of his patrimony'.[75] Rather than a 'moving song' of martyred heroes, Welsh history is a blood-stained record of fraternal violence.

Meredith symbolizes this theme through the embedded story, 'The Afanc King and the Sons of Teyrnon', told by Griffri's wife, Cristin. A version of an Algonquin myth, 'The Beaver Medicine Legend',[76] told in the style of the First Branch of the Mabinogi, it is set in Gwent Iscoed. Meredith envisaged this as 'a kind of play within the play, though the narrator himself wouldn't realise it' (*AF*, n.p.). Like the play in *Hamlet*, the story enacts the thematic crime of the text in symbolic form. While Griffri may miss its significance, the women Cristin tells it to do not (*G*, 185). Meredith borrowed the character of Teyrnon Twrf Liant, lord of Gwent Iscoed, from the First Branch of the Mabinogi where the childless Teyrnon and his wife find and bring up the lost Gwri Wallt Eurin, before restoring him to his rightful parents, Pwyll and Rhiannon.[77] In Meredith's tale, Teyrnon and his wife have twin sons, naming them 'Gwri' and 'Eurin'. The splitting of the name figures their status as doubles: when Gwri tries to kill Eurin the latter calls him, 'My other self' (*G*, 181) and when Gwri returns home he masquerades as Eurin. When Eurin reappears, having been succoured by the Afanc or beaver king, he is able to step back into his own identity after Gwri is drowned. This story of disputed patrimony and fratricidal intent plays out the themes of the novel in mythic form.

Using an Algonquin legend links Welsh history to that of the Native Americans, also subjected to brutal colonization and cultural theft. In the original story, it is Nopatsis's evil wife who manipulates him into abandoning his brother Akaiyan on an island and there is no substitution. The figure of the beaver, who teaches Akaiyan the mystery of the sacred songs and dances, resonates across the two histories. As Meredith notes, 'Afanc' is Welsh for beaver and since beavers were extinct or virtually extinct in Wales by the twelfth century they had become mythic creatures (*AF*, n.p.). In his *Journey Through Wales* Gerald of Wales claims that the river Teifi was the only place beavers could still be found in Wales or, indeed, south of the Humber.[78] He recounts the story that in eastern counties beavers hunted for musk would save themselves through self-mutilation: 'By some natural instinct [the beaver] knows which part of its body the hunter really wants. The creature castrates itself before the hunter's eyes and throws its testicles down.'[79] Within the context of Eurin and Gwri as doubles, the castration of Owain Pencarn suggests a similar self-mutilation of the Welsh as a people.

'The Afanc King' is a story which, in symbolic terms, can 'tell us what we are', exposing the hidden fratricide at the heart of Welsh history. Placed near the beginning of the second 'hearth', it provides a lens through which we can read the second half of the novel and re-interpret the events of the first half. While on first reading *Griffri* may appear to be a realistically confused representation of the chaotic mass of experience, it is actually constructed as a series of doublings and interweavings. Like a line of cynghanedd, it crosses over so that the second 'hearth' echoes and reworks the themes and imagery of the first. The first 'hearth' ends with Griffri established as *pencerdd* in Gwrgant's place: 'to become myself,' Griffri explains, 'I had to see the death of one mother and at least two fathers' (*G*, 149). Similarly, Iorwerth's murder of Morgan is doubled by Hywel's murder of Owain and mutilation of Owain Pencarn. The novel hinges around this shift between the first and second halves and the question of Griffri's own complicity in events. In this doubling and reversal, its structure is closer to that of medieval Welsh-language poetry than to the traditional linear plot of the realist novel.

Like *Snaring Heaven*, *Griffri* is rooted in Meredith's engagement with Welsh medieval poetry and history and it offers a way of thinking about the paradoxical power of poetry in times of historical conflict, past or present. Poetry is a 'craft' (*G*, 52) to be learned. It can be work done by a 'paid arselicker' (*G*, 9), even 'a kind of prostitution', done to 'provide satiety and the release of strong emotions' (*G*, 52). Griffri's battle song for Hywel orders the chaos of experience in order to whip up aggression: 'The kind of sieving off of what's not needed so that they don't see the moon except as a lamp, they don't see people but the enemy' (*G*, 163). The official *marwnadau* (elegies), *dadolwchau* (poems of reconciliation), battle songs and praise songs Griffri writes rework stock imagery and formulae. 'Hawk. Dragon. Wolf. Oak door of Gwynllwg' are the 'expected names' (*G*, 164) with which he will celebrate his prince, regardless of who that is. These draw on Gruffudd ab yr Ynad Coch's 'The Death of Llywelyn ap Gruffudd' where the prince is the 'Oaken door of Aberffraw', 'unshamed hawk', 'lion', 'thrusting wolf'.[80] This intertextual connection links *Griffri* to Meredith's 'Prisoners' and the context of the 1980s. But poetry can also be a way of making 'spaces for the spirit' (*G*, 52). Although Griffri never writes an official *marwnad* for Gwrgant, the fragment 'Intricate May' (*G*, 149) is presented here as a personal elegy which comes closer to a kind of truth. Meredith's translation omits the final three lines of the original which introduces a Christian framework ('From blest Christ there's no escaping'[81]), making Griffri's version a more modern individual meditation on grief. The monk who transcribes it thinks it 'too pessimistic' but Griffri notes: 'He didn't see that words that tell a grief can do more than tell' (*G*, 149). Words can whip up patriotic fervour, provide emotional release or therapy for trauma, but they can also (as in the story of the Afanc King) reveal truths beyond what is actually said.

The two figures in the novel who see more than Griffri are his wife Cristin, a storyteller and maid to Iorwerth's wife Angharad, and the madman Meilyr. Cristin is associated with the sacred through a nexus of imagery in the novel which links early Celtic Christianity, the natural world and sexuality. The novel opposes the Norman ecclesiastical establishment – epitomized by the stone cathedral at Llandâf with its arch 'Like the open mouth of a wolf' (*G*, 56) – and the 'true church' (*G*, 61) represented by Griffri and Cristin's love-making in the woodland. Both tree roots and Cristin's hair are compared to the interwoven carvings on Celtic crosses:

> Through a thicket of hair I could see the root plait. Living lines woven to the glory of god, like the old crosses . . .
> Here was the real church. How could god live in the belly of a wolf? (*G*, 61)

Dafydd Johnston suggests that this concept of native Welsh religion, 'located in the natural world and celebrating sexuality as an expression of divine love' anachronistically draws on 'popular ideas' about early Celtic Christianity and the fourteenth-century poetry of Dafydd ap Gwilym, particularly 'The Woodland Mass'.[82] In fact, Meredith was careful to use historically appropriate sources:

'For the bits of poetry in *Griffri* I used models only from roughly Griffri's era or earlier, sometimes much earlier. Dafydd ap G[wilym] was out of the question.'[83] Furthermore, the use of an unreliable narrator undercuts any attempt to take this concept as a source of either national or personal truth. For Cristin is entangled in the complicities which fracture this novel. She led Griffri into the woodland to be kidnapped by Ifor's men on the instructions of Iorwerth and Angharad, thus facilitating the deaths of Morgan and Gwrgant. Griffri's later comment – 'The true church. Even there we know nothing' (*G*, 244) – suggests that the narrative he has constructed around this is as false as any other.

Meilyr is based on a soothsayer in Gerald of Wales's *Journey Through Wales* who could allegedly 'explain the occult and foretell the future' as a result of madness brought on by an encounter with a beautiful girl who turned into a succubus.[84] Another double for Griffri – there is a 'bizarre resemblance' (*G*, 91) – he represents an alternative self. Meilyr speaks truth but slanted, in fragmented images which are reproduced as poetry in *The Meaning of Flight*: 'River rolling on the plain. A harvest full and certain' (*G*, 88; *MF*, 46); 'The butchered lie forgotten' (*G*, 90; *MF*, 46). As Meredith notes, the Welsh word for mad, *gwallgof*, translates as 'marred memory', therefore 'having a grip on memory is sanity'.[85] 'Soothing the memory marred,' Meilyr says, 'is a difficult art' (*G*, 92). Art should be the opposite of madness and Griffri's role as poet is to be the 'keeper of memory' (*G*, 9). Yet he is haunted by the fear that he's the same as Meilyr – or worse, that Meilyr sees more than he does: 'I would have liked his clarity, seeing through to what was needed' (*G*, 94).

After witnessing the final act of treachery in the novel, the massacre of Seisyll ap Dyfnwal and his men by Gwilym Brewys at Abergavenny, Griffri himself has a period of madness in the woodland. This culminates in the post-coital transformation of Sigfa (who appears in the first hearth as a young girl he wants to seduce) into a demon:

Tight together as we were she opened her eyes and I saw my own ghost in her pupils. *We ought to be dead* I thought. The pupils were an odd kind of slot . . . Against my palms the wattles grew hot, contorted and boiled into erupting horny skin and ringlets of fur and the claws dug into me . . . The thing was driving me into the earth, taking me where I ought to have been. (G, 234)

This is both a nightmare reversal of his woodland lovemaking with Cristin and an uncanny replication of Meilyr's encounter with a succubus: 'I looked into her wide eyes,' Meilyr remembers, 'and there was the glaucous, ravelled iris, my own ghost staring at me in it, and the pupil was a black slot' (G, 96). Unlike Meilyr, Griffri kills the woman.

On one level this replicates medieval thinking which positions women in misogynistic binary terms as either Madonna or demon. Meredith explains that:

I was thinking about what it would be like to live in a pre-rationalist society where there is no separation between an experience and the religious. There's a constant polarity in things – they are either sacred or profane. Griffri says that things are either 'miraculous or hellish'. It's a false polarity – a non-rational way of looking at the world and there's a mismatch with the ideological framework Griffri lives in.[86]

But it also suggests a psychological response to trauma. Bohata argues that the appearances of the succubus are connected to the violence of the Norman colonizers.[87] While this is true, the image of Griffri/Meilyr's 'ghost' in her eye suggests that this is a projection of their own fears onto a woman. Griffri's (possibly unconscious) plagiarism of Meilyr's story indicates that his tale is as much a cobbling together of the stock material of his culture as his battle songs.

On a symbolic level, the incident connotes death and rebirth. It takes place in a 'gaping mouth of earth' (G, 230), both womb and tomb, formed under the roots where a huge oak has fallen. Bohata reads this as a grotesque version of the cauldron of life from the Mabinogi which can transform a dead soldier into a living one: if Griffri's role as poet is to be 'the cauldron to contain a people', this is a metaphorical re-membering or re-vivifying of that people.[88] While Bohata reads the motif of the cauldron positively as figuring the possibility of 're-membering a people whole, not in the sense of returning them to an earlier state, but in (re)making them anew', it's also notable that in the Mabinogi the men thus reborn no longer have the power of speech.[89] Similarly, after these events Griffri loses the power to sing (G, 243–4).

Griffri's narrative ends with a 'meeting between two of the dead' (G, 245), suggesting that he is as much dead as reborn, and with a revelation of matrimony as well as patrimony betrayed. Walking back from Abergavenny, Griffri finds himself at the *hafod* over-looking the Gwedog valley where he grew up. There an unrecog-nizably old woman tells him that she lost a son who was 'taken to become a poet' (G, 247). We realize that Gwrgant bought Griffri as a substitute for Cadi, giving his brother a horse in return for telling Griffri's mother he was dead and himself telling Griffri that his mother had died. The system of fostering involves a symbolic matricide. Moreover, far from being a war hero Griffri's father was running away after impregnating his own daughter. The last words of the novel are Griffri's bald denial of his mother and his own identity:

> 'You might have known the little boy' [she said] 'He'd be about your age, I'd say, if he'd lived. Or no. A bit younger, I'd think. Do you remember him?'
> 'No' I said. (G, 248)

In this defeated, brutalized and fragmented country, the poet whose role is to be the 'keeper of memory' because song 'can tell us what we are' (G, 9) cannot bear to remember who he is and cannot escape the tissue of lies in which he is enmeshed.

Published just over a decade after the failed 1979 devolution referendum, *Griffri* comes out of the 1980s, that 'dark time' of internal divisions and strife, which Meredith has described as 'a beastly tangle when you don't know what to believe about yourself – your own locatedness in a position of inimical force –

about to pull apart whatever you are'.[90] As 'Prisoners' and '1985' show, Meredith was concerned with the question of complicity and betrayal in this contemporaneous context. In *Griffri* he presents the period of the Anglo-Norman incursions into Gwent as a 'pre-history of the present', when Wales was losing its independence.[91] It marked the beginning of a lengthy process of defeat, culminating in the 1536 Act of Union, which the devolution referendum failed to reverse. As Griffri tells us three times: 'a man who's freed can never be the same as one who's merely free' (*G*, 198). Whereas Walter Scott's *Waverley* folds Scottish defeat into a dialectical image of progressive British union,[92] *Griffri* depicts Wales as a country undergoing a traumatic process of conquest where brothers turn the brutality of the oppressor against their own kin. It ends with a fragmented brutalized country, and a poet who denies his own identity and his role as rememberer.

4

Space, place and time: *Sidereal Time* (1998) and *The Meaning of Flight* (2005)

Published in 1998, in the interval between the 1997 referendum in which the Welsh voted for devolution by just 50.3 per cent and the establishment of the Welsh Assembly in 1999, *Sidereal Time* is a condition-of-Wales novel.[1] The morning after the referendum, Meredith recorded in a 1999 piece for the *New Statesman*, he 'wandered around Brecon market in a blissful daze, accidentally bought a new guitar, then went home and gave my kids a tenner each before discovering I was broke'.[2] He went on to tease out the significance of the event:

> History, like geology, comprises small accretions and erosions, huge pressures shifting in slow motion. Then occasionally there are moments of immediately apprehended change, like this one. On that 18 September, *something* definitely happened, an Event.
> But what?[3]

For Meredith the referendum was about whether 'we wanted to reinvent ourselves in the arena of real politics'.[4] Published on the eve of that reinvention, *Sidereal Time* puts education at the centre of its exploration of historical process, as it was the centre of Tony Blair's election campaign in the run-up to Labour's landslide victory in the May 1997 election: 'Education, education, edubloodycation', as Meredith's teacher protagonist Sarah Bowen puts, 'Say a word often enough and it turns meaningless' (*ST*, 103).[5]

Perhaps the most underrated of Meredith's novels, *Sidereal Time* is a complex and self-consciously postmodern text. Both *Sidereal*

Time and *The Meaning of Flight* (2005) are the work of a mature writer who had attained, as Nicholas Murray noted in a review of the latter, 'an accomplished and enviable possession of the skills of [his] craft'.[6] Still grounded in materialist politics of local place, both novel and poetry look outward to a wider world that is in turn situated within a sense of deep space-time. Meredith's fascination with time in fiction, with how it can be manipulated in narrative and how that relates to time outside the text, connects to his representation of place and space and his interest in the relationship between historical process and event. In one sense, any form of writing, whether historiography or fiction, is a way of thinking about how we understand ourselves in time or as historically situated. While *Griffri* focuses on the subjective nature of historical narrative, *Sidereal Time* develops a sophisticated philosophical exploration of the relationship between space, place and time.

'It was in reading', Meredith writes in 'Secret Rooms' (1995), 'that I first became aware that time is elastic'.[7] As a child he found that:

> The real time for reading was the result of an unconscious collaboration between my skill and imagination and the author's . . . Reading was much more like performing a piece of music than listening to it. My dirty thumbmarks on the page edges left a kind of geological record of these struggles. Meanwhile, the time that ran in my head, the storytime, could stretch, concertina, divide, or loop back on itself like a Sopwith Camel doing an Immelmann Turn.
>
> With these loopings and divisions came the polyphony of shifting viewpoints and times.[8]

This captures the intensity of childhood reading – both its physicality (the 'dirty thumbmarks' on the page) and its dizzying interiority (the 'loopings and divisions' of interior time). Meredith's experimentation with 'shifting viewpoints' is evident in *Shifts* and *Sidereal Time* continues this. It also draws on Meredith's interest in time and narrative in film, explored in his surreal short story, 'The Woman on the Beach' (1991), a homage to Jean Renoir's 1947 film of the same name.[9] 'What books showed me of that other kind of time, history,' Meredith writes, 'is more complicated.'[10] Recognizing 'how books touched real history' through the connection between Orwell's *The Road to Wigan Pier* and his father's part in a sympathy strike for the Nine Mile Point miners was an important part of Meredith's politicization.[11] The complicated relationship between time/history, space/place and narrative is at the heart of *Sidereal Time*.

The question of time had a practical significance for Meredith as a writer in relation to his day job as a teacher at Brecon High School during the 1980s and early1990s. *Shifts* and *Griffri* were written in the context of a job which gave him very little time in which to write. During this time he and his wife, also a teacher, were bringing up a young family. While it clearly came out of his own experience, *Sidereal Time* had a long gestation period as Meredith recalled:

> When my first novel came out I remember a journalist asking me what I was working on now . . . I remember saying, 'I've got this phrase, "sidereal time", going round in my head'. It was about eight years and two books later that I wrote the first words of the novel *Sidereal Time*.[12]

By the time he began the serious writing of *Sidereal Time*, Meredith was no longer a secondary school teacher.

In 1993 Meredith became senior lecturer in creative writing at the new University of Glamorgan, based in Treforest, Pontypridd. This institution had been through a number of incarnations before it was awarded university status following the Further and Higher Education Act in 1992.[13] Under its first vice-chancellor, the Newport-born Professor Adrian Webb, the newly fledged Glamorgan aimed to be a university for the south Wales valleys during a period when student numbers were expanding rapidly. These close links with its local area made it a hospitable milieu for Meredith and other Wales-based writers.

At Glamorgan Meredith was joining an English department that was developing a reputation for pioneering the teaching of creative writing.[14] The poet Tony Curtis, influenced by his experience of the MFA at Goddard College, Vermont, and Rob Middlehurst, lecturer in communication studies, had begun teaching creative writing in the 1980s.[15] In 1993 an MA in writing was launched, led by Curtis. Taught on an innovative distance-learning basis, the MA (later an MPhil) proved extremely successful in nurturing writing talent. Other staff included the Birmingham-born poet Sheenagh Pugh, with whom Meredith shared an interest in language and translation. The poet and editor Meic Stephens, born in Treforest, began teaching at the university in 1994. As founding editor of the influential *Poetry Wales* between 1965 and 1973 and later as literature director of the Welsh Arts Council, Stephens had nurtured what he called the 'second flowering' of Anglo-Welsh poetry.[16] Many notable writers were tutors on the MA course including Helen Dunmore, Gillian Clarke, Siân James, Paul Henry and Stephen Knight. Later staff included the poet Jeremy Hooker, literary critic Jane Aaron (founding editor of the Honno Classics series), novelist and short story writer Catherine Merriman, poet Matthew Francis, Merthyr-born novelist Desmond Barry and Maria Donovan (a graduate of the MA in writing). Philip Gross joined the staff as professor of poetry in 2004.

An inspirational teacher, Meredith became a key player in this flourishing academic community. As subject leader for creative writing, he became responsible for leading a tightly knit if often independently minded team and he was promoted to professor in 2007. Among the local students he taught was Rachel Trezise from Cwmparc, whose semi-autobiographical novel, *In and Out of the Goldfish Bowl* (2000) won an Orange Futures prize. His postgraduate students included the Treorchy novelist Richard John Evans, whose *Entertainment* (2000) is a novel of disaffected youth in the 'post-everything' Rhondda,[17] and Emma Darwin, whose historical novel *The Mathematics of Love* (2006) alternated parallel narratives set in 1819 and 1976.[18] The Radnorshire novelist Tom Bullough, who completed a PhD at the re-named University of South Wales in 2014, is another writer who has paid tribute to Meredith, noting that in the writing of his novel *Addlands* (2016), Meredith's 'poem "Borderland" . . . was on my mind throughout'.[19]

As with *Shifts*, the writing of *Sidereal Time* seems to have benefitted from a retrospective view on a job that Meredith had already left behind. An image used by Meredith in an interview with Dai George for *Poetry Wales* is useful in thinking about this novel:

> I think of novels as like a Venn diagram. There are three circles: there's the self – and I don't mean *my* self; I mean the individual – then there are other selves, so the community or society, and then there's everything else . . . It moves through time as well as space. And we do sit in a bigger picture of historical process, political structures and the big natural, ecological processes – that's the third circle. I think the novel is brilliant at exploring between those spheres.[20]

Meredith used a similar image in his inaugural professorial lecture where he suggested that his novels attempted to 'bear witness to and to explore the relationship between the three realms of the inner, then the interpersonal, then the larger world of historical and natural forces'.[21] Both *Sidereal Time* and *The Meaning of Flight* are concerned with the relationship between the individual, his or her community, and those wider spheres of historical, political and universal processes. These relationships are situated in space/place and they are dynamic; that is, they move or change through or in time. 'Flight' is movement through time *and* space. The metaphor of 'spheres' is particularly apt in relation to *Sidereal Time* which engages with astronomy and the major shifts in understanding enabled by Nicolaus Copernicus's heliocentric model of the universe.

The 'gloopness of process': space, place and Sidereal Time *(1998)*

'Sidereal time' is star time; that is, time measured by the earth's distance from the fixed stars rather than the sun. A sidereal day is about four minutes shorter than a solar day.[22] As the title suggests, *Sidereal Time* is a novel obsessed with different kinds of time: clock time, body time, work time, family time, school time, historical time, narrative time, reading time, film time, drinking time, solar time, star time. The title also suggests a time to the 'side' of the 'real', an alternative time.[23] Meredith's childhood realization that 'time is elastic', an insight which underpins so much modernist experimentation, enables the novel's exploration of the ways in which time shapes and is shaped by narrative. Formally sophisticated and self-consciously intertextual, *Sidereal Time* is (like *Griffri*) a novel that explores the possibilities of making meaning out of the chaos of experience through patterns: 'the spilly slitheriness of process' (*ST*, 12) is given form by the markers of days, weeks, birthdays, timetables, diaries. This meditation on the different kinds of narratives we use to make sense of time – historiography, fiction, film, poetry, essay plans, CVs, obituaries – is located within a dynamic sense of geography so that the novel looks out from local 'place' to 'space' in the sense of the solar system.

The distinction between 'space' and 'place' is a complex one, as Phil Hubbard and Rob Kitchen acknowledge in their overview of theoretical approaches.[24] In relation to Meredith's work it is useful to think in terms of place as a distinctive type of space which is 'defined by (and constructed in terms of) the lived experiences of people'.[25] As such it is constructed in part through history and language (as Raymond Williams indicates), and connected to identity and belonging. In relation to space, I want to keep several meanings in play here, ranging from the interval between objects ('empty space') to 'outer space' (the solar system, universe or cosmos). Ultimately, *Sidereal Time* moves towards an understanding of what we can think of 'space-time' as the term is used by Doreen Massey to insist on the inseparability of these concepts.[26]

While *Shifts* takes place over nine months and *Griffri* covers forty years, *Sidereal Time* is set over five days of a working week. Meredith has suggested that this gives the novel 'a sort of five act structure' and that it fits the fact that the novel is 'partly about the drudgery of earning a living'.[27] The days of the week are given at the beginning of each section in Welsh: Llun, Mawrth, Mercher, Iau, Gwener. 'More transparently than in English', Meredith notes, 'these week-day names represent five "planets" – the moon, Mars, Mercury, Jupiter, and Venus'.[28] This structure maps work time onto astronomical and mythic time while the use of stream of consciousness represents the formlessness of interiority, or what Meredith calls the 'gloopness of process' (*ST*, 80). This is a very Joycean novel. Like *Ulysses* (1922), it encompasses the formlessness of the quotidian within a diurnal structure which references the epic or world-historical and it focuses on two protagonists who double each other (Leopold Bloom/Stephen Dedalus and Sarah Bowen/Steven Leyshon). Furthermore, it combines modernist techniques (stream of consciousness, allusion, parody and a mixture of realism and fantasy) with a self-reflexive postmodern irony.

Set in a comprehensive school in an unnamed post-industrial south Wales valley, *Sidereal Time* is focalized through Sarah Bowen, an over-worked English teacher, wife and mother, and Steven David Leyshon, a sixth-former from a run-down hilltop council estate. Like *Shifts* and 'Averted Vision', the text alternates points of view. Doubles and opposites, Sarah and Steve have very different relationships with time. Conscious of approaching the mid-life point (her thirty-fifth birthday is on the Friday), Sarah is what we would now call 'time-poor'. Pushed to the limit by her workload and forced by the suicide of the history teacher, Eileen, to cover sixth-form history classes, Sarah has to make a desperate attempt to keep one step ahead of the students, furtively reading the set textbook as she teaches. To use up lesson time, she asks the students to present their essay plans in class. In contrast, Steve is an intermittent attendee with a casual attitude to school time. Having been put back a year for 'Extra time' (*ST*, 204), he is seventeen and a half, exactly half Sarah's age. An autodidact (like his grandfather) fascinated by history, Steve becomes obsessed with the research for his presentation, composing a fiction about Nicolaus Copernicus (he never writes it down) which forms an embedded text within the novel.

The use of parallel historical narratives became a common technique in historiographic metafictions – such as Graham Swift's *Waterland* (1983), A. S. Byatt's *Possession* (1990) or Emma Darwin's *The Mathematics of Love* – as a way of exploring the nature of history and the impact of the past on the present.[29] In such novels, as Meredith noted in a review of Sam Adams's *Prichard's Nose* (2010), researching the past is often a trope for 'the puzzle of the knowability of other people'.[30] In *Sidereal Time* Meredith is doing something different. Steve's story is a parody of historical fiction but it is nevertheless an imaginative engagement with the past. Sarah's problem is that she has neither time nor space in which to address history in any meaningful way. For her, history is squashed into textbooks and reduced to arid fragments.

The 'black ink wafflegrid of her timetable' in the 'week to view diary' (*ST*, 13) which dominates Sarah's life symbolizes the rigid structures of the working school week. The novel opens as she wakes on Monday morning:

> Eight see nine tee eleven ee then, yes, then four ell, sorry, ten ell, and after grub seven see for a double and oh shit lower six double hist oh, oh Christ and enterprise denterprise in my dinner. That's the trouble. Once it's full on a Monday you're stuck the whole bloody year. Entist. Dentisprise Thursday. Dentist Thursday. (*ST*, 7)

In its rendering of female interiority, Sarah's stream of consciousness as she lies in bed next to Mel recalls Molly Bloom's famous soliloquy at the end of Joyce's *Ulysses*.[31] Whereas Joyce's frank depiction of female sexuality was shocking in its time, however, Sarah is a working mother with no time even for masturbation. While Joyce dispensed with punctuation and paragraphing to mimic the flow of consciousness in prose, Meredith uses unfamiliar spellings and sentence fragments to make 'strange' Sarah's anxious thoughts.

Making the ordinary 'strange' is a key theme in the novel. Later Sarah borrows the technique of defamiliarization from Craig Raine's 'A Martian Sends a Postcard Home', a classic example, in order to teach Ted Hughes's 'Pike' (*ST*, 59). Likewise, as readers we are jolted into seeing the ordinary as extraordinary: Year 10L as a 'three-toed sloth' (*ST*, 60), for instance. One of Meredith's most striking gifts as a writer is the ability to use the apparently mundane – an ordinary family waking on a Monday morning – to explore existential questions. The opening of the novel uses naturalistic detail – the banal details of sleeping, waking, farting, shaving, shitting, removing a tampon – to ground this philosophical exploration of time and space. Like *Shifts*, *Sidereal Time* has an 'ambitious symbolist heart' (*S*, 215) but the symbols are so ordinary, slipped in through mundane conversation or corny puns, that it is easy to miss them. Verbal wordplay is an important part of this layering and Meredith takes pleasure in what he has called 'the naffness of ordinary life'.[32]

Sarah's waking stream of consciousness becomes a meditation on the different kinds of time we use to give meaning to existence. There is the drudgery of the school day, neatly divided into lesson periods. There is clock time, no longer measured in the 'Jerky little jumps' of the ticking clocks of her childhood, but by the clock radio: 'Time comes down a wire now at two hundred and forty volts. A smooth passage of electrons' (*ST*, 8). There is her menstrual cycle, the 'Time of the Month' (*ST*, 134). The structure of the working week even dictates the rhythms of bodily desire: 'Sunday's fuckday as Monday's washday, or used to be' (*ST*, 8). Then there is her thirty-fifth birthday, signifying the mid-life point: 'Oh no not yet not half way yet' (*ST*, 7). Sarah wants a sense of occasion, something to give 'form and occasion to the spilly slitheriness of process', yet she knows that occasions like significant birthdays are 'just arbitrary markers' (*ST*, 12). Ageing is a movement through time as well as an un-ignorable signifier of mortality.

The physical process of ageing – 'When you get to thirty four your tits give up' (*ST*, 11) – makes the materiality of the human body explicit: 'That's what we are,' thinks Sarah, 'The inconsequential heaving processes at the bottom of muddy water. Gloop' (*ST*, 12). The novel's concern with bodily functions – Sarah's menstrual blood (*ST*, 10), Mel's 'matutinal fart' (*ST*, 10), Ben 'shitting' (*ST*, 13) – not only recalls Joyce (whose depiction of Leopold Bloom on the toilet famously caused outrage) but links the individual to the larger spheres of biological and historical process. Ben's proud announcement – 'Mummy I done two plops' (*ST*, 11) – represents the material body, what Yeats called, in a line from 'Byzantium' which echoes in Sarah's head, 'the mire of human veins'.[33] At the end of 'Mercher', Steve sees a graffitied word on the window of a broken-into house on the estate where he lives: 'it said SHIT, with the ess backwards' (*ST*, 140). The care with which it has been written in reverse shows that the writer is 'Sending his message to the world' (*ST*, 140). That life is at base a matter of 'SHIT' (as a house can be simply another 'nozzle . . . on the sewer' (*SH*, 29)) is one possible conclusion to the kinds of existential question Meredith is asking in this novel.

It is the tension between form and the 'spilly slitheriness of process' (*ST*, 12) which preoccupies Sarah. Her birthday offers one way of making the 'slither' of time meaningful but such occasions are, she knows, 'Fictions to make it bearable' (*ST*, 12). She wants 'Something nodal . . . Something fucking significant' (*ST*, 40). Meredith has said that:

> I'm suspicious of time-markers like centuries and decades . . . *Sidereal Time* is partly about that, about the tensions and complementarities between the concepts of 'event' and 'process' and how we perceive them, how we look for moments of significance that may or may not be there.[34]

That suspicion of 'time-markers' is evident in *Griffri*. In *Sidereal Time* the rigid structures of the school timetable are an equally arbitrary way of giving structure to time, masking the potential meaninglessness of existence. Sarah's week is a race either against time, or to fill time. Held open on her lap in the staff room, her diary conceals the 'twin planets of her knees' (*ST*, 13), suggesting how day-to-day drudgery obscures the larger cosmic picture. In this the novel continues the exploration of work begun in *Shifts*. Sarah's brother Kenny, facing redundancy, thinks: 'It's work, what it do to you. Destroy you. But what are you without it?' (*ST*, 171). In contrast to *Shifts*, *Sidereal Time* considers a culture in which women's employment has become a norm but this brings with it another set of problems.

Meredith's novels 'meditate on work and its meaning, or meaninglessness, and how it connects the individual, often unwittingly, with larger processes of politics and history'.[35] For Sarah, teaching is a job: '*Career* is something you do down a wet road without any brakes' (*ST*, 149). Just as using a poet as a protagonist in *Griffri* allowed Meredith to write about poetry as a vocation, using an English teacher in *Sidereal Time* gives him licence to think about the 'work' of teaching and how this relates to the 'meaning' of literature in a post-industrial capitalist society. Meredith shows what happens when fiction and poetry (usually opposed to work) become part of a daily job but he also shows the redemptive possibilities of art.

On one hand the relentless drudgery of teaching threatens to render art 'meaningless'. We see Sarah teaching poetry to class 10L – 'the educational equivalents of the three-toed sloth' (*ST*, 60). Conscious of her 'technique' (*ST*, 61), she hands out photocopies, talks through the importance of observation – 'When you look hard at anything it becomes strange' (*ST*, 64) – and reads the poem aloud. Reviewing her 'inner CV', she writes this class down as 'a halfway decent attempt, heroic but foolish, to overcome the gloopness of gloop in collaboration with a group of comatose fourteen year old three-toed sloths' (*ST*, 66). It is a feeling many teachers, at all levels, will recognize. It is exacerbated by innovations such as the '*Cycle of Assessment*' (*ST*, 129) promoted by a glib advisor from county hall. This will require a huge amount of what the advisor euphemistically calls 'nondirected time' (*ST*, 135), that is, time for which the teachers will not be paid, to implement: 'Six extra weeks a year fitted into the interstices of something which didn't have any interstices left' (*ST*, 136). The hollowing out of language, and time, by the corporatization of education is encapsulated in the advisor's platitudes: 'opportunities rather than obstacles' (*ST*, 136). Likewise, Tony Blair's phrase has already become an empty slogan: 'Education, education, edubloodycation, Say a word often enough and it turns meaningless' (*ST*, 103).

Conversely, *Sidereal Time* celebrates the value of teaching literature and the importance of observation, of close reading, in making meaning out of the ordinary. It was partly the experience of teaching that sent Meredith back to poetry in his twenties:

[I]t made me look at poetry again, harder – including poems I didn't much care for in some cases, though I had to be an advocate for them. Often it just seems like drudgery while you're doing it, but what you discover is that you learn how to read attentively . . . so that you see connections, interplays and patterns of imagery in texts.[36]

Likewise, Sarah is an advocate for the value of 'reading attentively' despite the drudgery and a range of intertextual allusions forms a pattern of connections in the novel. Many of these texts – the poems by Hughes and Raine, the 'Northern Realism' of Stan Barstow's *Joby* (*ST*, 56), Ian Serraillier's *The Silver Sword* (*ST*, 20), or D. H. Lawrence's 'Odour of Chrysanthemums' (*ST*, 35) – are the standards of secondary school teaching. As a piece of metafiction (fiction which self-consciously draws attention to its fictionality[37]) *Sidereal Time* makes them 'strange' for us. This is more than just postmodern game playing and Meredith makes clear how much is at stake in the 'work' of teaching literature in a post-industrial area.

Many of these intertextual allusions offer different ways of representing and structuring time from Homer's epithetic 'rosy-fingered dawn' (*ST*, 7) through the melodramatic ending of *The Mill on the Floss* (*ST*, 52) to Tennyson's 'The Kraken' (*ST*, 122) which layers together the biblical end-of-time with mythological and geological time. These allusions counterpoint the novel's theme, enriching and complicating it, but they also draw attention to the constructed nature of art as opposed to life. '[G]od is a boring author,' Sarah reflects, 'Every chapter starts like this with the cliché of waking' (*ST*, 7). The TV script of *Joby* is 'Beautifully constructed, unlike life' (*ST*, 56) while George Eliot is 'a better novelist than god' (*ST*, 186). Literature, like science, is one of many narratives we use to make sense of time. Thus watching a lath of light on Sarah's bedroom ceiling which fades 'in some precise Newtonian relation to its distance from the source' in turn suggests the poetic epithet 'rosyfingered dawn' (*ST*, 7). Poetic and scientific, the 'rosy sky finger' is the result of, and a figure for, the fact that Sarah's 'bit of the earth [is revolving] towards the sun' (*ST*, 10).

Another classroom favourite, Andrew Marvell's 'To His Coy Mistress', figures Sarah's desire to 'Make [time] stand or make it run' (*ST*, 39). There are points in the novel where time seems to stand still, demonstrating Meredith's sense that time – at least the time of reading or of a film – is 'elastic'. At the end of 'Iau' Meredith illustrates this as we read Sarah reading a short story in a woman's magazine, written 'modishly in the present tense' (*ST*, 163). The heroine's name, Penelope Weaver, recalls the Homeric Penelope, wife of Ulysses (revisioned as Molly Bloom in Joyce's *Ulysses*), who plays for time – or stalls time – by repeatedly failing to finish the weaving of a shroud for Laertes. As Sarah fails to finish the story, leaving Penelope and her lover stalled, the second hand on Sarah's watch stops and then snaps forward again: 'The film unlocked' (*ST*, 165).

Through Sarah's double, Steven Leyshon, Meredith explores the tension between process and form in relation to two other major narratives of time: astronomical or cosmic time and history. These represent the other part of the Venn diagram: the larger spheres of the historical and natural processes within which the individual and the community exist. Through Steve, Meredith develops his interrogation of the borderland between history and fiction but here he triangulates this in relation to solar time. Like the young Griffri, Steve is a would-be artist or, possibly, an artist manqué like Jack in *Shifts*. His given name recalls Stephen Dedalus in Joyce's *A Portrait of the Artist as a Young Man* (1916) and *Ulysses*.[38] As Meredith noted in his inaugural lecture, the Joyce- like Stephen Dedalus, the 'artist or would-be artist-figure', is named 'after the Daedalus of the Minotaur myth . . . an Athenian craftsman, an inventor or engineer'.[39] Although he never writes down his story about Copernicus, Steve is fascinated by the craft of writing, carefully negotiating the mechanics of word choice and narrative structure in his fiction: 'Aye, then that bit. What worms we are. Oops. Two worms . . . But how do I get them into the fucking village?' (*ST*, 46). This in turn draws attention to the constructed nature of the historiographic metafiction we are reading.

Steve's unwritten fiction is a parody of popular historical adventure novels such as those of Robert Louis Stevenson. Meredith remembers reading his father's copy of Stevenson's *The Black Arrow* (1888),[40] a novel set during the Wars of the Roses in which the protagonist, Dick, discovers that his guardian murdered Dick's father. There is a very faint echo of Stevenson's plot of betrayal in *Griffri* which suggests a long-absorbed influence from childhood. Stevenson's novel also includes a description of an 'earth cavern'[41] under the half-fallen roots of a beech tree, used as a hiding place by an outlaw, which recalls the 'gaping mouth of earth' (*G*, 230) under the roots of an oak where Griffri takes refuge.

Through Sarah's fumbling history classes and Steve's parodic historical novel, *Sidereal Time* stages a debate about history and time which contrasts two types of narrative, historiography and fiction, and two historical figures: the Welsh Henry VII, and Nicolaus Copernicus. Sarah sets her sixth-formers an essay question: 'Was Henry VII a modern or medieval king' (*ST*, 33). She's based this on their set textbook, D. M. Perrot's *The Dawn of our Times: Spirit and Structure of Tudor England* (*ST*, 15) which argues: '*with the accession of Henry VII to the throne of England, the first gleamings of what may with some justice be referred to as the modern age . . . began to flicker on the horizon*' (*ST*, 17). Perrot espouses the 'great man' theory of history as popularized in the nineteenth century by Hegel in *Lectures on the Philosophy of History* (1837) and Thomas Carlyle in *Heroes, Hero-Worship and the Heroic in History* (1841). As Beverley Southgate notes, it makes the single great hero figure, or what Hegel calls the 'World-Historical Individual', such as Caesar or Napoleon, the 'motor of history'.[42] (Such a figure is, of course, invariably male.) Thus Henry is, in Sarah's words, 'the Turning Point. Crux. Cusp. Fulcrum. The plop point at which what was one thing becomes something else. Henry the Node' (*ST*, 30).

Like significant birthdays, this is an attempt to give form to 'gloop' by structuring it as linear narrative. As Sarah tells her pupils, '1500 is often given as a convenient date to mark the end of the medieval period and the beginning of what's often called the modern period . . . But really [the] Battle of Bosworth [1485] could be a more appropriate marker' (*ST*, 29). Such historiographical narratives neatly divide the chaotic flux of the past into historical periods, the 'time-markers' of which Meredith is rightly suspicious. If human history is, in Carlyle's words, 'By its very nature . . . a labyrinth and a chaos' then narrative is always going to be unable to represent it adequately because 'Narrative is *linear*'.[43] Given the postmodern understanding that history and fiction are both kinds of narrative (as Hayden White argues), then Meredith's novel suggests that fiction which refuses the imperative of linearity offers another, possibly more fruitful way, of representing the 'gloopness of process'.

Just as *Griffri* destabilizes the idea that there can be one coherent account of history, Steve takes issue with Sarah's narrative, arguing 'It en just like one bloke or one moment. There's all sorts of factors going on' (*ST*, 32), including the fall of Constantinople, the Silk Road, the development of gunpowder and printing. Rather than Henry VII, Steve wants to put Copernicus's development of the heliocentric model of the universe in the centre of the picture. In a book Steve liberates from the library, *Nicolaus Copernicus* (1973), Fred Hoyle argues that Copernicus 'detonated an overwhelming explosion of human knowledge', making possible, for instance, the work of Isaac Newton.[44] As Steve puts it:

> [Copernicus] changed everything . . . Just by looking and thinking and saying. From then on they could work out dynamics and gravity. The lot . . . They go on about Darwin, but I reckon Copernicus gave god a hell of a bloody clout hundreds of years before him. (*ST*, 203)

Or to summarize this critique of standard historiography in Steve's own idiom: 'Some twat with a naff haircut wins a battle and gets to be kinglet. Nothing. Meanwhile, the universe changes shape' (*ST*, 48). The close observation that Sarah advocates in her lesson on reading poetry turns out to have wider applicability: 'Just by looking and thinking and saying,' Copernicus has changed the 'shape of the universe'.

Steve's historical fiction culminates in a blatantly anachronistic encounter between Copernicus and a spectral Henry VII which stages a debate about history, time and the function of fiction. Riddled with doubts about his achievements, Henry VII visits Copernicus in his tower saying: 'I no longer know myself . . . Give me back my certain path' (*ST*, 154). On the eve of confirming his theory and publishing *de revolutionibus* (1543), Copernicus tells Henry:

> 'We are alike. We have both changed the world. But I have had to kill no one, my friend, and I have nailed the sun to the sky, and made the Earth spin about it, simply by counting and looking.'

> '. . . All the premise of your life was wrong . . . And the dirt you devoted your life to is not at the centre. The earth beneath our feet is no more fixed than the soot that whirls in the chimney.' (*ST*, 155)

Copernicus's discoveries destabilize the known world and undercut the values of power, land and money which Henry has espoused. The shifting of the earth from the 'centre' of the universe is another version of defamiliarization, or 'making strange'. It enables a radical shift in point of view. At the end of their conversation, Henry crumbles into dust and Copernicus, left holding the stranger's empty cloak, realizes that it is his own – it is his own view that has changed.

It is through an imaginative engagement with the past, through fiction, that Steve comes to understand not only how Copernicus arrived at his heliocentric model of the universe but also 'How . . . you place the one life in the rolling of the big wheel' (*ST*, 137), whether the life is that of 'Aitch Seven' (*ST*, 137) or Steve himself. When Steve (drunk from testing his 'sip rate' theory of drinking time) finally delivers his presentation, he is able to tell Sarah, 'We do History . . . all wrong. We don' see it real . . . It's, like, it's somebody else's Now' (*ST*, 199). If you measure time by the fixed stars rather than the sun, 'you get a whole extra day every year. Star time' (*ST*, 201). Time, place and history are fluid and relative, a matter of patterns and perceptions rather than certainties. In many ways Copernicus's model of the heliocentric universe maps neatly onto Meredith's Venn diagram with the three circles of the individual, the community and the bigger picture of historical, natural or ecological processes. In thinking about the way in which his novels seek to represent the three realms of inner, interpersonal and the larger historical/natural world, however, Meredith noted that he had tried 'not to privilege any of these three as being *at the centre*'.[45] Just as Copernicus decentres the human, placing the sun at the centre, Steve decentres Henry VII and 'English' history, looking out instead to a wider universe.

Like *Griffri*, *Sidereal Time* is part of a wider trend in historiographic metafictions which use fiction to interrogate the politics of historiography. In *History Meets Fiction*, Beverley Southgate quotes Timothy Parrish's argument that 'fiction in the postmodern era has become both the primary medium for arguing about what history *is*' and 'the critical genre for understanding *how history is made*'.[46] As Southgate comments, this understanding has implications for our understanding of 'the ideological functions . . . of history' and the 'purposes of those who produce it'.[47] Similarly, Meredith uses fiction to ask 'what history *is*' and '*how history is made*'. Fiction enables Steve to look beyond a narrowly Anglocentric history which positions Henry VII as a world-historical figure (the maker of the modern nation state or the beginning of imperialism depending on your point of view), at the same time as it erases his Welshness, his connection to place.

Geography, an understanding that history happens *somewhere*, is the other crucial factor here. Sarah's history lessons take place in the geography room: 'What next?' asks Steve, 'Synchronised swimming in the car park?' (*ST*, 25). But above his head is a 'black globe with the continents in white lines, and the nets of latitude and longitude in finer lines. Degrees, minutes, seconds' (*ST*, 25) which maps the interconnections of time and space. A mundane accident of school timetabling symbolizes the relationship between geography, history and astronomy – or space, place and time – as inter-connected ways of making meanings. *Sidereal Time* asks how we can bring together history, geography and astronomy to understand our place in the different spheres in the Venn diagram. One answer, it suggests, is through fiction – or art more generally – which can enable us to look out from place to space through time. Steve's demonstration of the heliocentric universe during a history lesson in the geography room (with himself and then Sarah at the centre) suggests a dynamic and politicized concept of what Doreen Massey calls 'space-time':

> One way of thinking about all this is to say that the spatial is integral to the production of history, and thus to the possibility of politics, just as the temporal is to geography. Another way is to insist on the in-separability of time and space, on their joint constitution through the interrelations between phenomena; on the necessity of thinking in terms of space-time.[48]

Both Steve and Sarah learn 'the necessity of thinking in terms of space-time': time is contingent and 'elastic', but it is also intimately related to space and place, neither of which are static. The Welsh weekday names which provide section headings make visible the fact that our sense of time is shaped by the movement of the planets through space, the diurnal revolving of the earth as it circles the sun.

Our sense of space-time is also intimately linked to local place and to local communities. In her useful discussion of the importance of place in postcolonial theorizations of Welsh landscape, Kirsti Bohata begins with a definition of place (borrowed from Erica Carter, James Donald and Judith Squires) as 'space to which mean-ing has been ascribed'.[49] Even more than Meredith's earlier texts, *Sidereal Time* reinvents the landscape of his *bro*. The school is roughly located in the mid valleys area where two valleys join. (Meredith has said that he had a school he once visited in Trehafod vaguely in mind when he wrote the novel.[50]) Brynhelyg, the hilltop council estate where Steve lives, is like any number of such estates. This lack of specificity makes the novel more typical but also reflects the process of de-industrialization of the valleys, with the decline of religion, politics and other institutions. This has left what Sarah thinks of 'nonplace[s]': 'Where there used to be moorland and header ponds for the steelworks, now there was a nonplace sliced by overlit roads, a shedscape of windowless superstores with their carparks, and windowless factories' (*ST*, 71). Such 'non-places' (motorways, airports and shopping centres) are seen by Marc Augé as typical of the supermodern Western world where social bonds are broken down.[51] This is 'place' which no longer has meaning, which has reverted to being 'space' in the sense of being empty. Similarly, in the quarry where Mel works, the mountain has been 'hollowed like a drilled tooth' (*ST*, 93). Just as language and time are hollowed out by the glib advisor from county hall with his 'Cycle of Assessment', the landscape is being denuded of historical meaning by neo-liberal post-industrialization so that it loses its human significance as place.

This shift is also articulated in Richard John Evans's *Entertainment*. The 'post-everything' Rhondda valley, stripped of the industrial history which created community, is now 'a place where the primary meaning has been taken away and replaced with a multiplicity of fragmented and unconnected meanings'.[52] Villages with 'actual histories' are replaced with 'retail villages where no meaning is encoded apart from a purely commercial branding'.[53] For 'generation X', to which Evans's characters (and Steve) belong, the 'appropriate response to your milieu', whether the Rhondda or Seattle, is 'an exaggerated cynicism'.[54]

Geography is destiny in this small country. Facing redundancy and potentially suicidal Sarah's brother Kenny runs away, moving (like Jack in *Shifts*) through space not time, and ends up in a seaside town which looks very much like Aberystwyth. 'Trouble with this country is you can't have a road movie', he reflects (*ST*, 169). Yet the novel refuses to validate existential despair: Kenny's car keys are fished out of the ocean for him by a Welsh-speaking old man who represents the history Kenny has failed to acknowledge. Kenny concludes: 'And where is there other than back' (*ST*, 173).

Like 'View from the hill' or 'Another go at Hay Bridge', *Sidereal Time* triangulates the position of the individual in relation to the local, a particular 'place' with all the geographical and historical specificities which give it meaning, as well as 'space' in the sense of the solar system (rather than the emptiness of 'nonplace'). The novel stages a confrontation between the narratives we use to try to make sense of the chaos of human history and the vastness of solar or sidereal time, showing how even apparently abstract time is contingent on your point of view, on the place from which you measure it. Copernicus, Steve says, 'put energy in the middle. Light' (*ST*, 202). One of the most striking things about *Sidereal Time* is that Meredith takes two marginalized working-class figures, a woman teacher and a teenage boy, the opposite of what Hegel called 'world-historical individuals' (such as Henry VII or, indeed, Copernicus), and puts them at the centre. '[W]orking class communities exist and . . . history can happen here too. Some of us already knew these things' as Meredith remarked in a 1987 review.[55] His own achievement is to develop a sophisticated philosophical exploration of concepts of space, place and time (sidereal, solar and human) as ways of ordering the 'gloopness of process' (*ST*, 80) through a celebration of the ordinary.

The final page of the novel offers an affirmation, however tentative: of education, of art, of life, of ordinary people and of the connection between self and other, body and spirit. There may be 'no such thing as absolute space' (*ST*, 204) but 'Everything's important' (*ST*, 205). The significant birthdays – 17, 35, 70 – which ought to mean something but don't, make 'A pattern instead. A shape made in time, like a piece of music' (*ST*, 204). Like the 'harmonies of rain and light' in 'What's Certain', they compensate for the 'facts of meat and pain and nothing else' (*SH*, 51). In counterpoint to the graffitied 'SHIT' at the end of 'Mercher', 'Gwener' (after Venus, the goddess of love) ends with Sarah and Steve watching the patterns made by people going home from school. The image recalls an earlier redemptive insight from 'Margam Park': 'it's people animate this space/sculpt time with passing here/no art but being human' (*SH*, 74). In the final lines of the novel, Steve writes a word backwards on the misted window of the classroom: a 'backwards capital ee', a 'vee', an 'oh', and the missing final letter (*ST*, 207), which spells out ƎVO[L].

'The art of dying': The Meaning of Flight *(2005)*

The work of a mature writer experimenting with a range of forms and themes, *The Meaning of Flight* (longlisted for the Welsh Book of the Year), looks out from the local to the global. Movement – through air, water or space – is a central theme and is closely related to time, whether diurnal or historical. A sense of 'the turning earth' (*MF*, 16) which shapes our experience of space, place and time is never far from the surface. The inclusion of 'Meilyr's song' (*MF*, 46), from the madman's prophecies in *Griffri*, points to continuities with earlier concerns. The question of representation and reality, of how the artist 'snares' the world, runs through the collection, and as with *Snaring Heaven*, attentive reading reveals a series of patternings within and between poems.

Opening with 'What flight meant', which meditates directly on the title, the collection is then bookended by two groups of poems located mainly abroad. The initial group entitled 'The island hours' includes four poems which move through the key times of day – from early morning in 'Snorkel' (*MF*, 11–12) to 'Night' (*MF*, 16–17) – on a Mediterranean island or islands. The final group, 'Seven cities', comprises poems on cities present and past, real and mythic, ranging from Castell Dinas (an Iron Age hillfort and Norman castle on the edge of the Black Mountains) to Picasso's 'Antipolis'. In between are poems that revisit more familiar landscapes and subjects: Meredith's mother in 'My mother missed the beautiful and doomed' (*MF*, 38–9), his grandmother in 'Colour' (*MF*, 18), his father in 'Homecoming' (*MF*, 40), 'Owning' (*MF*, 41), 'Old' (*MF*, 42), and his *bro* in 'Sheep on the estate' (*MF*, 19) or 'Twyn yr Hyddod' (*MF*, 43).

The juxtaposition of the title, *The Meaning of Flight*, with a cover photograph showing a turtle swimming, its foreflippers raised like wings, offers a central paradox that is related to the making of art. Swimming and flying are figured as interchangeable in several poems. In the most extended use of this conceit, 'Magic hour' (*MF*, 14–15), a beached and upturned turtle is 'paddling air' with its

'legs or fins or wings, whatever they were, / revolv[ing] in absurd
syncopations'. When he is returned to the water:

> And they were wings
> after all, as he birded through warm sea
> and he was Daedalus
> we hoped, and not the other one.

Flight carries with it the risk of falling – as the 'other one', Icarus,
falls into the sea in the original Minotaur myth. It is also closely
connected to art, or making, through the figure of Daedalus, the
'Athenian craftsman, . . . inventor or engineer', who makes the
wings that allow himself and his son to escape from Crete, and
whose name is borrowed by Joyce for his artist-maker (Stephen
Dedalus).[56] Icarus dies because he flies too close to the sun; an
image of hubris. In 'Magic hour' the poet hesitates to take a picture
with his 'throwaway camera' because he 'can understand / the
faiths that make no images of god', suggesting the risks of art, both
failure and hubris. Yet art – the 'syncopations' or 'rag' 'struck up'
by the turtle's foreflippers – seems to come from the confrontation
with the risk of failure, even with death. The 'magic hour' of the
title is another liminal moment: in cinematography it is the period
just after sunset (or before sunrise) when there is still enough evenly
diffused light 'to get the shot'. 'Edges' – between light and dark,
beach and sea, land and air – are, as Meredith puts it in 'Borderland',
'where meanings happen' (*AH*, 8), where risks can be taken which
energize and enable art.

The (almost) title poem, 'What flight meant' (*MF*, 7–8), uses
brilliantly precise observation of a swallow, 'clouted by some wind-
screen out of air', to meditate on the metaphorics of flight in the past
tense. The unexpected opening line – 'I held the art of *dying* /
in my hand today'– suggests an unspoken but implicit rhyme (flying/
dying). It is perhaps only when flight is in the past, the poem implies,
that we can capture it in verbal or written human art. Only when
the swallow is dying, knocked into 'stillness', can the poet observe
at close quarters its materiality, the 'taut arrangement / of black

pins and scimitars', the 'thumbsized shoulders', and see the exact colour of her forehead, neither red nor black but 'minute scumblings of rust'. The legs which 'weren't there when she flew' are visible now as 'clean black needles', the claws are 'machines designed to clutch at straws'. As Matthew Jarvis notes: 'The organic is thus very effectively reduced to the mechanic, the nonhuman to the forms of human making.'[57]

What 'flight meant' to the swallow was fluidity and jouissance, an unthinking, natural and non-verbal art of living:

> ... the pulsing line of gorging and delight
> that drew the smooth blur
> of her x on air.

Jarvis usefully suggests that the bird in flight here stands 'as the rendition of movement as a metaphysical concept within the economy of the poem as a whole'.[58] This in turn suggests the way that movement, particularly flight, works as an image of the artist and their striving after an adequate mode of representation (an 'art of [flying]') within the collection. The poem moves towards an understanding that: 'When the world's smacked loose from meaning / all's knocked to fuss and artifice and pattern.' As in Meredith's earlier poem on his father's illness, 'What's Certain', all that is left in the face of mortality is pattern: 'random echoes / Making harmonies of rain and light' (SH, 51). Yet it is at the moment of death that the perceptions of the swallow and the poet blur together: her eyes 'clinical as an artist's', see the 'mad particularity' of the world which is 'so sharp and quick with colour, / so stopped'.

The image of flying recurs throughout *The Meaning of Flight*, figuring a human desire to move above, beyond or through boundaries – between sea and air, human and divine, life and death – and how this relates to the risky process of making art. In 'Snorkel' holidaymakers swimming are seen from below as 'gods' who 'hang crucified or fly / above their shadows' (MF, 11). In 'Colour' the black and white photograph of the poet's grandmother at Troedrhiwgwair is 'a lie', contrasted with the bright colours of the hang-gliders above Man Moel, 'signalling *we live, we live*' (*MF*, 18). The rope between Cessna and glider in 'My son on Castell Dinas' (*MF*, 57) figures the connection between father and son, which must be broken if the son is to establish a separate self and 'fly' on his own. In 'Twyn yr Hyddod', one of a group of poems about the poet's father which refuses to be an elegy, it is a skylark that is 'always on the brink of falling' yet 'climbs / singing up through daylight' (*MF*, 43). Both the art of making and the art of flying are 'always on the brink of falling'. Flight again offers a figure for the artist's endeavour in the short lyric, 'Seaward', where the poet has 'ridden out on / the gull's back' and 'snapped out patterns' from the glittering sea (*MF*, 54). The image evokes both natural patterns and the camera as an image of human art. Here the flight of the imagination and the 'patterning' of art have no more 'sense' or 'significance' than is 'in the ineluctable / present tense'. The experience of the world itself as evanescent is, perhaps, enough.

Another key theme is a concern with time which is produced by the planet's movement through space. The images from astronomy that are so important in *Sidereal Time* inform several poems about time here. 'Transitory' (*MF*, 26) uses a series of metaphors – trout-tickling, gold-panning, milking – to describe the process of watching the transit of Venus (its passage between the sun and a superior planet thus making Venus visible as a spot on the sun) on 8 June 2004. Occurring every 243 years, this is the kind of once-in-a-lifetime event on a cosmic scale for which Sarah yearns. The transit is rendered as a process controlled by the poet as he angles the image of Venus through field-glasses onto the 'blank page'. The poem can be read as an allegory for the process of writing (rather like Hughes's 'The Thought Fox'[59]), of teasing an image of reality into a verbal or visual representation: 'and there my star / bazookaed onto paper'. A love song to the planet named after the goddess of love, 'Transitory' is implicitly paired with the previous poem 'Red armchair' (*MF*, 25). An extended metaphor which hymns the beauties of the poet's chair, this ends by refusing the power of the figurative: 'she' is 'never so cheap as to yield / to any of my metaphors / but always was is just my red armchair'.

As in *Snaring Heaven*, the sequencing of the collection generates echoes between individual poems. 'Toy revolver' (*MF*, 49), for instance, detailing a child's fascination with a toy gun looks far more political read against 'Occupied' (*MF*, 48) and 'Homecoming' (*MF*, 40). 'Homecoming', as noted in chapter 1, depicts the father, a former soldier, giving his son a plastic gun but then turning aside, with the words, *'No. No. Don't point that thing / at me'*, suggesting wartime trauma.[60] 'Occupied' complicates the theme of flight by noting of the helicopters used by the army on manoeuvres near the Usk: 'They name them after beaten people. / *Apache. Iroquois. Chinook.*' Like 'The Afanc King', this makes the connection between Native Americans and the Welsh (and, indeed, the Gurkhas and the Scots who, like Meredith's Welsh father, are soldiers in the British army) as colonized peoples.

Similarly, 'The astronomer's daughter' and 'the very temple' gain from being read together. Both contrast the astronomical with the human, the solar/sidereal with the familial. In the former, the Astronomer Royal climbs upward in his tower to look out at 'unreachable stars' while his daughter gazes down and inward, 'back into her room' (*MF*, 50). The image of the moon 'wax[ing] to blood' suggests her movement into an adult woman's body with its monthly cycles. In 'the very temple' (*MF*, 52–3) a family drive from A Toxa up through Spain, crossing the Channel to witness a solar eclipse (that of 11 August 1999 was visible from the UK). What this poem brilliantly captures is the apocalyptic, otherworldly experience of witnessing a solar eclipse, the way in which the erasure of the sun 'makes strange' our everyday world. An unpunctuated series of unrhymed couplets linked with the conjunction 'and', the form of the poem initially conveys the movement of the humans travelling up the continent. But then, while they are stationary, it conveys the uncanny movement of the eclipse itself, as 'a bud of darkness' hardens and spreads over the sun, 'swallow[ing]' the landscape: 'and nature was struck dumb / just like the papers said'. Time seems to shift as the bud 'rushed like the ground when you fall'. The religious imagery of the poem – the moment of full eclipse is 'the very temple of totality' – suggests the human need to find meaning in such a cosmic event. The poem ends with an image of resurrection as the 'timerush regather[s]', the sun 'discover[s] the ordinary', and the 'stone of the moon is rolled away'. The sense of solar or cosmic time here as elastic, as 'rush[ing] like the ground when you fall', is frightening rather than exhilarating. While the poet in 'Transitory' is in control, here the family is threatened, although the resurrection imagery suggests a kind of redemption.

The role of the poet is the other major strand which weaves through these poems. Sometimes this is implicit as in 'Meilyr's song', 'Red armchair' or 'Seaward', and sometimes explicit as in 'Famous Czech poet in Dinbych y Pysgod', 'Life of the Poet (index)', or 'Application to the Arts Council'. The latter three all play with form in metatextual ways. 'Life of the Poet' (*MF*, 32–3) is arranged as an index, providing an ironic commentary on biographies as another reductive narrative (like historiography). Entries on 'debt' and a 'Civil Service post' suggest the perennial problem of financing a poetic career. This theme also underpins 'Application . . .' (*MF*, 29), structured as a letter to an arts council asking for money to write the poem, complete with 'unobtrusive control of rhythm and line/breaks' and a promise to provide 'capital investment'. 'Famous Czech poet . . .' (*MF*, 28) plays (bilingually) with the meanings of 'plaice'/place and 'fish'/'pysgod': 'Too much freedom', states the Czech poet, 'will be hard'.[61]

Meredith has acknowledged the importance of form as a paradoxically liberating force. Even attempting a form as restricting as the villanelle – as in 'The Message' (*MF*, 31) which adheres to the main rules while reworking the refrain – has been 'a means of releasing something that works'.[62] In interview with Sheenagh Pugh, a poet similarly interested in structure, Meredith has suggested that working with a form can 'help anchor your effort in the material rather than in the self. It makes the text the thing.'[63] Thus the strict form of 'The Message' enacts the restrictions that the writer-protagonist has imposed upon herself in the notebooks she conceals under a 'board': 'the message is the message is in code' (*MF*, 31). The only secret may be that there is a secret: 'what's on display's the fact that all is hidden' (*MF*, 31). The form itself is the point.

Some of the experimentation in *The Meaning of Flight* is less obvious than the formal structure of the villanelle. There is a structural irony in the fact that the gnomic lines of prose culled from *Griffri* to form 'Meilyr's song' fall into the regularity of two rhyming iambic sestets (*MF*, 46). Another song, 'Cân', uses a refrain pattern, alternating English couplets with a Welsh response but rhyming bilingually (*MF*, 27). It ends with the speaker looking in the mirror 'and a ghost looked at me. / *I berfedd tywyllwch, at gân eos ddu*' ('to the core of darkness, to a black nightingale's song'[64]) a doubling which recalls Griffri seeing 'my own ghost in [Sigfa's] pupils' (*G*, 234). 'Aubade in middle age' ironically reworks the dawn song (usually describing the regret of parting lovers) to outline the mid-life drudgery of 'resum[ing] yourself' each morning (*MF*, 45). 'Aubade. Oh, bad,' puns Sarah in *Sidereal Time* (*ST*, 174). Several of the narrative poems – 'The solitary reaper' (*MF*, 36–7), 'My mother missed the beautiful and the doomed' (*MF*, 38–9), 'Photograph of Captain Oates' (*MF*, 47) – layer past and present as part of an exploration of class structures across time. Reading these poems against the novels illuminates both.

The final section of the collection, 'Seven cities', begins in the Black Mountains with 'My son on Castell Dinas' and then moves out to ancient Crete, New York, Babylon, Europe and, finally, 'Sailing past Antipolis' ('the city opposite', the ancient Greek name for Antibes). This sequence focuses on the rise and fall of human civilizations, with past and present layered in each poem. In 'My son on Castell Dinas' (*MF*, 57–8), the different generations represented by father and son are seen against the historical landscape where the traces of both Iron Age fort and Norman castle are visible:

> . . . layered like the name –
> *castell* – men in helmets holding natives down,
> *dinas* – city before Rome breathed.

The use of Welsh words and place-names here figures the language that has been 'held down' but survives as traces in the landscape.

This poem anticipates the bilingualism of *Air Histories* which also takes its inspiration from the Black Mountains.

There is a strong sense of the apocalyptic in human history throughout this sequence, not so much as a single end time but as a process of repetition. Both 'Siesta time in the Labyrinth' and 'Gothic' look to the end of civilizations. The former looks back to the ancient Minoan civilization which is the context for the myth of Daedalus, catching it during the oppressive heat of a mid-day siesta which prefigures the coming end that 'will not be today / Not yet' (*MF*, 60). 'Gothic' (*MF*, 63) uses the swimming-flying motif of earlier poems, collapsing sky and sea imagery, to depict a New York cityscape as the scene of modern apocalypse: the planet is 'venting into space' in 'that thrilled uprush / of its own annihilation'. Civilizations repeatedly rise and fall, these poems suggest, as a result of human failings.

The superb 'Builders of Bab-ilu' (*MF*, 64–5), the most linguistic-ally experimental poem in the collection, invents a new form which reverses and breaks down normal syntax to mimic on the page the building of the Tower of Babel. In an account of its writing in 'Miller's Answer', Meredith emphasizes how long it took to solve the problem of an appropriate form for the poem which began with one phrase in a notebook: 'Nimrod ermined like a northern king'.[65] The two inspirations were the Old Testament story (Genesis 11: 1–9) and Pieter Brueghel the Elder's two famous paintings of the subject. (Nimrod, the king of Shinar, is traditionally credited as the originator of the tower.) Traditionally an explan-ation for the multitude of languages spoken by human beings, the Old Testament story depicts this multiplicity as divine punish-ment for man's hubris ('Bab-ilu – the 'gate of god' suggests the tower's encroachment on the divine) which brings in its wake confusion and disunity. The Tower of Babel is an especially sug-gestive image for a bilingual Welsh writer and two things resonated with Meredith. First, the oddness of the fact that God fragments the language of the builders rather than knocking down the tower. Secondly, the 'sheer beauty and strangeness of the paintings, with the tower portrayed as an immense coiling Romanesque ramp'.[66]

The ekphrastic nature of this poem is important since Meredith notes the political nature of Brueghel's paintings as 'a warning from the painter to the hubris of the governments of his day'.[67] The colonnaded structure of Brueghel's tower is reminiscent of the Colosseum in Rome, an architectural style adopted by the Normans (as in the Norman archway Griffri sees at Llandâf), thus linking it to the layering of successive colonizations Meredith identifies in Castell Dinas. Moreover, Nimrod in Brueghel's painting is 'ermined like a northern king'.

The speaker of Meredith's poem is a builder, working with his uncle and brother on the tower: they are 'tonguing' Nimrod's tower 'towards god'. The form of the poem echoes the work of building. Meredith has described it as 'an invented form that borrows from foreign and ancient ways of writing': the poem 'treats words as if they're the bricks of the Tower of Babel that have to be lifted into the sky by concerted human effort'.[68] He borrowed this form in part from boustrophedon script, an ancient Greek form where 'you read one line right to left and then the next left to right so that your eye winds down the page'.[69] His innovation was to start from the bottom to mimic the difficulty of writing the poem:

> The poem would become a flattened, two-dimensional picture of the helix of the tower. As the tower got near its breaking point at the top it would break into monosyllables. The heaviness, the thinginess of words, the breakdown of meaning came to be enacted in the structure of the poem.[70]

Thus the poem begins at the bottom of the page and alternate lines are reversed and ranged right so that the reading eye has to climb upwards, reading left to right and then right to left alternately. This layout foregrounds the work of attentive reading as well as the labour of making. Interestingly, it suggests the fall of the tower of words rather than just the confusion of language which the Bible records.

Moreover, Meredith weaves into the poem parallels with the myth of Daedalus, the craftsman/builder, suggesting a plurality of possible meanings. Like the tower, Icarus is an image of hubris.

As the builders of the tower get higher it is not the 'heat' of the wrath of god they feel, but the 'void of cold'. In this cold, wax would not melt but freeze for the '.fall to man ing / fly'. As the 'tower' of words on the page gets higher it begins to break down into monosyllables – 'pre po sit ions flake' and nouns 'loose work' – until the poem ends, at the top of the page, in pre-linguistic babble: 'b a b a ba barbar bar bar bare'. The 'fall' here is out of a monolingual Eden, not into multilingualism, but into meaningless sound. As Meredith has acknowledged, there are many possible meanings in the myth and the poem but what seems to interest him most is that: 'The materials and the form became its subject. I had no intention of bearing witness to anything in any direct way. That definitive quality of language, its ability to discuss itself, its reflexivity, was in play.'[71] In this, the poem resembles the villanelle 'The Message' (*MF*, 31) but, as Meredith also acknowledges, 'meaning is involuntary', and in 'Builders of Bab-ilu' a range of possible political meanings remain in play.[72]

From this biblical apocalypse, the sequence moves to modern European history as human catastrophe. Another ekphrastic poem, 'Europe after the rain' (*MF*, 66–7), takes its inspiration from Max Ernst's 1940–2 surrealist painting of the same name. Ernst's painting depicts two ambiguous figures – 'the giant madman in the zany's hat / and the statuebird / shut wings locked like armour on her flanks'– standing within a browny-greeny-mustard landscape which could be a bombed cityscape, or rotting vegetation/flesh, another planet, or an underwater scene. Meredith's poem takes the cue in Ernst's title to read this as an allegory of the destruction of Europe. The 'madman' and the 'statuebird' watch 'whatever there is / beyond them in the square' imaged as the space where the major events of Europe have taken place: from the scientific advances of Copernicus, Vesalius (father of anatomy) and Regiomontanus (astronomy), to the executions of Llewelyn the Last and Anne Boleyn, or Luther's theses nailed to the door of a church in Wittenberg, and the assassination of Archduke Franz Ferdinand. In contrast to these past events, the 'madman' and the 'statuebird' stare at 'an empty space' where 'nothing has ever been so still'. The static 'statuebird', with her 'shut wings', prefigures the 'chlorine sky' 'without a wing alive in it' at the end of the poem (*MF*, 67). The 'fall' of civilization here produces a 'poison[d]' sky where neither bird nor human can take flight. In the aftermath of 9/11 and the famously empty sky which followed the reduction of the Twin Towers in New York to a mass of skewed and buckled fragments, Ernst's painting takes on a new resonance to which this poem seems to gesture obliquely.

Within the global anxieties of the post-9/11 mid-2000s, Meredith's concern with apocalypse and ruined cities in this final sequence has a much wider depth of resonance than appears if he is merely read as a writer concerned with Wales. Like *Sidereal Time*, the collection ends with the possibility of redemption but it is far more qualified. The final poem is 'Sailing past Antipolis' (*MF*, 69) 'After' Picasso's 1946 'Joie de vivre'. An antique fantasy, Picasso's painting features an abstract depiction of his then lover Françoise Gilot joyously dancing naked with a pipe-playing centaur and faun and two kids. In Meredith's poem movement and music become an expression of jouissance and creativity and a tentative self-identification: the piper 'blowing his notes into bright blue air . . . could be me'. But there are two movements here: the dancing woman and her 'kids', and the ship which is 'sailing *past* Antipolis' so that the dancing figures 'slide leftwards, dancing, out of frame / and past'. This is a fleeting glimpse of a place, possibly a home, recognized, desired, but lost: 'I think I might have lived / in this town once'. If *The Meaning of Flight* opens with a poem about flying which turns out to be a poem about dying, then it closes with a poem celebrating the 'joy of living' which turns out to be a poem about loss.

5

'Edges are where meanings happen': *The Book of Idiots* (2012) and *Air Histories* (2013)

A sense of place is integral to the making of meaning in Christopher Meredith's writing. His work always has its feet firmly in 'the earth of [his] own home patch', but that home patch has widened over the last few years.[1] For much of his adult life, Meredith has lived in Brecon, close to the Black Mountains which mark the border between Wales and England. His most recent books at the time of writing, *The Book of Idiots* (2012) and *Air Histories* (2013), write across the 'edges' between that mountainous landscape of sheep and bog cotton and the post-industrial south Wales valleys that are his natal 'heartland'. From Tredegar to Brecon is around 26 miles by road and less – around 13 miles – as the crow flies. In one sense the two places are geographically very close; in another, separated by the Brecon Beacons and by very different histories, they might be different countries. While working at the University of Glamorgan between 1993 and 2013, this was a shift in landscape Meredith negotiated regularly in his commute to work.

Landscape as linguistic palimpsest has been a consistent motif in Meredith's writing and some of his earlier work had drawn on material from the Black Mountains, as in 'My son on Castell Dinas' (*MF*, 57–8). Several elements, however, suggest an intensification of Meredith's engagement with this landscape which connects to the interplay between his two languages. One is his part in the Bog~Mawnog project, which fed into poems published first in *Black Mountains: Poems and Images from the Bog~Mawnog Project* (2011) and then in *Air Histories*. A central strand of *The Book of Idiots* is also set during a walk to Carreg y Dial (the Revenge Stone, scene of a Welsh-Norman assassination) in the Black Mountains. A second important element is Meredith's ongoing work as a translator: his English translation of Mihangel Morgan's Welsh-language novel, *Melog* (1997), came out in 2005. Although Meredith must have been working on it alongside *The Meaning of Flight*, its influence is discernible in *The Book of Idiots*. A third important experience is his stint as Writer in Residence in Finland and Slovenia in the winter of 2012–13, during which he was editing the poems for *Air Histories*.

The Bog~Mawnog project was set up by the artist Pip Woolf as part of her Woollen Line scheme started in 2009. In the 1970s some of the upland peat bogs of the Black Mountains were scarred by fire damage which led to extensive erosion. ('Mawnog' translates into English as 'peat bog'.) A fire in 1976 burned away a 70,000 metre area of Pen Trumau leaving what looked like a huge wound on the ridge. Left exposed, the peat was swept away by rain and wind: 'At its upper edge', Meredith writes, 'the Pen Trumau site has eroded down to the mineral soil, and there are places where whitened rocks like fragments of bone stick through the mud and peat' (*BM*, 3). When she saw the damage more than thirty years later, Pip Woolf's idea was to try to heal the wound on the land-scape: 'There's a black space,' she thought, 'if we covered it in wool it would turn white, and the long term picture would be that it would turn green.'[2] The wool would hold the peat in place and allow plants to grow again, as well as preventing carbon loss. Using low-grade sheep's wool Pip and a team of volunteers, including Meredith, pegged lines of wool felt embedded with heather and grass seeds onto the mountain. The result was a white line over the scar which could be seen from the air.

The *Bog~Mawnog Project* was a collaboration between five visual artists (Pip Woolf, Elizabeth Adeline, Lin Charlston, Kirsty Claxton and Deborah Aguirre Jones), and Meredith, who all responded to the project and the place in their chosen media. The work led to an exhibition, first shown at Brecknock Museum and Gallery in summer 2011, and the book: *Black Mountains: Poems and Images from the Bog~Mawnog Project*. Both poems and images gain from their juxtaposition and Meredith notes how his writing meshes with the concerns of the artists: Elizabeth Adeline's concern with memory, Lin Charlston's interest in 'the quasi alphabetic or calligraphic shapes' she found in peat and mosses, and Deborah Aguirre Jones's interest in belonging/unbelonging all resonate with his work (*BM*, 3).

In the introduction to *Black Mountains* Meredith identifies a theme which becomes increasingly important in his writing, encapsulated in the villanelle 'Borderland', first printed in this collection: '[T]he Black Mountains, as Raymond Williams famously had it, are border country. The edges are not just between countries, but between earth and air, between languages, between language and silence, between human and other' (*BM*, 4). At the start of his unfinished historical fiction, *People of the Black Mountains*, Williams describes the 'scarp and ridges of these hills in hypnotic detail as if they were an outstretched human hand' (*BM*, 4). In *Black Mountains* Meredith notes the 'strange familiarity' which comes from picking up a handful of the 'curious black earth that's made of the same carbon as your own body' (*BM*, 4). Edges – between earth and air, language and silence, human and other, and between Welsh and English – become a powerful theme in *Air Histories*: 'Edges are where meanings happen' as he puts it in the refrain to 'Borderland' (*BM*, 9; *AH*, 8).

'Borderland' invokes the landscape around Capel y Ffin. The central conceit – 'We see what is when we see what it's not' (*AH*, 8) – is central to post-structuralist theory: meaning, or definition, in language is generated through the contrast between (binary) oppositions, the contrast (or edge) between black/white, good/bad and so on. In this villanelle, a form which itself foregrounds the constructedness of language, Meredith riffs on the meanings of 'Ffin': this is, as the epigraph notes, '*the Welsh for* border. *It occurs inside* diffiniad which *means* definition, *and in* Capel y Ffin ['chapel of the border or boundary']' (*BM*, 9; *AH*, 8).[3] While this is another palimpsestic location inscribed with human history – 'Live rock can yield to mortared stone, / a city to a castle, then a shepherd's hut' – it is also a place where the human self 'blurs into annihilation'

(*AH*, 8) in the face of the natural world. There is a sense of transcend-ence here which connects to that of 'The slurry pond' (*AH*, 26). Borders – between mountain and sky, lithic and human, earth and air, English and Welsh – are defined in being crossed. Meredith's use of Welsh in 'Borderland', as in much of his writing, connects him to a history of the loss and recovery of a language that was his 'own' but which he had to learn as an adult. Linguistically, as well as figuratively, the poem crosses borders.

One way of thinking about translation is as a negotiation across the borders, or 'edges', between two languages. (There are other equally productive metaphors which I will discuss below.) Another important shift in Meredith's writing during this period is an increasing bilingualism which is connected to his work as a trans-lator and his engagement with the landscape. As early as *Shifts* his working notes were written in Welsh,[4] but several of the Black Mountain poems were originally written in Welsh in response to a request from Pip Woolf and then translated into English. Meredith found writing in response to a commission took the pressure off and enabled him to write in Welsh.[5] Although *Black Mountains* includes only one poem in Welsh – 'Enwau'r mynydd' (*BM*, 7) which is, as the name suggests, a list of the names of mountains – *Air Histories* includes five poems in facing-page Welsh and English versions. Four of these were originally published in English in *Black Mountains*. Interestingly, although 'Borderland' takes its inspiration from a Welsh word, this is not one of the poems for which Meredith provides a parallel Welsh version; the play across the languages is part of the point of the poem.

One important catalyst for Meredith's thinking about the inter-play between the two languages seems to have been his translation of Mihangel Morgan's brilliantly strange postmodern Welsh-language novel *Melog*. In the Afterword Meredith invokes Umberto Eco's description of translation as a 'negotiation' between 'the encyclopedias of two cultures' (*M*, 234). This is, as he notes, a particularly appropriate metaphor for a text in which the pro-tagonist, Dr Jones, an unemployed *soi-disant* academic, spends much of his time studying *Y Gwyddoniadur Cymreig* (the Welsh encyclopedia) edited by John Parry and Thomas Gee in ten volumes from 1854 to 1878 (*M*, 234). A novel that plays with 'the borders between the real and the imagined' (*M*, 234), *Melog* was problematic to translate because of its linguistic complexity as well as its range of cultural reference. Its translation was clearly the labour of a novelist who recognized qualities that chimed with his own interests.

Set in a valleys town, Morgan's novel focuses on Dr Jones's obsessive relationship with Melog, a white-haired, pale-skinned young man with sapphire-blue eyes, who claims to come from Laxaria, a small country conquered by its larger neighbour, Sacria. The political parallels are spelt out: 'I see Wales as quite like Laxaria before the Sacrians turned against her', Melog tells Dr Jones (*M*, 33). But just as Dr Jones is never sure whether Laxaria really exists, we are never sure that Melog exists. Dr Jones may not be who he appears to be either: he failed to obtain his doctorate and has spent time in a mental hospital. While Dr Jones maintains that 'Every novelist reflects reality', Melog asks 'What is reality?' (*M*, 79).

Literary translation, Meredith discovered, is 'partly an intense and interrogative kind of *reading*' which '*force*[s]' the translator to be attentive to the patterning of themes and images, the linguistic choices, manipulation of point of view, and cultural references in the source text.[6] In translating *Melog*, Meredith became intensely aware of its tightly controlled 'thematic coherence' which works around the doubling of Dr Jones and Melog.[7] As well as coding unspoken homoerotic desire, this binary opposition foregrounds questions of truth and reality through a range of improbable stories and parodic literary/academic projects: 'Jones and Melog look at one another as if looking into a distorting mirror of their cultural selves.'[8] These elements – doubling, alternating point of view, patterns of theme and imagery, and a concern with narrative as representation – are all strongly evident in Meredith's own fiction. He also notes Morgan's subtle use of 'apparently casual conversational preambles', such as '"*a dweud y gwir*" ("to tell you the truth")', to point up themes of truth and authenticity.[9] Again, this is a technique – an exploitation of the symbolic significance of the ordinary – that Meredith uses himself, and which he develops further in *The Book of Idiots*. It is similar to a technique he notes in the work of Dorothy Edwards, where her stories are so stripped down that 'what *is* used almost inevitably acquires symbolic weight or at least a feeling of significance'.[10] Thinking about these techniques in relation to translation, however, focuses our attention on the meanings that are made when the edges of two languages rub up against each other.

Meredith's interest in translation was also evident in a conference he co-convened with Katja Krebs on 'The Politics of Literary Translation' at the University of Glamorgan in 2003. Several papers from this, including one by Claudine Tourniaire (who translated *Griffri* into French in 2002), were published as *Five Essays on Translation* (2005). As he noted in the introduction, translation is both vital and invisible in our culture: 'It's arguable,' he suggests, 'that Copernicus was able to change our notion of the universe not only because of his grasp of maths and astronomy, but because he could read Greek.'[11]

A Europe where multilingualism is the norm was the context within which Meredith edited the poems for *Air Histories* during a period as Writer in Residence in Finland and Slovenia between October 2012 and February 2013. Funded by a HALMA/Translator's House Scholarship, both these periods were productive: he edited the collection and wrote some new poems while he also saw several of his pieces translated into Slovene or Finnish. His blogs repeatedly return to the question of language and two connected realizations. First, that while much of Europe is multilingual, 'English has become the lingua franca and is becoming a modern kind of Latin for academic discourse'.[12] Secondly, he finds that in a country like Slovenia, the 'meeting place of four major language groups', people are self-conscious about the experience of 'living inside a "small" language' in ways that resonate with the Welsh experience.[13] This awareness of the politics of language – 'A dialect with tanks,' remarks his translator at one point, 'is a language'[14] – can be a source of enrichment. The thoughtful attitude of the translators and broadcasters he worked with in Slovenia put 'the pains of language at the centre' and this brought the discovery that 'Babel can be a place of connections.'[15]

Ironically, this focus on the possibilities of bi- and multilingualism in a European context runs alongside Meredith's illumination of the increasing hollowing-out of language within university administrative systems. His blogs record the endless form-filling entailed in his role as professor of creative writing. Such forms, he notes wryly, have to be filled with 'Boring Sentences' which 'should usually contain nothing at all': 'This is tricky. But occasionally you have to sneak some meaning into them unnoticed, and this is tricky too.'[16] Both these facets of language – the rich but politically fraught complexity of bilingualism and the hollowness of bureaucratic language – are important themes in *The Book of Idiots*.

Falling and flying: The Book of Idiots *(2012)*

In the opening chapter of *The Book of Idiots*, the narrator Dean recalls a childhood game called 'Best Man's Fall'. The object was to perform a dying fall as authentically and aesthetically as possible when 'shot' by the one chosen to be 'On It'. As Dean remarks, 'It seemed to me that all the art was in dying rather than being On It' (*BI*, 2). A meditation on 'the art of dying' which returns to some of the questions raised in *The Meaning of Flight*, *The Book of Idiots* explores masculinity and mortality through a series of images of flying and falling. The cover image – Martin Barrett's 'We all fall with Icarus', depicting a collapsing tower of industrial debris, ancient statuary and alphabet letters – visually encapsulates the novel's fusing of Meredith's interests in Daedalus and Icarus, the Tower of Babel, the fall of civilizations, the nature of work and the construction of masculinity.

As Dean's allusion to the '*art*' of dying suggests, *The Book of Idiots* is also an exploration of the difficulties of narrative and language. It is 'an adventure in meaning' as Hooker puts it (*BI*, cover), which measures the conventions of tragedy, farce, romance and ghost story against the messiness of experience and, in Meredith's own words, 'argues almost constantly with [Aristotle's] idea of dramatic unity'.[17] Like *Griffri*, this intricately constructed novel is an exercise in that most testing of forms, the first person narrative, which interrogates the act of memory. And, like *Sidereal Time*, it is a densely patterned metafiction in which ordinary daily life and casual conversations carry symbolic significance. While the characters struggle to make meaning from the monotonous patterns of their lives, their days are rendered with sympathy and conveyed through the sharp ear for dialogue which is one of Meredith's major strengths.

Addressed by the narrator, Dean Lloyd, to an unnamed 'you' with whom he is, or was, having an extra-marital affair, the novel twists together three narrative strands and moves back and forward between past and present. The main strand recounts Dean's daily life as he drives to and from work, goes swimming and is involved in interviewing a new colleague. Woven into the story are Dean's encounters with other men, all 'idiots' in one way or another: Graham, the colleague whose retirement is hastened by an incident when he is locked in a toilet; Matt Owen, interviewed as Graham's replacement; Jeff Burridge, a former colleague, now retired from teaching in FE after hitting a student; Meirion Walker, who has an allotment on the same site as Jeff; and an unnamed man who falls from a railway revetment. Embedded within this is the second strand, Dean's account of a walk to Carreg y Dial in the Black Mountains with Wil Daniel nearly two years earlier. During this Wil tells Dean a story about an affair he had – or may have had (as with *Melog* it is unclear) – with Annette Protheroe, a former school girlfriend he bumps into at the hospital while undergoing treatment for lung cancer. Much of this section is in dialogue and, as with *Griffri*, it is a kind of confessional, as Wil implies through his joking references to Dean as 'Reverend Judge' (*BI*, 150) and 'spiritual advisor' (*BI*, 70). *The Book of Idiots* is, like *Shifts*, a 'butty novel' which explores male friendships through dialogue. The third strand is a series of recollections of games Dean played when he was a child – 'Best Man's Fall' (*BI*, 1), throwing things (*BI*, 51), 'flights' (*BI*, 63) and soccer or 'Three Goals and In' (*BI*, 160) – which culminates in the drowning of Dean's schoolfriend, Clive Wise.

Each of the chapters includes a fall of some kind, whether real or metaphorical, intended or accidental.

At first glance, this novel seems the least 'Welsh' of Meredith's books. But there is an extraordinary moment three-quarters of the way through that forces us to reassess our reading of it. Dean and Wil have been talking in the pub at the end of their walk, and a German man comes over to ask a question: 'My friends were discussing what language you are speaking . . . Forgive me for asking what language is this please?' (*BI*, 185). Wil's answer – 'It's Welsh' (*BI*, 185) – throws into question the identity of the novel we have, up to that point, been reading. If they have been speaking Welsh, then is what we have been reading an English translation, in part if not in whole, of a Welsh original? The novel thus takes on a narrative duality, and duplicity: it is not the book we thought we were reading, but possibly a quite different book in another language about people who are not what we thought they were. Are Wil and Dean first- or second-language Welsh speakers? In which language have the novel's other conversations been conducted?

The subsequent exchange between the German and his wife repositions the novel within debates about Wales as a postcolonial country in relation to language loss. 'Die sprechen Walisisch', he tells her, 'Die Sprache der keltischen Ureinwohner' ['They speak Welsh. The language of the Celtic native inhabitants'] (*BI*, 185).[18] The use of 'Ureinwohner' – also meaning 'aboriginal', and covering Native Americans and indigenous peoples – suggests the parallel between the Welsh and Native Americans already made in Meredith's 'Occupied' (*MF*, 48) and 'The Afanc King'. The wife's reply and his rejoinder position Wil and Dean as representatives of a near-extinct people:

> 'Echt?' the wife said. 'Gibt's die Sprache den überhaupt noch?' ['Really? Does the language actually exist still?']
>
> 'Anscheinend schon . . . Das müssen einige der letzten Sprecher sein' ['Apparently so. They must be some of the last speakers.'] (*BI*, 185)

Hence the German insists on photographing Dean and Wil like 'a couple of coelacanths . . . just hauled from the deep' (*BI*, 186). When he compliments Wil on his 'excellent' English, Wil's bitter response, 'Call me Caliban' (*BI*, 185), invokes postcolonial readings of *The Tempest* as an account of Prospero's usurpation of the island from its original inhabitant.[19] Moreover, the German connects the word 'Welsh' with the German '*Kauderwelsch* [meaning] jargon [or] babel' (*BI*, 186). *Kauderwelsch*, meaning 'speaking foreign', can cover a foreign language, or a hybrid or nonsense language ('babble'), but is a derisive/derogatory term. The erudite Wil immediately connects this, via the hilltop ruins they have visited, to the 'Tower of Babel' (*BI*, 186) which thus becomes a symbol of the derogatory labelling of 'small' languages as 'babble'. It is at the 'edges' between languages that their unequal status becomes sharply visible.

These questions of bilingualism and translation illuminate the novel's concern with living on the edge between languages, cultures and countries, figured in the doubling of the narrative. Most of the major characters – Dean, Wil, Matt, Edith, Annette – are living a double life in the sense that they are having illicit affairs. This duplicity is enacted in Dean's own narrative which withholds details of either his family or his lover. Moreover, Dean discovers (like Griffri) that he has misread key moments in the past, that there are other possible narratives: Matt, the favourite candidate during the interview process, wanted the job because he was having an affair with Edith; Jeff, initially a comic figure lusting over his blonde swimming instructor, becomes a tragic figure after his probable suicide; Clive Wise drowns because his friends did not know that he was an epileptic. This is a novel about living a double life, linguistically, emotionally, professionally and personally.

Among the metaphors for translation to which I alluded earlier are several that are apposite here. In his essay, 'Sleeping with the Enemy: The tensions of literary translation', in the collection Meredith co-edited, Grahame Davies discusses the ways in which translation has been figured: as adultery, addiction, warfare, civil war, colonial appropriation, exploitation, antagonism and a bridge.[20] As Davies notes, *The Adulterer's Tongue* was the title given to

Robert Minhinnick's 2004 selection of Welsh verse in English trans-lation.[21] *The Book of Idiots* brings together several of these metaphors, including adultery, warfare, the bridge, as well as the border/frontier and the palimpsest. In her essay in the same collection, Claudine Tourniaire remarks that translating *Griffri* into French (the language of the Norman invaders), 'somehow felt like trans-lating into enemy language'.[22] Yet she also notes the 'linguistic duplicity' of the source text, given that Griffri speaks only Welsh and his addressee, the chronicler Idnerth, would have transcribed the narrative in Latin or French:

> Indeed, the English in *Griffri* is not so much an 'enemy language' as an interloper, requiring as much suspension of disbelief as the story itself, *duplicitous* because it refers to words beyond itself, yet by the same token, exposing itself as a translating tool.[23]

Duplicity, then, is a key trope for thinking about the inequalities involved in translating. Tourniaire goes on to suggest that 'the Welsh language haunts *Griffri* more effectively than if the entire text had been written in Welsh'.[24] The same could be said of *The Book of Idiots* which uses the metaphor of adultery to write about the duplicity of translation and bilingualism, exposing the suspen-sion of disbelief in which we have been engaged. Conversely, it uses the metaphor of translation to think about the duplicities of narrative and infidelity: like the betrayed spouse we have been deceived. The metaphor works both ways.

The novel's geographical setting in the border country, the edge between Wales and England, provides another figure for trans-lation. Lisa Lewis uses M. Wynn Thomas's description of translating as '"*cynnyrch cyffindir iaith*", that is the product of living on the frontier of language', to discuss her experience of bilingualism.[25] This involves the complex negotiation of a 'dual identity' through translation which is never neutral:

> I am constantly translating within myself and hiding or disclosing this process . . . my very existence is one that may be read as treading a

continuum of translation. Or perhaps *a palimpsest* is a better word – as though one language is inscribed on top of the other, endlessly.[26]

The possibility of duplicity is implicit in the notion of 'hiding or disclosing'. Lewis also invokes Homi Bhabha's description of translation as 'an *act* resulting from living on borderlines'.[27] Border-lines, frontiers, edges are scenes of warfare. The doubly named Carreg y Dial/Revenge Stone to which Wil and Dean walk is a suggestive symbol of the violent conflict over the frontier or border, now almost forgotten: 'A Norman on a horse got killed by some Welsh blokes with bows and arrows' (*BI*, 57) as Wil puts it. The dual identity of bilingualism, the 'hiding or disclosing' of the process of translation, connects to the palimpsest of the border landscape where one language hides or displaces another. Tellingly, Wil's affair with Annette takes place in liminal places, including a village 'just the other side of the border' (*BI*, 117). As he puts it, 'Edges turn into centres with this kind of thing' (*BI*, 117).

This action of turning an edge into a centre is also evident in the way Meredith's novel foregrounds the narratives of ordinary lives and the 'comedy of hidden suffering'.[28] The original title Meredith had in mind was *The Torturer's Horse*, a reference to Auden's 'Musée des Beaux Arts'.[29] The Old Masters, Auden suggests, knew:

That even the dreadful martyrdom must run its course
Anyhow in a corner, some untidy spot
Where the dogs go on with their doggy life and the torturer's horse
Scratches its innocent behind on a tree.[30]

Thus in Brueghel's *Icarus*, 'everything turns away' from the 'boy falling out of the sky'.[31] As Wil knows only too well from his experience of the numb waiting rooms and cafes in hospitals, 'Misery happens quietly in corners, next to coffee machines and things' (*BI*, 58). As in *Icarus*, it may be observed but not recognized by onlookers. Later, Wil echoes Auden even more directly: 'Big things happen anyhow, in a corner' (*BI*, 156). In a more gruesome echo, the blood and brains blown through a hedge when Jeff shoots himself are lapped up by the dog Soot going on with his 'doggy life' oblivious to human tragedy.

The ordinariness of human suffering – Jeff's suicide, Wil's cancer, Dean's unlived life, the smash-up caused by Matt's infidelity – is specifically male in a novel where we only ever see women through men's eyes. Meredith's interest in the construction of masculinity is another thread in his work that comes clearly into focus again in this novel. As feminist theorists from Simone de Beauvoir on-wards have pointed out, in Western society masculinity is both ubiquitous *and* under-interrogated; it is taken for granted as a norm from which femininity represents some kind of deviation.[32] In contrast, Meredith's novels trace the predicament of men caught in historical shifts which expose masculinity, particularly working-class masculinity, as just as constructed and historically contingent as femininity. While Judith provided 'perhaps the crucial view-point' in *Shifts*, in writing *The Book of Idiots* Meredith consciously 'imposed formal limitations on [himself], partly in order to focus more deliberately on the men'.[33] In a percipient review of Alun Lewis's *Collected Stories* in 1991 Meredith noted a sense in Lewis's fiction that 'real life' continues elsewhere 'and many of the male characters . . . cannot catch the trick of it'.[34] Similarly, the male characters in *The Book of Idiots* cannot 'catch the trick of' a world in which the older forms of masculinity associated with manual labour are no longer available. Like Icarus, they find themselves in free fall. Their 'idiocy' – if Icarus is one kind of 'idiot' as Meredith posits,[35] Dean is merely 'differently idiotic' (*BI*, 206) – is an ex-pression of their failure to transform that fall into flight.

The crisis in masculinity Meredith maps is the result of changes in the type of work available to men in south Wales due to de-industrialization. In *The Book of Idiots* assumptions about the nature of 'work' exist as a kind of folk memory for men too young to have experienced that earlier culture directly: 'Even now I can't think of being in an office as work', the forty-something Dean says (*BI*, 16). Coming out of a communal history of masculine labour in coal mines and steelworks, he retains a sense that 'work' is manual; it is 'what an engine does', or 'what Jeff Burridge did in his workshop turning chair legs or in his allotment turning earth' (*BI*, 16). A decade or so older, Jeff leaves the Foundation because he wants to 'bloody make something' (*BI*, 16). In contrast, Edith belongs to the new 'call centre generation' for whom work is 'electrons or photons or whatever they are moving on screens, in phones, or in the head' (*BI*, 16). This is the problem that Meredith addressed in 'Breaking Wood' and 'Miller's Answer': even writing is not 'proper' work. As in *Shifts* or *Sidereal Time*, Meredith illuminates how this new concept of work alters our experience of time: 'Flexitime fuzzes the edges,' Dean thinks, 'Work is an oily noisy place you run from through lorry-sized gates when a hooter goes. Not this' (*BI*, 20). Work is part of what connects us as individuals to those other parts of the Venn diagram, to the sphere of community and to the larger processes of time, history, political structures and the big natural, ecological processes.

Part of the irony of the book is that we never know exactly what it is Dean does at the ambiguously named 'Foundation'. It involves driving, both to and from the Foundation itself, and out to site visits, and we are told that he 'draw[s] plans and elevations, inspect[s] things and write[s] reports' (*BI*, 4). When the candidates for Graham's replacement are interviewed we are not told the content of what they do, only whether they use PowerPoint for their presentations. In our post-industrial society, Meredith suggests, some work has become so detached from 'making and extracting' that it is 'virtually content-free': 'The continual effort to measure performance, plan staffing, assess how we're doing and so on actually replaces the work . . . content-free work is here, and some people are working themselves into the ground doing it.'[36]

Meredith's analysis here chimes with that offered by the anthropologist David Graeber in 'On the Phenomenon of Bullshit Jobs' (2013) and *The Utopia of Rules* (2015). As Graeber points out, the automation of productive jobs has resulted, not in the fifteen-hour week predicted by John Maynard Keynes, but in the creation of what he calls 'bullshit jobs':

technology has been marshalled, if anything, to figure out ways to make us all work more. In order to achieve this, jobs have had to be created that are, effectively, pointless. Huge swathes of people, in Europe and North America in particular, spend their entire working lives performing tasks they secretly believe do not really need to be performed. The moral and spiritual damage that comes from this situation is profound.[37]

The number of 'professional, managerial, clerical, sales and service workers' has tripled, inflated by 'the creation of whole new industries like financial services or telemarketing, or the un-precedented expansion of sectors like corporate law, academic and health administration, human resources, and public relations'.[38] While '[r]eal, productive workers are relentlessly squeezed and exploited' (and are the first to be laid off), the remainder are either unemployed or 'basically paid to do nothing' in positions that 'make them identify with the perspectives and sensibilities of the ruling class'.[39] Graeber suggests that the explosion of administrative work in universities (where administrative staff now outnumber academics) is one example of this phenomenon.[40] In his role as professor of creative writing, Meredith had experienced this at first hand as his blog about form-filling indicated.

The 'moral and spiritual damage' done to the post-industrial generation of men in the south Wales valleys by the 'bullshit' jobs that have replaced productive work is one theme in Meredith's novel. Wil's assertion that, 'work gets you in the end . . . You are what you do, if you're not careful' (*BI*, 218–19) echoes *Shifts*. But what does it mean for men like Dean, Wil and Jeff to be defined by jobs that they do not believe in? Like Jack and Steve, Wil could be seen as an artist manqué and he shares Keith's autodidactic interest in history but his prodigious memory for facts is frittered away on the equivalent of a pub quiz in his conversation with Dean. Working in the planning department, Wil has attempted to make himself 'workproof' (*BI*, 218). 'Wemmicking' (*BI*, 219) he calls this, after John Wemmick in Dickens's *Great Expectations* (1860–1), who embodies the split between public and private selves necessitated by modern work: 'the office is one thing, and private life is another', Wemmick tells Pip, 'When I go into the office, I leave the Castle [his ironically fortified home in Walworth] behind me.'[41] But this duality is dangerous and delusive. Having failed to plan his own life (he has been 'looking the wrong way for twenty-five fucking years' (*BI*, 77)), Wil finds that 'I've turned into the thing I thought I was shutting out' (*BI*, 219) – and scripts his own funeral meticulously.

Work is only part of a wider inability to grasp 'the trick' of real life. In her commentary on Graeber's essay, Eliane Glaser pushes its implications further, suggesting that neo-liberalism 'simultaneously overinvests work with meaning and drains it of meaning, via automation and audit'.[42] Does collusion with the deracination of our working lives, she asks,

> provide a way to avoid intimacy with our children and family? A way to avoid facing difficult problems and truths? Our ability to be properly alive is intimately connected to our acknowledgment of mortality, and bullshit work is deadening – which helps us avoid thinking about death.[43]

This is perhaps the key to Meredith's novel which is concerned with that failure to be 'properly alive' on all levels – professionally, personally, emotionally and politically – the tendency to fall rather than fly. It's worth noting the etymology of the word 'idiot', which comes from the Greek *idiōtēs* meaning 'private person, layman, ignorant person'.[44] This suggests a failure to engage with others, and with 'difficult problems and truths', but also implies the loss of the collective radical politics associated with those older manual jobs.

As a narrator Dean Lloyd embodies this failure to engage. His surname – Lloyd is an anglicization of the Welsh *llwyd* ('grey')[45] – is appropriate for his role as a semi-transparent narrator but it also suggests a colourless life. Dean is an observer, rather than a participant, who twice leaves the scene of an accident, and repeatedly tries to avoid engaging with Jeff Burridge. Worse than this, Wil associates Dean with the chainmail-clad Normans in a line which recalls the 'cool thug' in 'By Bronllys Castle' (*T*, 35): 'there you are up in Castle Lloyd, peeping round the chainmail curtain, keeping an eye on what you're doing' (*BI*, 116). Wil's own given name suggests the force of 'will' Dean lacks while his surname, Daniel, is the name of a Hebrew prophet, meaning 'God has judged'.[46] Although Wil calls Dean 'Reverend Judge' (*BI*, 150), Dean's failure to provide any details of his wife and children or his lover suggests that lack of intimacy Glaser identifies. Indeed, the affairs in the novel repeatedly suggest an attempt to escape real intimacy. Dean's lover has made some kind of an affirmation/commitment – 'Yes, you said. Yes' (*BI*, 6), an echo of Molly Bloom's life-affirming 'yes I said yes I will yes' which ends *Ulysses*[47] – to which Dean has failed to respond.

Wil himself articulates this evasion of the real when he tells Dean, 'we don' actually experience our lives, not most of the time' (*BI*, 77). He makes a distinction between 'the higher brain, the really smart bit' which focuses on 'Remembering and planning and making stuff up', and the 'mechanical bit' which does the everyday stuff (*BI*, 76). Most of the time it is only the mechanical bit which is engaged. As an example of this he cites the war film *Ice Cold in Alex* (1958), in which two soldiers, the war-traumatized Captain Anson (John Mills) and Sergeant-Major Tom Pugh (Harry Andrews) together with a nurse, Diana Murdoch (Sylvia Sims), have to make their way across the Libyan war zone to Alexandria in a dilapidated ambulance. On the way they pick up a tall and extremely strong Dutch South African, Van Der Poel (Anthony Quayle), who turns out to be a German spy with a radio transmitter in his bag. Obsessive and alcoholic, Anson focuses throughout the journey across the desert on his dream of ice-cold beer in a bar in Alexandria. Like Anson, Wil is addicted to alcohol and cigarettes, involved in a love triangle and emotionally inept. His obsessive behaviour likewise borders on the hysterical, particularly when he encounters Annette's husband. We watch the film, Wil argues, with the smart brain but 'we'd go mad if the smart brain was always on. Think, if every beer was like those couple John Mills downs' (*BI*, 77).

As an intertext, *Ice Cold in Alex* illuminates several themes that are important in the novel, including post-war masculinity and nationality in crisis, obsession and duplicity. Raymond Durgnat sees *Ice Cold in Alex* as an account of 'Britain's sense of inferiority in the post war world' and Meredith similarly portrays Welsh masculinity in crisis.[48] Yet both film and novel celebrate male solidarity: Wil and Anson embody a kind of inverted heroism in their refusal to conform to stereotypes. In a climactic scene in the film the quartet crank the ambulance painstakingly up a sand-covered escarpment in reverse using the starting-handle. Just as they reach the top, the men take a break leaving Diana to hold it alone without the brake on. The ambulance plummets to the bottom of the slope and they have to push it all the way up again. It is another version of falling and flying but it is also 'real work', of the kind no longer available to Dean and Wil's generation, which is rewarded with the ice-cold beer of intense experience.

Art – 'making stuff up' and reading or watching films – is part of what the smart brain does and as such it involves absolute engagement but this is only attainable for brief moments. Meredith glosses this in an interview:

> the shape of the novel is related to its interest in the extent to which we pay attention to, are engaged with, the lives of other people and our own lives. Wil engages this head-on, perhaps because his illness and his encounter with Annette force him to it. For him, the smart brain . . . when engaged completely with the immediate experience before it, can apprehend it with extraordinary intensity. He craves it, as he craves another of his cigarettes, and perhaps is scared by it.[49]

This connects, Meredith argues, to the narrative strand which deals with games since they represent 'formalised ways of focusing the engaged brain on intense moments of experience', while some (like the parachute jump), 'confront mortality in a moment of intense, lived apprehension'.[50] The arc of the trajectory also suggests the inevitability of the fall. This in turn connects to the theme to do with drama since a play 'formalises and enacts moments of significance'.[51] Yet this is perhaps too neat, as Meredith acknowledges when he notes that there is an ambiguity as to whether the games, like the cigarettes and alcohol Wil craves, are merely a drug-like displacement of the craving for direct engagement. Even Wil's affair with Annette arguably constitutes a way to avoid a confrontation with his own mortality.

Place and space are another important part of the symbolic patterning of the novel and are closely linked to work, time, gender and nationality. Meredith's consciousness of the ways in which a geographical setting can be used for symbolic purposes is articulated in his analysis of the 'time-space structure' of A. J. Cronin's best-selling *The Citadel* (1937), based on Cronin's experience as a doctor in Tredegar.[52] As Meredith points out, *The Citadel* combines ostensibly naturalistic description with a chronotopic shaping of time and place which serves a specific ideological viewpoint. Despite shifting the time of the novel to the late 1920s so that his protagonist's stay in Wales does not coincide with his own, Cronin never mentions the events of 1926 (the lockout, the General Strike and the miners' strike). The novel thus espouses a notion of heroic individualism which is at odds with the kind of radical collectivism (epitomized by Aneurin Bevan) which was evident in Tredegar during these years.

While Meredith similarly shapes the time-space structure of *The Book of Idiots* to convey symbolic significance it carries a very different political freight. The landscapes of the novel are both real and re-imagined versions of the south Wales valleys, the Black Mountains and the border areas. What Dean calls the 'map of [his] life' is exactly re-imagined in both senses of the word:

> The Foundation, on the edge of the city, is twelve point three miles from where I live . . . I'm one of those people who plead that there's no direct route in order to explain why I don't travel to work on the train. But it's true. The map of my life lies across the grain of these places. The railway lines run from the city up a few of the valleys. (*BI*, 15)

Despite the apparent exactitude here ('twelve point three miles'), the 'map' of Dean's life does not fit neatly onto the terrain of

Meredith's own 'home patch', not least because there are so few place-names given. Dean's home town is never named. The effect is to reinforce the 'greyness', the hollowed-out lack of specificity, in Dean's life. The places he inhabits have been reinvented, with the exception of the walk he takes over the Black Mountains, as unnamed non-places, spaces which lack meaning.

Much of the novel takes place in transitional or generic non-places – 'edges' – such as bridges, roads between places, cafes, waiting rooms, the pub, a petrol station, a hedge between allotments, even the toilet in which Graham is trapped. It is when an accident causes Wil to detour through 'urban edge stuff ' (*BI*, 111) that he finds where Annette lives. Many of these spaces half-invoke real places. The interior description of the Foundation with its 'core of staircases and liftshafts [and] windowless service rooms [with glimpses of] galv ducts, fuseboxes, sheaves of copper pipe, silver-lagged heating pipes and electric cable' (*BI*, 21–1) recalls Forest Hall, the building where English staff had their offices at Glamorgan when Meredith was on the staff. Similarly, the petrol station tucked under the revetment where Dean witnesses a man fall from the railway line resembles one that used to be situated in Treforest. There is only one domestic interior in the novel (when Dean visits the dying Wil) and this focus on public, impersonal spaces is part of the formal constraint Meredith imposed on himself.

Conversely what seems like the marker of a real place, the name 'Llanwedog', is deceptive in that it is invented. It combines the common prefix 'Llan' (church or parish) with a form of Gwedog, the name Meredith borrowed from that of an old Tredegar farmhouse, Llyswedog, and gave to the valley in *Shifts* and *Griffri*. This is where Dean encounters Matt on the bridge. Dean remembers a lecturer telling him that bridges are 'points of significance' or 'pinch points':

> Bridges turn up in spy films as border places when dodgy deals are done. In wars we blow them up or build them ... They're the trajectory of a flight through space, the lecturer said, solidified into wood or stone or metal or concrete. They're places where one stream of stories is laid crosswise over another. (*BI*, 109–10)

Bridges, then, mark borders or 'edges' where 'meanings happen'. The blowing-up of a bridge is the catalyst for the journey in *Ice Cold in Alex*. This passage brings together the imagery of flight and narrative which runs through the novel. As Dean comments metafictionally at this point, halfway through the novel: 'when you come to a bridge like the one in my story, even if you aren't interested in the place on the other side, something makes you go half way, and you look at that other stream passing crosswise' (*BI*, 110). This is the point when two stories cross, although Dean (like Griffri) does not realize this until later. It also recalls Meredith's poems about Hay Bridge, where different times – past and present, human and sidereal – connect. Finally, the bridge also works as an image of translation where two languages cross over each other.

In contrast to the non-places of Dean's working life and Wil's affair, the landscape of their walk in the Black Mountains – the 'edge' between England and Wales – is rendered in the novel with far more authenticity. This is a landscape that is imbued with layers of historical, cultural and linguistic meaning and with which Meredith engages in the poems of *Air Histories*. Within this landscape Wil and Dean are able to talk with more honesty and reach some kind of authentic engagement with each other. Through the black humour of Wil's death games they also confront mortality. Even this, however, is ambiguous since Dean is never sure whether Wil is 'playing [him] like a fish with this story' (*BI*, 60) or even if the story about Annette *is* a fiction, whether it is tragedy, comedy or ghost story. As a story it lacks the 'straight line' (*BI*, 46) Aristotle's unities were supposed to secure.

Like Wil, Dean craves the loss of self which comes with direct apprehension of experience but he aims at this through swimming lengths rather than cigarettes or alcohol. The perfect length, Dean believes, should achieve a 'sort of emptiness . . . You'd collapse into the line of your own movement, become a point' (*BI*, 83) but this is as difficult to achieve as the unified story Wil's life refuses to adhere to. The imagery of lines, of flight and falling, which runs through the novel, connects through Dean's sense that swimming lengths has a 'sort of trajectory, a climb and fall' (*BI*, 83) to Wil's concept of the 'smart brain': 'Somewhere near the line, thought stops in the face of the moment. Think of Wil's idea of Alexandria. All the freight of being, condensed into droplets running down a glass in some hot bar' (*BI*, 84). Dean connects this to a TV commentary on wild dogs which notes that they are 'extraordinarily observant of their environment': 'He meant that they saw, smelt, heard, felt the things around them with intense particularity. Briefly, when I swim well, I'm raised somewhere near the one-dimensional emptiness of a wild dog' (*BI*, 84). Dean returns to this cluster of images later:

> I thought of swimming, pushing used water behind me, resolving myself into a pure line, achieving the perfect sentience of a wild dog. I thought of Wil, fixing on how people aspire to some grand drama but actually get something like plotless farce. (*BI*, 142)

This is a good example of Meredith's ability to infuse the ordinary experiences of life – childhood games, mundane conversations, swimming lengths, a film or documentary, even the ringtone on a phone (both the Flight of the Valkyries (*BI*, 79) and the William Tell Overture (*BI*, 145) are used in this way) – with symbolic significance. This dense network of imagery laces the novel together and illuminates key questions about art and narrative and their relationship to experience.

At the end of the novel, after scattering Wil's ashes, these themes come together in a final image of flying and falling. Dean books a flight in a glider and flies over the Black Mountain landscape he has walked with Wil, seeing the ruined fortress, the Revenge Stone, the pub, the reservoir where Wil met Annette and, finally, his own town in 'a fold in the earth' (*BI*, 237). The glider's eye view gives him a completely different perspective on this landscape, an aerial panorama which takes in all these layers of history, both personal and political. As he flies, he becomes aware of the air itself with its eddies and thermals as space or, rather, place. Flying is a 'sort of controlled fall' (*BI*, 223) and in the glider he is 'close to the edge of nothing' (*BI*, 224), between earth and sky: 'the planet peeled from us and did a complicated curve down and to our left' (*BI*, 217). This makes him aware of himself within space, that largest part of the Venn diagram.

The metaphors of life as flight, art as flight, come together here as Dean learns to pilot the glider. 'Flying in a straight line', the pilot tells him, '[is the h]ardest thing in the world' (*BI*, 238). Yet it is the line of flight that gives shape to the world. Just as Clive Wise's throws 'made the sky visible' (*BI*, 52), the glider and the towplane 'describe . . . a piece of the sky with their movement' (*BI*, 217). Daedalus as a 'planner' or a 'maker' (*BI*, 221) is a key figure here. In their last conversation, Wil and Dean discuss the latter's trip to Knossos and the labyrinth while on a family holiday in Crete. Wil asks a question which Meredith considered as another possible title for the novel: 'Who killed Icarus?' (*BI*, 221). Both art and life are, as the myth of Daedalus and Icarus suggests, an attempt at flight which 'makes the sky visible' but which always hold within them the possibility of falling. In light of this, the ending of the novel is ambiguous. Told by the pilot to 'Fly towards home', Dean finds that: 'The fold of earth and blur of air were no longer in front us [*sic*]. I wasn't sure where we were' (*BI*, 238). Is he flying, or falling? Daedalus, or Icarus? Living, or dying? Asked whether *The Book of Idiots* is a comedy or a tragedy, Meredith's reply invokes the metaphor of a trajectory through air, with its possibilities of flying or falling, for the novel's own form: 'The complexity and tension of the forces in this piece, I hope, hold it in the air.'[53] The ending of the novel, too, is held 'in the air'.

'A shape made in time': Air Histories *(2013)*

The title of Meredith's fourth collection of poetry offers a paradox: how can anything as insubstantial as air have a history? Air is 'space', surely, in the sense of non-place or no-thing, the blank or interval between or around material things? Interestingly, the diversity of Meredith's poetry still seems to baffle some reviewers.

In an otherwise positive review of *Air Histories*, Cato Pedder expressed frustration with the 'variety of form and content [which] can make this collection hard to handle'.[54] In fact, reading *Air Histories* against *The Book of Idiots* makes clear not only the coherence of the collection but also how it develops concerns which run through Meredith's *oeuvre*.

The plural 'Histories' connects back to ideas about narrative and historiography which Meredith first explored in *Griffri* and suggests his concern with what Hooker calls the 'shaping effects [of history] on land, people and language'.[55] 'Air' is more complex: it is the element we live in and breathe, so familiar we don't see it unless, like Dean in the glider or Clive throwing a ball, we are engaged in an activity (a movement in time) that makes it 'visible'. The word 'air' is onomatopoeic: it 'is a breath,' as Meredith says, 'and poetry itself is a breath in some senses'.[56] In 'The record keepers' (which was selected for the *Forward Book of Poetry* (2014)) the twelfth-century chronicler Brother Cynan watches butterflies flying over a barley field: 'They wrote the history of air' (*AH*, 12) we are told. 'History' suggests temporality while 'air' suggests a spatiality which, as Doreen Massey points out, we tend to think of in antithetical terms as stasis or nothingness.[57] Yet, as Dean's experience in the glider shows, air has its own aerial topography and thus its history. The conjunction in 'Air Histories' prompts us to think of air in terms of a dynamic 'space-time' rather than as nothingness.

There are layers of meaning here. The poem's epigraph is taken from *Brut y Tywysogyon*: '*One thousand one hundred and thirty was the age of Christ when there were four years in succession without there being any history . . .*' (*AH*, 12). The 'history of air' stands for the experiences that do not get recorded: butterflies in a field, the yawn of a wicket-keeper or the Minotaur in George Frederic Watt's 1885 painting who may be waiting on the battlements for the consignment of virgins but may not: 'Perhaps there's no more narrative / than watching sky'. These are moments, as in *Sidereal Time*, when process and narrative pause. But the Minotaur with his hoof on the crushed bird (foreshadowing the fated virgins and the death of Icarus) links to another monstrous figure in the poem, the Anglo-Norman Henry I who died, infamously, of a surfeit of lampreys in 1135: 'a monster battened on bad meat / and found it good, till / suddenly he stopped'. As Wil argues in *The Book of Idiots*, Henry I's death initially appears to be 'appropriate' because it is the result of greed (*BI*, 49, 94), but it is actually another form of fate (like the falling tortoise which kills Aeschylus). Like the lamprey, or hagfish, which appears in both novel and poem, Henry is a parasite – 'Lampreys are nothing but brainless jawless mouths at the end of a strip of muscle. Hagfish' (*BI*, 48) – but his death only accidentally provides the illusion of history as a shaped narrative. Nevertheless, Henry's death in 1135 led to a civil war over the succession during which the Welsh took the opportunity to carry out the assassination at Carreg y Dial. There is a sequence of cause and effect here which links twelfth-century history to Wil and Dean's own lives: 'We owe this day – maybe even the fact that we aren't talking English – or French – to something really mouldy some twat ate a very long time ago' (*BI*, 195). In 'The record keepers', Meredith revisits this moment. For Brother Cynan, the death of Henry I kick-starts history: 'Process stiffened to event and story woke / and plot and consequence began again' (*AH*, 13). The king's death is recorded, the butterflies are not, although they, like other inconsequential things, will stay within Cynan till he dies: 'small scriptless books that eddied in still air'.

But 'air' has other meanings, notably it is a tune or a melody and music is a central motif in this collection. In *Sidereal Time* Sarah, approaching the age of thirty-five, characterizes the pattern created by significant birthdays as 'A shape made in time, like a piece of music' (*ST*, 204). In 'Y grib'/'Ridge' the words of the poems on the page make the shape of the ridge which is also an arpeggio:

> Na. Llinell alaw ydyw
> o graig
> a phridd
> ffiwg o rythmau (*AH*, 14)[58]
> . . .

> No. It's a line
> of music
> made in stone
> and earth . . . (*AH*, 15)

Finally, the line of music/earth/stone resolves into 'y distawrwydd / ar diwedd y gân'[59], 'almost-silence in / white noise of / living air'.

The imagery of music as/from air is approached from a different angle in 'Daedalus with a paramotor' (*AH*, 55), written in response to the cover photograph of a paraglider by V. Meredith, which reworks the aerial perspective from *The Book of Idiots*. In the air the paramotorist's parachute, fanblade and motor become a musical instrument:

> the whole thing an Aeolus lyre
> over us its
> wires singing that
>
> escape is just a tune
> is just this flight's small hour

As the reference to Daedalus suggests, this brings together some of the key motifs of *Air Histories* and *The Book of Idiots*: the human being as maker whose art and life are an attempt at flight, a 'shape' made in time and space, hanging between earth and air.

'Making' in all its forms – the making of music, art, landscape, history or war, an arrowhead or a metaphor, a poem or gravy – is the central concern of *Air Histories*. As Hooker notes, Meredith is 'acutely aware of process, of what goes to the making of a landscape or a people or a personal identity, of life as flight, the winged phenomenon, rather than the finished corpse ready for autopsy'.[60] The collection itself traces a 'shape made in time', opening with a poem on a 5,000-year-old Neolithic arrowhead (*AH*, 7), uncovered by the environmental damage in the Black Mountains, and closing with 'The wool of the sheep that bit you' (*AH*, 58–61) which urges environmental activism for the future.

From early in his career, Meredith was fascinated by the idea that writing 'satisfies the primitive urge to make something': 'the satisfaction is all the more intense', he argued, when using pen and paper rather than a computer so that 'the thing seems to be made, like a piece of music, out of air, out of almost nothing'.[61] In *Air Histories* he returns repeatedly to the idea that music is 'made of air and time' (*AH*, 29) as a way of thinking about the paradoxical materiality/non-materiality of the act of making in sound and language. '[M]atter matters' as he puts it in 'The fiddler's frown' (*AH*, 54) which traces sound coming up from the ground, spreading through the wood floor and fiddler's flesh and 'out along the woodwork springboard/into air'. In 'The guitar maker Antonio de Torres in old age described by the priest Juan Martínez Sirvant' (*AH*, 20–2), Juan describes the materiality of guitar-making: the wood and glue which form 'the ribs and soundboards / and the backs and inlays and rosettes' of the instruments Master Torres makes. Asked to reveal 'the secret of your art' before he dies, however, Master Torres merely holds up his fingertips and thumb: 'A pinch of air / was all he had'. Air 'matters' too but we forget this when we think of it as mere empty space.

'The guitar maker Antonio de Torres' is one of several narrative poems about history in the collection, some of which write 'histories of air' in the sense of music. Like Brother Cynan, the priest Juan Martínez Sirvant is a recorder of history. Just as Master Torres's 'work is his witness', 'witness was [Juan's] work'; the chiasmus draws attention to the 'work' of art and of history and the importance of witness or the 'work' of seeing. The materiality of music and the labour that goes into its making, both the construction of instruments from fine wood and the physicality of playing, are also explored in 'The strange music' which looks back to the great luthiers René François Lacote and Lovis Panormo: '*For the song is worth / the ache in the hands / the agony, the work*' (*AH*, 33). In 'Daniel's piano' (*AH*, 27), it is silence which draws attention to a failure to witness the atrocities of history. In an Israeli household, a dead boy's unplayed piano is a marker of civilization and a long-past grief. But the greater silence is that surrounding the Palestinian village which was emptied in order that the Jewish settlement might be built: 'No one talks of the village's going. / Its old name is silenced.' The parallels made with the historical oppressions of the Native Americans and the Welsh elsewhere in Meredith's work are perhaps more powerful for not being spoken here.

In a more contemporary mode 'Guitar' (*AH*, 28–9) is a love song to the poet's own instrument, a poem which, like 'Red Armchair' (*MF*, 25), elaborates an erotics of things. In a sentence that stretches teasingly over fifteen couplets, the poet meditates on how man and guitar 'play' each other, climaxing in the brief occasions when they 'forget [they] are two': 'how close we get to something right / that's made of air and time'. Singing appears as a motif in other poems: in the arrow which sings through the air in 'Arrowhead' (*AH*, 7), or the songs sung by the women in 'What earth thought' (*AH*, 10). Made of 'air and time' but grounded in earth, wood and flesh, music negotiates the edge between sound and silence and thus writes its own kind of history.

In several poems Meredith riffs on the edge between music and language as different ways of making meaning. 'The business of language is to convey meaning' he writes in an appraisal of Dorothy Edwards's use of musical patterning in *Winter Sonata*.[62] In contrast, music is 'shapes in the air, that don't have meaning as language does, but rather structure and perhaps mood'.[63] In the concrete poem 'At Colonus' (*AH*, 16–18), as in 'Builders of Bab-ilu', language fragments into ostensibly meaningless shapes which the reader has to rebuild into meaning through the work of reading. In contrast, 'Twobeat deathsong' (*AH*, 42) and 'The wool of the sheep that bit you' (*AH*, 58–61) are almost nursery-rhyme-like in their use of emphatic ballad stresses. Meredith exploits the musicality of language as well as the shapes it makes on the page to explore its relation to spatiality and temporality, often translating these into motifs of air, earth, stone and wood within the landscape. 'Borderland' with its insight that 'Edges are where meanings happen' (*AH*, 8) points us to the borders these poems cross – between air/ earth, England/Wales, sound/silence. As Hooker suggests, this borderland is 'also a poetics', a way of thinking about meanings.[64]

Form and metaphor here make, and unmake, meaning. The
formal experimentation of these poems is another way in which
they cross borders, between poetry and prose, sound and silence,
English and Welsh. Many – like the fractured sonnet 'The slurry
pond' (*AH*, 26) or the divided ballad, 'Twobeat deathsong' (*AH*,
42) – are shaped to incorporate an 'edge' within the poem itself.
The words of 'Twobeat deathsong' form two columns which seem
to fall down the page like the 'falling   fountains' and 'failing
hours' the poem invokes. In contrast, 'Daedalus with a paramotor'
(*AH*, 55) and 'We dream of snow' (*AH*, 53) are shaped poems which
use what Meredith calls 'river rhyme' (borrowing the term from
printers' terminology for words that directly underlie each other
on successive lines):

> the filmy *glimmer* of the not-there disc
> > *shimmering* on his back (*AH*, 55; emphasis added)

Rather than being broken, the form is held together by a rich seam
of central rhymes while the edges fragment. With others, such as
the opening poem, 'Arrowhead' (*AH*, 7) or 'Y grib'/'Ridge' (*AH*,
14, 15), we become aware of the relationship between the printed
word and the border or 'edge' of the page. In 'Arrowhead' the
poem, shaped like the eponymous arrow, points us like a cursor
to the edge between words and blank page and to the possibility
of flight beyond. The shaping of 'Y grib'/'Ridge' makes us aware
of the relationship between word and the white space of the blank
page, the 'air' around the poem like the sky around the ridge. The
sestina 'What earth thought' (*AH*, 10–11) uses a restricted vocabulary taken from the Dyen List, a compilation of around two hundred
words which is used by researchers to assess the inter-relatedness
of languages and the possibility of a lost European protolanguage
(*AH*, 63). Within those constrictions of both form and language the
complexities of meanings push at the boundaries or edges of the
poem.

Still other forms are 'edgy' in a different sense. 'At Colonus'
takes a line from Dorothy Edwards's story 'A Garland of Earth'

(in *Rhapsody* (1927)[65]), 'One may not rest yet', and fragments it so that the words appear to rain down the page (*AH*, 16–18). The speaker is the blind Oedipus, a man at the edge of sanity, and this concrete poem gives 'visual form to [his] psychological disintegration'.[66] Meredith noted that critics hated this poem because they had to work at reading it: the work, however, is the point.[67] The shape both distracts the reader from and lays bare the transparency of language which we tend to take for granted. 'Borderland' uses another 'edgy' form, the villanelle, which, in Hooker's words 'calls attention to artifice, verbal pattern-making, and simultaneously orders precariousness, as the reader thinks: will the poet make it, will he complete the form?'[68] Will the poet fly or fall? The metaphor of art, or life, as flight takes on another set of possibilities here.

The poems that appear in facing-page Welsh and English versions – 'Y grib'/'Ridge' (*AH*, 14, 15), 'Stori'r mynydd'/'Under the mountain' (*AH*, 36, 37), 'Peth doeth'/'You were right to come' (*AH*, 40, 41), 'Dim byd'/'Nothing' (*AH*, 44, 45), 'Bro Neb: yr arweinlyfr'/'An outline description of Nihilia' (*AH*, 46, 47) – incorporate another kind of 'edge' or 'border'. The two languages are separated, literally, by the gutter between the pages. Although the Welsh version comes first, and the acknowledgements make it clear that they were 'the original' versions (*AH*, 62), which version of these poems the reader reads first and how depends on their own linguistic history, whether they are mono-, bi- or multilingual, English or/and Welsh speakers. Moreover, as the titles indicate, these are not literal translations: 'Stori'r mynydd' ('story of the mountain') becomes 'Under the mountain'; 'Peth doeth' ('wise thing') becomes in English the more prosaic 'You were right to come'. The Welsh title of one of the poems about environmental damage in the Black Mountains, 'Dim byd' ('nothing'), contains within it 'byd' ('world', thus literally 'no world'). As Meredith has noted, the word 'byd' occurs four times in 'Dim byd', forming an embedded metaphor which is lost in the English version, one layer of which concerns the 'erosion of the Welsh language, potentially into nothingness, along with the vanishing peat'.[69] The work of translation, the negotiation across the borders of language, becomes visible here and the resonances generated as the 'edges' of the language rub against each other make their own palimpsest of meanings.

As Hooker has suggested, the notion of borderland becomes a poetics in *Air Histories*. The strands which bind this collection together – place, flight and falling, music, language and narrative, history and time, earth and air – are woven lightly through the individual poems but gather resonance as the collection itself moves through time. Meanings are generated through a dialogue between poems. 'The churches', for instance, written as a response to aerial photographs in the archive of the Royal Ancient Monuments Commission for Wales, emphasizes their earth-bound nature, their 'downhereness' (*AH*, 19). Whether in 'low places' or mountaintops, it is their affiliation with mud and stone which is stressed: 'at the base all's earth'. An aerial viewpoint is revisited in 'Earth air' (*AH*, 56) but here the earth itself is 'a billowing pavilion' pegged down by the stone churches 'hammered' into it like tent pegs. The Welsh names – 'Patricio, Cwmiou, Cwmdu, Capel y Ffin' – anchor the poem in the reality of place, but 'their grip's uncertain'. The border between earth and air seems insubstantial here as the earth itself threatens to take flight:

> One day the earth will wake and stretch and sigh
> and each church will pop its button
>
> and she'll fly.

The border between earth and human is similarly blurred in 'Peth doeth' / 'You were right to come' where a visit to the doctor becomes a reminder of mortality, of the movement of time:

> Pridd ydwyf
> fy nghorff ar fainc meddyg
> yn grib mynydd
> a gwenwyn yn anadlu
> o'r rhwyg du. (*AH*, 40)[70]

> I am becoming earth
> the ridge of me this mountain
> its lesions breathing poison into air. (*AH*, 41)

This is one of several English-language poems in the collection which end with either 'air' ('Ridge' (*AH*, 15) , 'The fiddler's frown (*AH*, 54), 'The near myth' (*AH*, 57)), or related words ('fly' in 'Earth air' (*AH*, 56), 'sky' in 'Birch' (*AH*, 51), 'daylight moon' in 'Daedalus with a paramotor' (*AH*, 55), 'light' in 'Trees on Castell Dinas' (*AH*, 9)). But this air is 'poison', a reminder of the history of environmental damage done by humans, and of the lung diseases which were often the result of working in the coalmines. The notion of 'becoming earth' recalls the funeral service and Wil's ashes, 'chunky and granular' (*BI*, 234) which Dean pours off a sea cliff to the sound of *Smokehouse Blues*. It reminds us that our bodies are made of the 'same carbon' as the 'curious black earth' of the mountains (*BM*, 4). Just as we are made of earth and air, our lives are a shape made in time and space.

Discussing the phenomena of poet-novelists in an interview, Meredith argues that to see poetry and prose as 'actual opposites is lazy thinking'.[71] Instead, he compares the difference to a musician turning from playing the piano to playing a guitar. The musician may feel a sense of cohesion rather than opposition between the instruments: 'When it works, the tension between them is creative rather than obstructive. It's all making the air vibrate in the end.'[72] Just as Meredith sequences his poetry collections like a piece of music so that we can hear the echoes between poems, the echoes between his fiction and his poetry are there if we take the trouble to listen for them. This is perhaps particularly true of *The Book of Idiots* and *Air Histories*, connected by their concern with place, boundaries and edges, language and form, and the motifs of flying and falling. Meredith has said of *The Book of Idiots*: 'I think [it] reflects a little of where we are in Wales nowadays, but I hope it's understated.'[73] The novel depicts a neo-liberal, post-industrial and affectless twenty-first-century south Wales, where people work at 'content-free' jobs and collude in an avoidance of intimacy or connection with others. It's through an engagement with the land-scape of the Black Mountains and a call to recognize and, perhaps above all, try to repair the damage done to it by humans that *Air Histories* offers the possibility of a way into the future. For all its nursery-rhyme rhythms, 'The wool of the sheep that bit you' (*AH*, 58–9) posits making – 'Let's knit a mountain' – as art which offers both reparation and redemption.

Afterword

Christopher Meredith is a major writer *because* of, not despite, the fact that he writes in and out of a 'small' country and across the 'edges' between a 'small' language and what has become the lingua franca of our globalized age. If he wrote about London rather than Tredegar, Wessex rather than Gwent, his reputation might be rather different. Like Thomas Hardy, Emily Brontë or D. H. Lawrence, he is a novelist-poet grounded in his place whose work addresses universal themes precisely because of its location in an intimately rendered geographical and historical specificity. The realism of his work, its humour and its concern with the quotidian, should not distract us from its sophisticated formal experimentation, the richness of its symbolism and the ambitious philosophical ideas with which it plays. Meredith's writing benefits from attentive reading of his *oeuvre* as a whole, a reading across the 'edges' between poetry and prose, English and Welsh, mountain and valley, past and present, rural and post-industrial.

Any critical work on a living writer can only be a very partial assessment of the *oeuvre* so far, qualified by acknowledgement that subsequent work may require a radical reassessment of all that has gone before. At the time of writing Meredith's work seems to be moving in two directions. The first is the new collection of poems, *Still Air* (2016).[1] Produced in collaboration with the artist Sara Philpott, and hand printed as a limited edition of fifty copies, it includes nine poems with accompanying linocuts. Both poems and linocuts are responses to landscape, trees, birds and plants: Philpott's to the area around Newtown, Meredith's to the area around his home in Brecon. A particular inspiration for Meredith was Allt yr Esgair, a wooded hill topped by an Iron Age hillfort near the home of the seventeenth-century metaphysical poet Henry Vaughan.

The sequence opens with 'Allt spring', a 'birthsong and an elegy', and moves through the seasons to close with 'Winter woods' which meditates on 'the alchemy of snow' as it forms and falls, 'rid[ing] down the zigzag / seesaws of the half-sustaining air'. There is also an upwards movement to the sequence. It opens at ground level with poems that focus on the 'felled trees' of 'Allt spring' and low-growing woodland plants ('Dogs' Mercury' and 'Fumitory'), and moves through 'Nettles', where the eponymous plants are 'tall as men', to poems about trees ('Ash trees' and 'In this stilled air the turning trees').[2] It finishes in 'Winter woods' with the snow 'conjured' 'miles up' in the atmosphere, falling downwards to the earth.

Still Air develops themes and techniques from *Air Histories*, where the unrecorded moments of history – butterflies flying over a barley field, sparrows on a path – are described as 'small scriptless books that eddied in still air' (*AH*, 13). As a title, *Still Air* suggests, first, that Meredith is 'still' concerned with the ongoing project of writing air. Secondly, it connects notions of time and space. To be 'still' is to be motionless, to lack movement through time or space, or to be quiet/silent. But as an adverb – 'still it sounds' – or a verb – 'stilled' – it holds within it the possibility of both endurance and movement. It reminds us that if air can be 'still' it can also be 'stirred'. It is not simply empty or static space but has its own aerial topography which can be mapped through movement, an aerography of eddies and thermals: 'the calms and freshes / of the liquid sky' as the birds experience it in 'Village birds'.

The majority of the poems here are shaped or concrete, with subtle use of sound echoes on key words. 'In this stilled air . . .' uses the words 'stilled', 'still' or 'stillness' six times in different modulations (as verb, noun, adjective and adverb). And it similarly shifts from 'air' as in atmosphere to 'air' as in music. In the 'stilled air' of autumn both sap and blood slow, like an orchestra, becoming almost mute:

and *still* it stands
and *still*, as Galileo almost said, it moves
this music of the shape we make in time
the almost
       *still*ness of the air
we have to play. (*SA*; emphasis added)

Here Meredith develops his use of what he calls river rhyme. Thus poems cohere around a central stem or trunk of echoing words: variations on 'still' in 'In this stilled air . . .' or a series of feminine half-rhymes in 'Fumitory': burning/cleansing/ending/frettings/counter-pointing/condensing. Their edges are formed to echo the shapes made in air, or earth, or time, by the objects described: the 'zigzag/seesaws' of snow falling through the air in 'Winter woods' or the shimmeying of 'Ash trees' 'danc[ing]/ a trembling striptease'.

This is, on the whole, an 'unpeopled' collection: in 'Nettles' the eponymous plants mark the places where people no longer live – 'ruins', 'broken houses', *'rubble'*. They *'chok[e] the stone gates where /your children passed'*, suggesting the natural world taking back the landscape as it did in Troedrhiwgwair. The exception is 'Village birds', a brilliant example of defamiliarization, of making strange, which takes its cue from an epigraph from the nature writer William Condry: *'Villages are communities of birds as well as of people.'* 'Village birds' offers us the human world seen through the eyes of birds whose 'miles-deep parish is / the teeming air'. Like the glider's eye-view in *The Book of Idiots*, this refigures the world from above. To the birds, humans are 'landtrapped monsters' or 'bottom-dwellers' who try to 'rear into the third dimension' on 'heaps of stone' or 'strange wings of fire'. Human buildings are 'heapings of curious rocks' which are given 'meaning' when the birds use them, as they use the privet hedges or the telegraph wires, for their own purposes. This bird's-eye view puts us in our place, at the edges of their world. We co-exist with the natural world, this poem suggests, and recognizing this would both humble and enrich us.

The second development in Meredith's writing is a focus on short stories. While he published individual stories earlier in his career

– 'Opening Time', 'Averted Vision', 'The Woman on the Beach' – I have, for space reasons, only been able to touch on these very briefly. His recently published stories, 'Somavox' (2014) and 'Progress' (2009), and the new stories, 'The Cavalry' and 'The Enthusiast', suggest that his short fiction merits careful attention.[3] The powerful 'Somavox', collected in *Best European Fiction 2015*, brings together many of Meredith's interests – language, landscape, space, ageing – to provide an unsettling glimpse of a possible future.[4]

Framed by epigraphs from the Romantic poets and notes on the development of a new 'interactive system' from 'G. Pallander, MD Somavox Corp', the story details three intensely physical encounters between an unnamed young couple as they meet and make love in a rural cabin by the sea.[5] The vivid descriptions of the landscape and of their physical apprehensions during these sexual encounters are rendered with intimate and tender detail. Their heightened sensuality suggests a Romantic understanding of the ability of humans to apprehend the natural world through immediate indi-vidual physical experience: *'Energy is eternal delight'*, as the epigraph from Blake has it.[6] And yet it becomes apparent that the couple are elderly, each sitting alone in some kind of geriatric care home, and experiencing through Somavox, a voice-activated system which crosses the 'linguistic/physical barrier', a virtual reality which is constructed of their memories and language.[7] As the final epigraph from G. Pallander tells us, this new system is being trialled by gerontologists for its 'potential in palliative care'.[8] What we think of as the most intimate and sensual of human experiences has become corporatized, marketed as a drug to alleviate the tedium and loneliness of senility.

'Somavox' interrogates the ambiguities in the epigraph from Wordsworth: 'Language is the incarnation of thought'.[9] On the one hand it explores the ways in which bodily and physical experience are always mediated by language. The descriptions repeatedly figure the physical in terms of writing: the grass is 'frosted white like a blank page'; lopped trees are 'pothooked and seriffed'; dried leaves are 'effs and ees and curly jays'.[10] 'I can read you like a book', he tells her.[11] In this virtual world there is nothing except language.

On the other hand, the story suggests a bodily experience of ageing – the loss of everything except speech – in which language becomes a palliative against an unbearable reality. 'Soma', from the Greek *sōma* (body) recalls the drug used in Aldous Huxley's *Brave New World* (1931), an antidepressant or opiate used to keep the populace of his dystopian Fordian future in a state of unquestioning contentment. Pallander's name suggests not only 'palliative', but also 'pander' (a procurer or go-between in clandestine affairs).

What drives the couple is the desire to 'occupy the same space', which they can do now only virtually.[12] At the end they appear to merge in a union which is more complete than 'the mechanical inhabitings of sex': 'All the space that matter is made of suddenly understood itself, and was generous and let the other in. Their different grammars and lexicons didn't just blend into a creole. They atomised as they crossed and reconfigured.'[13] The edges between the physical and linguistic are crossed. Bodies become a metaphor for languages and vice versa. The final image of snow falling suggests a crossing of the edges between life and death:

> The snow fell in tiny pieces on his dark jacket. Eventually it would white him out. But for now it was a scattering, and it wasn't true, what they said about the flakes. They weren't all unique. Each was a word and they were identical.
>
> 'Yes' they said. 'Yes. Yes.'[14]

In 'Winter woods' Meredith asks with regard to snow, 'Was there ever a lousier metaphor / for death?' adding, 'The cold catch in the throat says we're alive' (*SA*, n.p.). 'Somavox' picks up the same paradox. While the affirmative 'Yes' recalls Molly Bloom, the image of snow falling recalls the ending of Joyce's 'The Dead': '[Gabriel's] soul swooned slowly as he heard the snow falling faintly through the universe and faintly falling, like the descent of their last end, upon all the living and the dead.'[15] This is the 'unironic blanket that Joyce spread / over his one green love' as Meredith puts it in 'We dream of snow' (*AH*, 53). Snow here stands for the affirmative recognition of death as what shapes and gives meaning to life.

In the story of his origins which Meredith fashions (however ironically) in 'Birth myth' it is the snow that both 'marks [him] ordinary' and transforms the topography of Market Street into something mythic: 'A woman with a baby in a whitened street / ... walking towards eternity from the clock / uphill, in the cold' (*AH*, 24–5). Just as snow makes 'a living sculpture of our breath' in 'Winter woods', death makes visible 'the shape we make in time' (*SA*, n.p.). In 'We dream of snow', Meredith brings these images together as he asks for 'Definitive annihilation' to 'blur us into earth / erase us to completion' (*AH*, 53). And he identifies this process with writing: 'the better rhyme / that restores this page's room with / white' (*AH*, 53). Reading across Meredith's fiction and poetry in turn makes visible how he builds a poetics made of the ordinary – fashioned of time and air – which offers art as an affirmation.

Notes

I

1. Biographical information is based on an interview conducted with Christopher Meredith on 23 June 2016. Hereafter indicated in the text by the abbreviation I. Further information drawn from e-mail correspondence is indicated in the notes with the abbreviation CM.
2. William Shakespeare, *Henry IV*, Act 3, scene 1, ll. 13–14.
3. Shakespeare, *Henry IV*, Act 3, scene 1, l. 41. Depicted by Shakespeare as a self-aggrandizing Welsh wizard, the historical Owain Glyndŵr was the leader of the last attempt to establish Wales as an independent country.
4. Michael Foot, *Aneurin Bevan: A Biography, Vol. 1: 1897–1945* (London: MacGibbon and Kee, 1962), p. 23.
5. Roger Howe, 'Welshness and the human condition: interview with Christopher Meredith' *Zeitgeist Diagram, http://zeitgeist-diagram.com/index.php/interviews/8-welshness-and-the-human-condition* (accessed 21 October 2017).
6. Ieuan Gwynedd was the bardic name of Evan Jones, an independent minister who defended Welsh women from the strictures of the infamous 1847 report into education in Wales (the so-called 'Treachery of the Blue Books').
7. Christopher Meredith, 'Review: Tony Curtis, *Letting Go*', *Poetry Wales*, 19/4 (1984), 77–9, 77.
8. The term was popularized by D. J. Williams. See Dafydd Johnston, *The Literature of Wales* (1994; Cardiff: University of Wales Press, 1999), p. 99.
9. Jeremy Hooker, '"Heartlands": on some poems by Ruth Bidgood and Christopher Meredith', *Scintilla: The Journal of the Vaughan Association*, 17 (18 December 2013), 186–200.
10. William Wordsworth, 'Ode: Intimations of Immortality from Recollections of Early Childhood', in W. H. Auden and Norman Holmes Pearson (eds), *The Portable Romantic Poets: Blake to Poe* (Harmondsworth: Penguin, 1977), pp. 197–203, p. 199.

11 Hooker, 'Heartlands'; Matthew Jarvis, *Ruth Bidgood* (Cardiff: University of Wales Press, 2012), p. 34.

12 Christopher Meredith, 'Dai Greatcoat, Insectman, and Alun Lewis', *Poetry Wales*, 22/4 (1987), 59–65, 61.

13 Meredith, 'Dai Greatcoat, Insectman, and Alun Lewis', 63.

14 Meredith, 'Dai Greatcoat, Insectman, and Alun Lewis', 63.

15 CM, e-mail correspondence, 20 May 2016.

16 Christopher Meredith, 'Averted Vision', *Planet*, 81 (June/July 1990), 24–8.

17 CM, e-mail correspondence, 20 May 2016.

18 Meredith, 'Averted Vision', 25.

19 Meredith, 'Averted Vision', 27, 26.

20 Meredith, 'Averted Vision', 27.

21 Meredith, 'Averted Vision', 28.

22 Meredith, 'Averted Vision', 28.

23 Meredith, 'Averted Vision', 28.

24 Meredith, 'Averted Vision', 26.

25 Samuel Taylor Coleridge, 'The Rime of the Ancient Mariner', in Auden and Pearson (eds), *The Portable Romantic Poets*, pp. 130–52, p. 139.

26 Christopher Meredith, 'Opening My Palms I Saw', *The New Welsh Review*, 1/1 (summer 1988), 16.

27 Christopher Meredith, 'Progress', in A. Arjanee, M. Jenkins and K. Vadamootoo (eds), *Dodos and Dragons: An Anthology of Mauritian and Welsh Writing* (Mauritius: Atelier d'écriture, 2016).

28 Howe, 'Welshness and the human condition'.

29 CM, e-mail correspondence, 25 June 2016.

30 For an account of the residents' struggle to remain in Troedrhiwgwair see *Wales This Week, How safe was my valley?*, ITV Cymru Wales report, 1 April 2013, available online: *www.itv.com/news/wales/2013-04-01/wales-this-week-how-safe-was-my-valley/* (accessed 12 July 2016).

31 Seamus Heaney, *Death of a Naturalist* (1966; London: Faber, 1969), pp. 15–16.

32 The word 'panic' comes from the Greek god Pan (*OED*). See Ernest Rhys (ed.), *A Smaller Classical Dictionary* (1910; London: Everyman, 1920), p. 377.

33 See *Wales This Week, How safe was my valley?*, ITV Cymru Wales report.

34 Jane Mulvagh, *Madresfield: The Real Brideshead* (2008; London: Black Swan, 2009).

35 Hooker, 'Heartlands', 186–200.

36 This would have been Sir John Simon, 1st Viscount Simon (1873–1954), Secretary of State for Foreign Affairs between 1931 and 1935 (I). He held the positions of Home Secretary (1915–16, 1935–7) and Chancellor

of the Exchequer (1937–40) under Neville Chamberlain and was one of those responsible for the policy of appeasement.

37   William Wordsworth, 'The Solitary Reaper', in Auden and Pearson (eds), *The Portable Romantic Poets*, pp. 189–90.

38   Karl Marx, *Capital: A Critical Analysis of Capitalist Production, Vol. 1*, trans. Samuel Moore and Edward Aveling and ed. Frederick Engels (1887; Moscow: Progress, n.d.), p. 682.

39   Christopher Meredith, 'Up the Mountain', *Planet*, 106 (August/ September 1994), 36–9, 37.

40   Raymond Williams, 'The Welsh Industrial Novel' (1979), in *Who Speaks for Wales? Nation, Culture, Identity*, ed. Daniel Williams (Cardiff: University of Wales Press, 2003), pp. 95–111, p. 105.

41   Meredith, 'Up the Mountain', 37.

42   Meredith, 'Up the Mountain', 37.

43   Meredith, 'Up the Mountain', 37.

44   Meredith, 'Up the Mountain', 37.

45   Meredith, 'Up the Mountain', 37.

46   Meredith, 'Up the Mountain', 38.

47   Meredith, 'Up the Mountain', 38.

48   Meredith, 'Up the Mountain', 38.

49   Gary Meredith was a founder member of Gwent Theatre in 1976 and artistic director for both Gwent Theatre and its youth branch Gwent Young People's Theatre, founded in 1956. Both companies closed as a result of Arts Council cuts. Gary has worked in television, film and radio, appearing in *That Uncertain Feeling* (1985), *I Was Born in Rhymney* (1990) as Idris Davies, and *Intimate Relations* (1996).

50   CM, e-mail correspondence, 25 June 2016.

51   Christopher Meredith, 'Secret Rooms', *Planet*, 109 (February/March 1995), 51.

52   Meredith, 'Secret Rooms', 52, 53.

53   Meredith, 'Secret Rooms', 53.

54   Meredith, 'Secret Rooms', 54.

55   Meredith, 'Secret Rooms', 54.

56   George Orwell, *The Road to Wigan Pier* (1937; Harmondsworth: Penguin, 1962), p. 106.

57   Meredith, 'Secret Rooms', 54.

58   Meredith, 'Secret Rooms', 54. The 'fat owl' is Billy Bunter, the schoolboy who appeared in the stories of Greyfriars School written by 'Frank Richards' (Charles Hamilton) for *The Magnet* from 1908 to 1940.

59   See Chinua Achebe, 'An Image of Africa: Racism in Conrad's *Heart of Darkness*' (1975/7), in Andrew Michael Roberts (ed.), *Joseph Conrad*, Longman Critical Reader (London: Longman, 1998), pp. 111–17.

60 Christopher Meredith, 'Foreword', in Christopher Meredith (ed.), *Moment of Earth: Poems and Essays in Honour of Jeremy Hooker* (Aberystwyth: Celtic Studies Publications, 2007), pp. xiii–xv, p. xv.

61 Dai George, 'Interview: Christopher Meredith', *Poetry Wales*, Blog Archive: Interviews, 28 July 2015, *http://poetrywales.co.uk/wp/2531/interview-christopher-meredith/* (accessed 20 April 2016).

62 George, 'Interview: Christopher Meredith'.

63 James Joyce to Grant Richards, *Letters*, II, p. 134, quoted in *Dubliners* (1914; Harmondsworth: Penguin, 1992), p. xxxi.

64 Sheenagh Pugh, 'Interview with Christopher Meredith', 22 June 2011, 'Good God! There's writing on both sides of that paper!', *Live Journal*, *http://sheenaghpugh.livejournal.com/68450.html* (accessed 5 September 2013).

65 Pugh, 'Interview with Meredith'.

66 Pugh, 'Interview with Meredith'.

67 Pierre Bourdieu, *Distinction: A Social Critique of the Judgement of Taste* (1979; Abingdon: Routledge, 2010).

68 Pugh, 'Interview with Meredith'.

69 Glyn Jones, *The Dragon Has Two Tongues*, ed. Tony Brown (rev. edn, Cardiff: University of Wales Press, 2001), p. 127; Hooker, 'Heartlands', 186–200.

70 Hooker, 'Heartlands', 186–200.

71 Christopher Meredith, 'Unbroken on the Wheel' (review of Ned Thomas, *The Welsh Extremist*), *Planet*, 93 (June/July 1992), 89; emphasis added.

72 Meredith, 'Unbroken on the Wheel', 90; emphasis added.

73 Meredith, 'Unbroken on the Wheel', 90; emphasis added.

74 Meredith, 'Unbroken on the Wheel', 90; emphasis added.

75 Meredith, 'Up the Mountain', 37, 39.

76 Meredith, 'Up the Mountain', 38.

77 Meredith, 'Up the Mountain', 39.

78 Meredith, 'Up the Mountain', 39.

2

1 Raymond Williams, 'The Welsh Trilogy: *The Volunteers*' (1979), in *idem*, *Who Speaks for Wales? Nation, Culture, Identity* (Cardiff: University of Wales Press, 2003), p. 117.

2 Letter from Christopher Meredith to Richard Poole, 3 November 1995, quoted in Richard Poole, 'Afterword' (*S*, 231).

³ *Church of St Cynog, Defynnog: A brief history* (Defynnog: PPC of the Church of St Cynog, 2015).

⁴ Christopher Meredith, 'Scintilla Poets in Conversation', contribution, *Scintilla: The Journal of the Vaughan Association*, Blogspot, *http://vaughanassociation.blogspot.co.uk/p/scintilla-poets-in.html* (accessed 20 February 2014).

⁵ *The Defynnog Yew: An ancient and venerable tree* (Defynnog: PPC of the Church of St Cynog, 2015).

⁶ Meredith, 'Scintilla Poets'.

⁷ Meredith, 'Scintilla Poets'.

⁸ John Barnie, 'Christopher Meredith: *This*', *Poetry Wales*, 20/4 (1984), 98–100, 99, 98.

⁹ Barnie, 'Christopher Meredith: *This*', 98.

¹⁰ Barnie, 'Christopher Meredith: *This*', 98.

¹¹ Barnie, 'Christopher Meredith: *This*', 98.

¹² Seamus Heaney, *Death of a Naturalist* (1966; London: Faber, 1969), pp. 13, 24.

¹³ Heaney, *Death of a Naturalist*, p. 14.

¹⁴ Heaney, *Death of a Naturalist*, p. 23.

¹⁵ Heaney, *Death of a Naturalist*, p. 23.

¹⁶ Barnie, 'Christopher Meredith: *This*', 100.

¹⁷ 'The Pwca of the Trwyn', in W. Jenkyn Thomas, *The Welsh Fairy Book* (1907; Cardiff: University of Wales Press, 1952), pp. 248–52.

¹⁸ Christopher Meredith, 'Saying it in Saesneg', *Poetry Wales*, 20/1 (1984), 12.

¹⁹ Meredith, 'Saying it in Saesneg', 13.

²⁰ Meredith, 'Saying it in Saesneg', 12, 13.

²¹ Meredith, 'Saying it in Saesneg', 13.

²² Meredith, 'Saying it in Saesneg', 14.

²³ Meredith, 'Saying it in Saesneg', 14.

²⁴ Meredith, 'Saying it in Saesneg', 14.

²⁵ Emyr Humphreys, *The Taliesin Tradition: A Quest for the Welsh Identity* (1983; Bridgend: Seren, 1989), p. 19.

²⁶ Dafydd ap Gwilym, *Poems*, trans. Rachel Bromwich (1982; Llandysul: Gomer, 1987), pp. 106–8, 74–5.

²⁷ Glyn Jones, *The Dream of Jake Hopkins* (London: Fortune, 1954), pp. 4–41, 40.

²⁸ Christopher Meredith, 'Telling and the Time', in Maura Dooley (ed.), *How Novelists Work* (Bridgend: Seren, 2000), pp. 56–70, 56. See chapter 3 for discussion of the Cardiff conspiracy trials.

29 Christopher Meredith, 'Miller's Answer: Making, Saying, and the Impulse to Write', *New Writing: The International Journal for the Practice and Theory of Creative Writing*, 8/1 (2011), 71–89, 81.

30 Ian Jack, 'In Port Talbot in 1980 I found growing resentment at rulers who were "out for themselves"', *The Guardian*, 4 April 2016, 11.

31 Meredith, 'Telling', p. 56.

32 Meredith, 'Telling'.

33 Dai George, 'Interview: Christopher Meredith', *Poetry Wales*, Blog Archive: Interviews, 28 July 2015, *http://poetrywales.co.uk/wp/2531/interview-christopher-meredith/* (accessed 20 April 2016).

34 Christopher Meredith, 'The Dance of Misunderstanding' (interview with Richard John Evans), *New Welsh Review*, 53 (spring 2001), 7–10, 9.

35 Raymond Williams, 'Working-class, Proletarian, Socialist' (1982), in *idem, Who Speaks for Wales?*, pp. 147–58, 148.

36 Meredith, 'Telling', p. 56.

37 Stephen Knight, *A Hundred Years of Fiction* (Cardiff: University of Wales Press, 2004), p. 180.

38 Williams, 'The Welsh Industrial Novel' (1979), in *idem, Who Speaks for Wales?*, pp. 95–111, 103.

39 Williams, 'The Welsh Industrial Novel', p. 104.

40 Williams, 'The Welsh Industrial Novel', p. 108.

41 Raymond Williams, 'Wales and England' (1983), in *idem, Who Speaks for Wales?*, pp. 16–26, 20.

42 Christopher Meredith, 'Two from the Heart' (review of Gwyn Thomas, *Sorrow for Thy Sons* and *All Things Betray Thee*), *Planet*, 59 (October/November 1986), 98–99, 99.

43 James Joyce, *Ulysses* (1922; Harmondsworth: Penguin, 1971), p. 40.

44 Karl Marx, *The Eighteenth Brumaire of Louis Bonaparte* (1852; New York: International Publishers, 1998), p. 15.

45 Meredith, 'Two from the Heart', 99.

46 Meredith, 'Two from the Heart', 99; emphasis added.

47 Meredith, 'Two from the Heart', 99.

48 Derrick Price, '*How Green Was My Valley*: a romance of Wales', in Jean Radford (ed.), *The Progress of Romance: The Politics of Popular Fiction* (London: Routledge, 1986), pp. 73–94, 92.

49 Meredith, 'Telling', p. 64.

50 Meredith, 'Telling', p. 64.

51 Meredith, 'Secret Rooms', 53.

52 Williams, 'Welsh Industrial Novel', p. 105.

53 See Evan Powell, *History of Tredegar* [1884; repr. 1902], chapter 2, 15, *www.mike-jones.ukfsn.org/phot/* (accessed 21 July 2017).

54 Williams, 'Welsh Industrial Novel', p. 100.
55 Robert Lewis, *Wenglish: The Dialect of the South Wales Valleys* (2008; Talybont: Y Lolfa, 2016).
56 See Arthur Gray-Jones, *A History of Ebbw Vale* (Risca: Starling Press, 1970); R. Protheroe-Jones, *Welsh Steel* (Cardiff: National Museum of Wales Press, 1995); John Elliott, 'The Iron and Steel Industry', in Chris Williams and Sian Rhiannon Williams (eds), *The Gwent County History, Volume 4: Industrial Monmouthshire, 1780–1914* (Cardiff: University of Wales Press on behalf of The Gwent County History Association, 2011), pp. 73–86; John Elliott and Colin Deneen, 'Iron, Steel and Aluminium', in Chris Williams and Andy Croll (eds), *The Gwent County History, Volume 5: The Twentieth Century* (Cardiff: University of Wales Press on behalf of The Gwent County History Association, 2013), pp. 59–74.
57 Elliott and Deneen, 'Iron, Steel and Aluminium', p. 59.
58 Elliott and Deneen, 'Iron, Steel and Aluminium', p. 60.
59 Kirsti Bohata, *Postcolonialism Revisited* (Cardiff: University of Wales Press, 2004), p. 124.
60 Bohata, *Postcolonialism Revisited*, p. 124.
61 See Jane Aaron, 'Post-industrial resilience in south Wales valleys' fiction: A regional case study', in Britta Caspers, Dirk Hallenberger, Werner Jung and Rolf Parr (eds), *Theorien, Modelle und Probleme regionaler Literaturgeschichtsschreibung* (Essen: Fritz Hüser Institut, 2016), pp. 75–92, 86–7.
62 Meredith, 'Secret Rooms', 54.
63 Ann Pettit, *Walking to Greenham* (Dinas Powys: Honno, 2006).
64 Robin Morgan, *The Word of a Woman: Feminist Dispatches* (1992; Open Road Media, 2014), p. 33.
65 Meredith, 'Scintilla Poets'.
66 Knight, *Hundred Years*, p. 180.
67 Dylan Moore, 'Greatest Welsh Novel # 3: *Shifts* by Christopher Meredith', *www.walesartsreview.org/greatest-welsh-novel-3-shifts-by-christopher-meredith/* (accessed 27 July 2016). 'The Winner of the Greatest Welsh Novel is . . .', *www.walesartsreview.org/the-winner-of-the-greatest-welsh-novel-is-un-nos-ola-leuad-by-caradog-prichard/* (accessed 2 August 2016).

3

1 Gwyn Williams (ed.), *The Burning Tree* (London: Faber, 1956); English translations only reprinted as Gwyn Williams (ed. and trans.), *Welsh Poems Sixth Century to 1600* (London: Faber, 1973).

2   Christopher Meredith, 'Telling and the Time', in Maura Dooley (ed.), *How Novelists Work* (Bridgend: Seren, 2000), pp. 56–70, 57.

3   Sheenagh Pugh, 'Interview with Christopher Meredith', 22 June 2011, 'Good God! There's writing on both sides of that paper!', *Live Journal*, *http://sheenaghpugh.livejournal.com/68450.html* (accessed 5 September 2013).

4   Pugh, 'Interview with Christopher Meredith'.

5   Tony Conran, 'Sadness in Springtime', in *idem*, *Welsh Verse* (1967; Bridgend: Seren, 1992), p. 139.

6   CM, e-mail correspondence, 14 November 2016.

7   Jill Farringdon, 'Christopher Meredith: *Snaring Heaven*', *Poetry Wales*, 26/2 (September 1990), 60–1, 60.

8   Wayne Burrows, '*Snaring Heaven*, Christopher Meredith; *The Black Goddess*, Norman Schwenck', *New Welsh Review*, 13 (IV/1) (summer 1991), 57–8, 57.

9   Christopher Meredith, 'Opening Time', *Anglo-Welsh Review*, 85 (1987), 75–9.

10 CM, personal communication.

11 Meredith, 'Telling', p. 57.

12 Seamus Heaney, *Death of a Naturalist* (1966; London: Faber, 1969), p. 24.

13 Heaney, *Death of a Naturalist*, pp. 13–14.

14 Christopher Meredith, 'Miller's Answer: Making, Saying, and the Impulse to Write', *New Writing: The International Journal for the Practice and Theory of Creative Writing*, 8/1 (2011), 73.

15 Meredith, 'Miller's Answer', 74.

16 Seamus Heaney, *Preoccupations: Selected Prose, 1968–1978* (New York: Farrar, Strauss and Giroux, 1981), p. 138.

17 Farringdon, 'Christopher Meredith', 60.

18 Gerald of Wales, *The Journey Through Wales and The Description of Wales*, trans. Lewis Thorpe (1978; London: Penguin, 2004).

19 Raymond Williams, 'Welsh Culture' (1975), in *idem*, *Who Speaks for Wales? Nation, Culture, Identity*, ed. Daniel Williams (Cardiff: University of Wales Press, 2003), pp. 5–11, 9.

20 'Bedo' is a diminutive of 'Meredith'; Meredith lived in Bronllys.

21 Jeremy Hooker, '"Heartlands": on some poems by Ruth Bidgood and Christopher Meredith', *Scintilla: The Journal of the Vaughan Association*, 17 (18 December 2013), 186–200, 191.

22 Heaney, *Death of a Naturalist*, p. 57.

23 Thomas Campbell, 'Hohenlinden', in Francis Turner Palgrave (ed.), *The Golden Treasury* (1861; London: Oxford University Press, 1941), p. 213.

24 Diana Wallace, interview with CM, 1 April 2014.

[25] John Osmond, *Police Conspiracy* (Talybont: Y Lolfa, 1984).

[26] Peter Berresford Ellis, *The Celtic Revolution: A Study in Anti-Imperialism* (Talybont: Y Lolfa, 1985), p. 93.

[27] See Williams, *The Burning Tree*, and Williams, *Welsh Poems*, pp. 46–7.

[28] Williams, *Welsh Poems*, p. 47.

[29] Williams, *Welsh Poems*, p. 5.

[30] Williams, *Welsh Poems*, p. 9.

[31] Christopher Meredith, 'Two from the Heart' (review of Gwyn Thomas, *Sorrow for Thy Sons* and *All Things Betray Thee*), *Planet*, 59 (October/ November 1986), 98–9, 99.

[32] Avrom Fleishman, *The English Historical Novel: From Walter Scott to Virginia Woolf* (Baltimore and London: Johns Hopkins Press, 1971).

[33] Georg Lukács, *The Historical Novel*, trans. Hannah and Stanley Mitchell (1936/7; Lincoln and London: University of Nebraska Press, 1983).

[34] Raymond Williams, 'Working-class, Proletarian, Socialist: Problems in Some Welsh Novels', in *idem, Who Speaks for Wales?*, pp. 147–58, 158; emphasis added.

[35] Williams, 'Working-class, Proletarian, Socialist', pp. 157–8.

[36] Raymond Williams, 'Introduction', in Gwyn Thomas, *All Things Betray Thee* (1949; London: Lawrence and Wishart, 1986), p. viii.

[37] Williams, 'Introduction', p. vi.

[38] *Wales on Sunday*, back cover blurb, Raymond Williams, *People of the Black Mountains: Vol. 1: The Beginnings* (1989; London: Paladin, 1990).

[39] See Beverley Southgate, *Fiction Meets History* (Harlow: Pearson, 2009), pp. 174–5.

[40] *Brut y Tywysogyon or The Chronicle of the Princes, Red Book of Hergest Version*, ed. and trans. Thomas Jones (Cardiff: University of Wales Press, 1955), p. 137.

[41] Dai George, 'Interview: Christopher Meredith', *Poetry Wales*, Blog Archive: Interviews, 28 July 2015, *http://poetrywales.co.uk/wp/2531/ interview-christopher-meredith/* (accessed 20 April 2016).

[42] Wallace, interview with CM, 2014.

[43] George, 'Interview'.

[44] Gerald, *Journey*, p. 261.

[45] Gerald, *Journey*, p. 267.

[46] Gerald, *Journey*, p. 273.

[47] Hayden White, *Tropics of Discourse: Essays in Cultural Criticism* (1978; Baltimore and London: Johns Hopkins Press, 1985), p. 82.

[48] White, *Tropics of Discourse*, p. 83.

[49] White, *Tropics of Discourse*, p. 83.

[50] White, *Tropics of Discourse*, p. 85.

[51] White, *Tropics of Discourse*, p. 84.

[52] George, 'Interview'.
[53] Christopher Meredith, 'FS+LI=N or How to be a Novelist', *Planet*, 104 (April/May 1994), 46–9, 49.
[54] CM, e-mail correspondence, 22 January 2016.
[55] Wallace, interview with CM, 2014.
[56] Linda Hutcheon, *A Poetics of Postmodernism: History, Theory, Fiction* (New York and London: Routledge, 1988), p. 5.
[57] Lukács, *Historical Novel*, p. 53.
[58] Dafydd Johnston, 'Making History in Two Languages; Wiliam Owen Roberts's *Y Pla* and Christopher Meredith's *Griffri*', *Welsh Writing in English: A Yearbook of Critical Essays*, 3 (1997), 118–33, 123.
[59] Johnston, 'Making History', 123.
[60] Wallace, interview with CM, 2014.
[61] Wallace, interview with CM, 2014.
[62] Wallace, interview with CM, 2014.
[63] Kirsti Bohata, *Postcolonialism Revisited* (Cardiff: University of Wales Press, 2004), p. 152.
[64] Bohata, *Postcolonialism*, p. 149.
[65] John T. Koch (ed.), *Celtic Culture: A Historical Encyclopedia, Vol. 2* (Santa Barbara CA: ABC-Clio, 2006), pp. 771–2.
[66] Gerald, *Journey*, p. 261.
[67] Wallace, interview with CM, 2014.
[68] White, *Tropics*, p. 87.
[69] White, *Tropics*, p. 87.
[70] Southgate, *History*, p. 76.
[71] Southgate, *History*, p. 76.
[72] Bohata, *Postcolonialism*, pp. 146–56.
[73] Gerald, *Journey*, p. 203.
[74] *Brut y Tywysogyon*, p. 163.
[75] *Brut y Tywysogyon*, pp. 131, 151, 163, 165.
[76] Lewis Spence, 'Beaver Medicine Legend', *North American Indians* (1914), reprinted as *North American Legends* (London: Mystic Press, 1987).
[77] *The Mabinogion*, trans. Gwyn Jones and Thomas Jones (1949; London: Dent, 1978), p. 19.
[78] Gerald, *Journey*, p. 174.
[79] Gerald, *Journey*, p. 176.
[80] Williams, *Welsh Poems*, pp. 46–8.
[81] Conran, 'Sadness', p. 139.
[82] Johnston, 'Making History', 126.
[83] CM, e-mail correspondence, 24 November 2016.
[84] Gerald, *Journey*, p. 116.
[85] Wallace, interview with CM, 2014.

86 Wallace, interview with CM, 2014.
87 Bohata, *Postcolonialism*, p. 151.
88 Bohata, *Postcolonialism*, p. 187, n. 68.
89 Bohata, *Postcolonialism*, p. 156; *Mabinogion*, p. 29.
90 Wallace, interview with CM, 2014.
91 Lukács, *Historical Novel*, p. 53.
92 Lukács, *Historical Novel*, pp. 30–63.

4

1 The term 'condition-of-England novels' refers to the new novels of social consciousness by writers such as Elizabeth Gaskell and Benjamin Disraeli which emerged in the 1840s.
2 Christopher Meredith, 'Do we really want to be Welsh?', *New Statesman*, 3 May 1999, 33–4, 33.
3 Meredith, 'Do we really want to be Welsh?', 33.
4 Meredith, 'Do we really want to be Welsh?', 34.
5 Tony Blair used the phrase in his leader's speech at Blackpool in 1996: 'Ask me my three main priorities for government and I tell you: education, education and education.' *www.britishpoliticalspeech.org/speech-archive.htm?speech=202* (accessed 15 October 2017).
6 Nicholas Murray, 'Looking to the World: Sheenagh Pugh, *The Movement of Bodies*. Christopher Meredith, *The Meaning of Flight*, Jeremy Hooker, *Arnolds Wood*', *Planet*, 174 (December 2005/January 2006), 97–9, 97.
7 Christopher Meredith, 'Secret Rooms', *Planet*, 109 (February/March 1995), 51–4, 52.
8 Meredith, 'Secret Rooms', 52–3.
9 Christopher Meredith, 'The Woman on the Beach', *Planet*, 87 (June/July 1991), 51–4.
10 Meredith, 'Secret Rooms', 53.
11 Meredith, 'Secret Rooms', 54.
12 Sheenagh Pugh, 'Interview with Christopher Meredith', 22 June 2011, 'Good God! There's writing on both sides of that paper!', *Live Journal*, *http://sheenaghpugh.livejournal.com/68450.html* (accessed 5 September 2013).
13 Originally established as the South Wales and Monmouthshire School of Mines in 1913, it became Glamorgan Technical College in 1949 and then Glamorgan Polytechnic in 1970. Following a merger with Glamorgan College of Education in Barry the institution was re-named the Polytechnic of Wales in 1975, before becoming the University of Glamorgan in 1992.

[14] See Sam Adams, 'Letter from Wales', *PN Review*, 144, 28/4 (March–April 2002), *www.pnreview.co.uk/cgi-bin/scribe?item_id=1153* (accessed 22 October 2017).

[15] See Tony Curtis, 'Centenary Essay: From Barry to Treforest via Vermont', *http://centenary.southwales.ac.uk/essays/tony-curtis/* (accessed 16 October 2017).

[16] Meic Stephens, 'The Second Flowering', *Poetry Wales*, 3/3 (winter 1967), 2–9.

[17] Richard John Evans, *Entertainment* (Bridgend: Seren, 2000); Christopher Meredith, 'The Dance of Misunderstanding' (interview with Richard John Evans), *New Welsh Review*, 52 (spring 2001), 7–10, 7.

[18] Emma Darwin, *The Mathematics of Love* (2006; London: Headline, 2007).

[19] Tom Bullough, *Addlands* (2016; London: Granta, 2017), p. 295. Both writers featured in a 'Sound Walk' by Horatio Clare, BBC Radio 3, Monday, 29 May 2017, *www.bbc.co.uk/mediacentre/proginfo/2017/22/sound-walk* (accessed 29 May 2017).

[20] Dai George, 'Interview: Christopher Meredith', *Poetry Wales*, Blog Archive: Interviews, 28 July 2015, *http://poetrywales.co.uk/wp/2531/interview-christopher-meredith/* (accessed 20 April 2016).

[21] Christopher Meredith, 'Miller's Answer: Making, Saying, and the Impulse to Write', *New Writing: The International Journal for the Practice and Theory of Creative Writing*, 8/1 (2011), 71–89, 84.

[22] *OED*.

[23] I am indebted to Jeni Williams for this point.

[24] Phil Hubbard and Rob Kitchen (eds), 'Introduction', *Key Thinkers on Space and Place*, 2nd edn (2004; London: Sage, 2011), pp. 1–25.

[25] Hubbard and Kitchen (eds), 'Introduction', p. 8.

[26] Doreen Massey, *Space, Place and Gender* (Cambridge: Polity, 1994), p. 269.

[27] Pugh, 'Interview with Meredith'.

[28] Pugh, 'Interview with Meredith'.

[29] Graham Swift, *Waterland* (1983; London: Picador, 1996); A. S. Byatt, *Possession: A Romance* (1990; London: Vintage, 1991). See Kate Mitchell, *History and Cultural Memory in Neo-Victorian Fiction: Victorian Afterimages* (Basingstoke: Palgrave, 2010).

[30] Christopher Meredith, 'Knowing the Unknowable' (Review of Sam Adams, *Prichard's Nose*), *PN Review*, 195, 37/1 (September–October 2010), 65–6, 66.

[31] James Joyce, *Ulysses* (1922; Harmondsworth: Penguin, 1972), pp. 659–704.

[32] Christopher Meredith, 'Robert Crawford, *Masculinity*', *Poetry Wales*, 32/1 (July 1996), 62–3, 63.

[33] W. B. Yeats, 'Byzantium', in *idem*, *Selected Poems* (London: Pan, 1974), p. 153.

[34] Gwen Davies, 'Interview: Chris Meredith', *New Welsh Review*, 95 (2013), online, *www.newwelshreview.com/article.php?id=136* (accessed 4 September 2013).

[35] Davies, 'Interview: Chris Meredith'.

[36] George, 'Interview: Chris Meredith'.

[37] Patricia Waugh, *Metafiction* (London and New York: Routledge, 1984).

[38] His second name, David, perhaps recalls D. H. Lawrence. Leyshon is an anglicized version of the Welsh name Lleision, probably from Lleisiol meaning 'belonging to the voice', appropriate for a would-be-writer. Trefor Rendall Davies, *Book of Welsh Names* (n.p.: Read Books, 2016). E-book.

[39] Meredith, 'Miller's Answer', 73–4.

[40] CM, personal communication.

[41] Robert Louis Stevenson, *The Black Arrow* (1888; London: Bloomsbury, 1994), pp. 156–7.

[42] Beverley Southgate, *History Meets Fiction* (Harlow: Longman, 2009), p. 108.

[43] Thomas Carlyle, *The Letters and Speeches of Oliver Cromwell*, quoted in Southgate, *History Meets Fiction*, p. 30.

[44] Fred Hoyle, *Nicolaus Copernicus* (London: Heinemann, 1973), p. 37.

[45] Meredith, 'Miller's Answer', 84; emphasis added.

[46] Southgate, *History Meets Fiction*, p. 156.

[47] Southgate, *History Meets Fiction*, p. 156.

[48] Massey, *Space, Place and Gender*, p. 269.

[49] Kirsti Bohata, *Postcolonialism Revisited* (Cardiff: University of Wales Press, 2004), p. 80.

[50] CM, personal communication.

[51] Hubbard and Kitchen, *Key Thinkers on Space and Place*, p. 29.

[52] Meredith, 'Dance of Misunderstanding', 10.

[53] Meredith, 'Dance of Misunderstanding', 10.

[54] Meredith, 'Dance of Misunderstanding', 7.

[55] Christopher Meredith, 'From the Wordface' (review of Duncan Bush, *Black Faces Red Mouths* and Mogg Williams, *The Wastelands*), *Planet*, 61 (February/March 1987), 99–100, 100.

[56] Meredith, 'Miller's Answer', 74.

[57] Matthew Jarvis, 'Christopher Meredith, *The Meaning of Flight* and Sheenagh Pugh, *The Movement of Bodies*', *Poetry Wales*, 41/1 (summer 2005), 57–60, 57.

[58] Jarvis, 'Christopher Meredith', 57.

[59] Ted Hughes, 'The Thought Fox', in George MacBeth (ed.), *Poetry 1900–1975* (Harlow: Longman, 1979), p. 279.

60 An earlier version of 'Toy revolver' included the final words 'he doesn't understand'; see *Planet*, 95 (August/September 1992), 47.

61 The Czech poet was Miroslav Holub; see Roger Howe, 'Welshness and the human condition: interview with Christopher Meredith', *Zeitgeist Diagram*, *http://zeitgeist-diagram.com/index.php/interviews/8-welshness-and-the-human-condition* (accessed 21 October 2017).

62 Pugh, 'Interview with Meredith'.

63 Pugh, 'Interview with Meredith'.

64 Thanks to Jane Aaron for this translation.

65 Meredith, 'Miller's Answer', 86.

66 Meredith, 'Miller's Answer', 86.

67 Meredith, 'Miller's Answer', 86.

68 Pugh, 'Interview with Meredith'.

69 Meredith, 'Miller's Answer', 86.

70 Meredith, 'Miller's Answer', 86.

71 Meredith, 'Miller's Answer', 86.

72 Meredith, 'Miller's Answer', 86.

5

1 'Christopher Meredith wins international scholarship', *Wales Literature Exchange*, 2012, *http://waleslitexchange.org/en/news/view/christopher-meredith-wins-international-scholarship* (accessed 20 April 2016).

2 Helen Babbs, 'The Woollen Line', *The Guardian*, 17 April 2013, *www.theguardian.com/lifeandstyle/gardening-blog/2013/apr/17/woollen-line-pip-woolf* (accessed 28 July 2017).

3 Meredith reverses the italicization of this epigraph in *Air Histories* where the English is given in italics and the Welsh in upright Roman.

4 Christopher Meredith, 'Telling and the Time', in Maura Dooley (ed.), *How Novelists Work* (Bridgend: Seren, 2000), p. 58.

5 Diana Wallace, 'Interview: Christopher Meredith talks about *Air Histories*', University of South Wales, *https://soundcloud.com/universityofsouthwales/professor-christopher-meredith* (accessed 19 January 2018).

6 Christopher Meredith, 'Double Acts and Distorting Mirrors: *Melog*', *New Welsh Review*, 73 (autumn 2006), 7–12, 10, 11.

7 Meredith, 'Double Acts and Distorting Mirrors', 8.

8 Meredith, 'Double Acts and Distorting Mirrors', 8.

9 Meredith, 'Double Acts and Distorting Mirrors', 11.

10 Christopher Meredith, 'The window facing the sea: the short stories of Dorothy Edwards', *Planet*, 107 (October/November 1994), 64–7, 65.

11 Christopher Meredith, 'Introduction', in Katja Krebs and Christopher Meredith (eds), *Five Essays on Translation* (Pontypridd: University of Glamorgan, 2005), p. 7.

12 Christopher Meredith, 'Dispatch#6 Pictures, Tongues, Cities', 'Chris Meredith (Wales→Finland)', *Wales Literature Exchange, http://waleslitexchange.org/en/translator's-house-wales/blog/christopher-meredit-* (accessed 20 April 2016).

13 Christopher Meredith, 'Dispatch# 3 I am not an elf', 'Chris Meredith Reporting from Slovenia', *Wales Literature Exchange, http://waleslitexchange.org/en/news/view/christopher-meredith-reporting-from-slovenia* (accessed 20 April 2016).

14 Meredith, 'Dispatch# 1 A Bend in the River', 'Chris Meredith Reporting from Slovenia'.

15 Meredith, 'Dispatch# 3 I am not an elf'.

16 Meredith, 'Dispatch# 2 Dogs and Toddlers', 'Chris Meredith Reporting from Slovenia'.

17 Gwen Davies, 'Interview: Christopher Meredith', *New Welsh Review*, 95 (2013), online *www.newwelshreview.com/article.php?is=136* (accessed 4 September 2013).

18 With thanks to Jane Finucane for translation expertise.

19 For another reading of this scene see Lisa Sheppard, 'Pulling Pints Not Punches: Linguistic Tensions in the Literary Pubs of Wales', *International Journal of Welsh Writing in English*, 3 (2015), 75–101.

20 Grahame Davies, 'Sleeping with the Enemy: The tensions of literary translation', in Krebs and Meredith (eds), *Five Essays on Translation*, pp. 10–21.

21 Davies, 'Sleeping with the Enemy', p. 17.

22 Claudine Tourniaire, 'Translating Welsh Historical Fiction into French: Politics of War and Peace', in Krebs and Meredith (eds), *Five Essays on Translation*, pp. 53–71, 54.

23 Tourniaire, 'Translating Welsh Historical Fiction', p. 56; emphasis added.

24 Tourniaire, 'Translating Welsh Historical Fiction', p. 56.

25 Lisa Lewis, 'Between Word and Worlds: The performance of translation', in Krebs and Meredith (eds), *Five Essays on Translation*, pp. 33–41, 33.

26 Lewis, 'Between Word and Worlds', p. 34.

27 Lewis, 'Between Word and Worlds', p. 35.

28 'Christopher Meredith reveals how his latest novel got its name', *Wales Online*, 18 August 2012, *www.walesonline.co.uk/lifestyle/christopher-meredith-reveals-how-latest-2057* (accessed 25 November 2013).

29 'Christopher Meredith reveals'.

30 W. H. Auden, 'Musée des Beaux Arts', in George MacBeth (ed.), *Poetry 1900 to 1975* (Harlow: Longman, 1979), p. 158.

31 Auden, 'Musée des Beaux Arts'.

32 See Simone de Beauvoir, *The Second Sex*, trans. H. M. Parshley (1949; Harmondsworth: Penguin, 1983).

33 Davies, 'Interview with Meredith'.

34 Christopher Meredith, '*Alun Lewis: Collected Stories*', *New Welsh Review*, 13, 18/1 (summer 1991), 31–2, 32.

35 'Christopher Meredith reveals'.

36 Davies, 'Interview with Meredith'.

37 David Graeber, 'On the phenomenon of bullshit jobs', *Strike! Magazine* (summer 2013). Reprinted https://libcom.org/library/phenonmenon-bullshit-jobs-david-graeber (accessed 17 July 2017).

38 Graeber, 'On the phenomenon of bullshit jobs'.

39 Graeber, 'On the phenomenon of bullshit jobs'.

40 David Graeber, *The Utopia of Rules: On Technology, Stupidity, and the Secret Joys of Bureaucracy* (2015; Brooklyn and London: Melville, 2016), pp. 133–4.

41 Charles Dickens, *Great Expectations* (1860–1; London: Penguin, 1985), p. 231.

42 Eliane Glaser, 'Beyond bullshit jobs', *Soundings: A Journal of Politics and Culture*, 57 (summer 2014), 82–94, 87, *www.lwbooks.co.uk/sites/default/files/s57_08glaser.pdf* (accessed 17 July 2017).

43 Glaser, 'Beyond bullshit jobs', 92.

44 *OED*.

45 *Collins Gem Dictionary of First Names* (London and Glasgow: Collins, 1975).

46 *Collins Gem Dictionary of First Names*.

47 James Joyce, *Ulysses* (1922; Harmondsworth: Penguin, 1972), p. 704.

48 Raymond Durgnat, *A Mirror for England* (1970), cited in John Pym, *Time Out's Film Guide*, 8th edn (London: Penguin, 2000), p. 486.

49 Davies, 'Interview with Meredith'.

50 Davies, 'Interview with Meredith'.

51 Davies, 'Interview with Meredith'.

52 Christopher Meredith, 'Cronin and the Chronotope: Place, time and pessimistic individualism in *The Citadel*', *North American Journal of Welsh Studies*, 8 (2013), 50–65.

53 Davies, 'Interview with Meredith'.

54 Cato Pedder, '*Air Histories*: Christopher Meredith', *Write Out Loud*, 13 November 2013 *www.writeoutloud.net/public/blogentry.php?blogentryid=39687* (accessed 19 February 2014).

55   Jeremy Hooker, '*Air Histories:* Christopher Meredith', *Planet*, 212 (winter 2013/14), 157–8, 157.
56   Wallace, 'Interview: Christopher Meredith talks'.
57   Doreen Massey, *Space, Place and Gender* (Cambridge: Polity, 1994), p. 251.
58   A literal translation would be: 'No. A line of tune [air] it is / of rock / and soil / a fugue of rhythm'. With thanks to Nigel Wallace.
59   'the silence at the end of the song'.
60   Hooker, '*Air Histories*', 158.
61   Meredith, 'Telling and the Time', p. 58.
62   Meredith, '*Rhapsody*'s Lost Story', in Christopher Meredith (ed.), *Moment of Earth: Poems and Essays in Honour of Jeremy Hooker* (Aberystwyth: Celtic Studies Publications, 2007), pp. 159–70, 160.
63   Meredith, '*Rhapsody*'s Lost Story', p. 160.
64   Jeremy Hooker, '"Heartlands": on some poems by Ruth Bidgood and Christopher Meredith', *Scintilla: The Journal of the Vaughan Association*, 17 (18 December 2013), 186–200, 190.
65   Dorothy Edwards, *Rhapsody* (1927; Cardigan: Parthian, 2007), p. 138. My thanks to Claire Flay-Petty for identifying the line.
66   Hooker, '*Air Histories*', 157.
67   Wallace, 'Interview: Christopher Meredith talks'.
68   Hooker, 'Heartlands', 189.
69   Christopher Meredith, 'Scintilla Poets in Conversation', contribution, *Scintilla: The Journal of the Vaughan Association*, Blogspot, 2014, *http:// vaughanassociation.blogspot.co.uk/p/scintilla-poets-in.html* (accessed 20 February 2014).
70   A literal translation would be: 'Earth I am / my body on the doctor's bench / a mountain ridge / poison breathing from the black wound.' With thanks to Nigel Wallace.
71   Dai George, 'Interview: Christopher Meredith', *Poetry Wales*, Blog Archive: Interviews, 28 July 2015, *http://poetrywales.co.uk/wp/2531/ interview-christopher-meredith/* (accessed 20 April 2016).
72   George, 'Interview: Christopher Meredith'.
73   Davies, 'Interview with Meredith'.

6

1   *Still Air* includes no page numbers.
2   'Nettles' appeared in an earlier version as 'Nettles, Cwmorthin' in Paul Henry and Zed Nelson (eds), *The Slate Sea* (London: The Camden Trust, 2015), p. 32.

3   See *Brief Lives*, a collection of Meredith's short fiction, forthcoming from Seren in 2018.

4   Christopher Meredith, 'Somavox', in West Camel (ed.), *Best European Fiction 2015* (Champaign, London, Dublin: The Dalkey Archive, 2014), pp. 246–56. Republished as 'Haptivox' in *Brief Lives*.

5   Meredith, 'Somavox', p. 246.

6   Meredith, 'Somavox', p. 250.

7   Meredith, 'Somavox', p. 246.

8   Meredith, 'Somavox', p. 254.

9   Meredith, 'Somavox', p. 254.

10 Meredith, 'Somavox', pp. 246, 249, 255.

11 Meredith, 'Somavox', p. 256.

12 Meredith, 'Somavox', p. 256.

13 Meredith, 'Somavox', p. 256.

14 Meredith, 'Somavox', p. 256.

15 James Joyce, *Dubliners* (1914; Harmondsworth: Penguin, 1992).

Bibliography

Primary texts by Christopher Meredith

Novels
Shifts (Bridgend: Seren, 1988; repr. in Seren Classics series with Afterword by Richard Poole, 1997, 2005).
Griffri (Bridgend: Seren, 1991; revd edn 1994).
Sidereal Time (Bridgend: Seren, 1998).
Griffri, trans. into French by Claudine Tourniaire (Rennes: Terre de Brume, 2002).
The Book of Idiots (Bridgend: Seren, 2012).

Poetry collections
This (Bridgend: Poetry Wales Press, 1984).
Snaring Heaven (Bridgend: Seren, 1990).
The Meaning of Flight (Bridgend: Seren, 2005).
Black Mountains: Poems and Images from the Bog~Mawnog Project, with images by Elizabeth Adeline, Lin Charlston, Kirsty Claxton, Deborah Aguirre Jones and Pip Woolf (Cardiff: Mulfran, 2011).
Air Histories (Bridgend: Seren, 2013).
Still Air, images by Sara Philpott, (n.p.: Singing Nettle Press, 2016).

Short fictions
'Opening Time', *Anglo-Welsh Review*, 85 (1987), 75–9.
'Averted Vision', *Planet*, 81 (June/July 1990), 24–8. Reprinted in Tony Curtis (ed.), *After the First Death: An Anthology of Wales and War in the Twentieth Century* (Bridgend: Seren, 2007), pp. 197–201. Broadcast on BBC Radio Wales, producer Ceri Meyrick, 24 January 1994 and 25 January 1994.

'The Woman on the Beach', *Planet*, 87 (June/July 1991), 51–4.
The Story of the Afanc King and the Sons of Teyrnon (Newtown: Gwasg
   Gregynog, 2006).
'Progress', *The Interpreter's House*, 41 (June 2009), 47–51. Reprinted in
   A. Arjanee, M. Jenkins and K. Vadamootoo (eds), *Dodos and Dragons*:
   An Anthology of Mauritian and Welsh Writing (Mauritius: Atelier
   d'écriture, 2016).
'Somavox' in West Camel (ed.), *Best European Fiction 2015* (Champaign,
   London, Dublin: The Dalkey Archive, 2014), pp. 246–56.
'The Cavalry', forthcoming in *Brief Lives* (Bridgend: Seren, 2018).
'The Enthusiast', forthcoming in *Brief Lives* (Bridgend: Seren, 2018).

Play
The Carved Chair: A play for radio, *Planet*, 65 (October/November 1987),
68–92. Performed by Made in Wales Stage Company, directed by Jamie
Garven, Sherman Theatre, Cardiff, May 1986.

Radio drama
Gruffudd ap Llywelyn, commissioned by BBC Education, producer
   Sioned Roberts, Broadcast BBC Radio Wales, February 1993.

Selected individual poems: uncollected or translated poems
and anthology contributions
'Opening My Palms I Saw', *The New Welsh Review*, 1/1 (summer 1988), 16.
'Toy revolver', *Planet*, 95 (August/September 1992), 47.
'Christening Pot Boiler' and 'Plasnewydd Square' in Dannie Abse (ed.),
   Twentieth-Century Anglo-Welsh Poetry (Bridgend: Seren, 1997),
   pp. 247–8, 248.
'Desk', 'On Hay Bridge', 'She Plans a Purchase', 'Red Armchair', 'My
   Mother Missed the Beautiful and Doomed', 'Occupied', in Meic
   Stephens (ed.), *Poetry 1900–2000*, The Library of Wales (Cardigan:
   Parthian, 2007), pp. 740–8.
'My mother missed the beautiful and doomed', and 'Occupied', in Tony
   Curtis (ed.), *After the First Death: An Anthology of Wales and War in
   the Twentieth Century* (Bridgend: Seren, 2007), pp. 110, 252.

'The Churches', Ancient Monuments and Present Words – 3
(Commissioned by *Planet* and the Ancient Monuments Commission
for Wales), *Planet*, 189 (June–July 2008), 62–3.
'Two-hander', *New Welsh Review*, 84 (summer 2009), 39.
'Temppeli' ('the very temple' translated into Finnish by Marko Niemi),
in M. Niemi (ed.), *Valo kajahtaa* (Jyväskylä: Keski-Suomen Kirjailijat
r.y., 2013), pp. 78–81.
'The record keepers' (from *Air Histories*), *The Forward Book of Poetry 2014*
(London: Faber, 2013).
'Nettles, Cwmorthin', 'There could be temples' and 'North Coast
Swing', in Paul Henry and Zed Nelson (eds), *The Slate Sea* (London:
The Camden Trust, 2015), pp. 32, 42–3, 2–4.

Translation

Morgan, Mihangel, *Melog* (1997), trans. Christopher Meredith with
Afterword (Bridgend: Seren, 2005).
'Naffaa', Nawal, 'Enough', 'Stillness', trans. from the Arabic by the
author and Christopher Meredith, *Poetry Wales*, 43/1 (summer
2007), 48–9.

For children

Nadolig Pob Dydd (Llandysul: Gomer, 2000; repr. 2005).
Christmas Every Day (Llandysul: Pont, 2006).

Criticism, essays, reviews and blogs

'Laurie Lee, *Selected Poems*, and Padraic Fallon, *Poems and Versions*',
Poetry Wales, 19/1 (summer 1983), 102–5.
'Review: Tony Curtis, *Letting Go*', *Poetry Wales*, 19/4 (1984), 77–9.
'Saying it in Saesneg', contribution to 'The Welsh Language and
Anglo-Welsh Poets', *Poetry Wales*, 20/1 (1984), 12–14.
'Two from the Heart' (review of Gwyn Thomas, *Sorrow for Thy Sons*
and *All Things Betray Thee*), *Planet*, 59 (October/November 1986),
98–9.
'Chris Broadribb, *Prepositions*, Christopher Mills, *The Bicycle is an Easy
Pancake*, and Ifor Thomas, *Giving Blood*', *Poetry Wales*, 22/2 (1987),
93–5.

'Dai Greatcoat, Insectman, and Alun Lewis', *Poetry Wales*, 22/4 (1987), 59–65.

'From the Wordface' (review of Duncan Bush, *Black Faces Red Mouths* and Mogg Williams, *The Wastelands*), *Planet*, 61 (February/March 1987), 99–100, 100.

'Tussle with Images' (review of Eleanor Cooke, *A Kind of Memory*, Tim Liardet, *Clay Hill*, Kathy Miles, *The Rocking-stone*, and Mavis Howell, *Annwn*), *Planet*, 72 (December/January 1988–9), 106–8.

'The Browsability Factor' (review of Alan Llwyd (ed.), *Y Flodeugerdd o Ddyfyniadau Cymraeg*), *Planet*, 75 (June/July 1989), 95–6.

'More for the Tourists' (review of Alice Thomas Ellis (ed.), *Wales, An Anthology*), *Planet*, 79 (February/March 1990), 103–4.

'Voices in the Village: The Hay on Wye Festival of Literature', *Poetry Wales*, 26/2 (September 1990), 56–7.

'Alun Lewis: *Collected Stories*', *New Welsh Review*, 13, 18/1 (summer 1991), 31–2.

'Robert Crawford, *A Scottish Assembly*', *Poetry Wales*, 27/2 (September 1991), 64–5.

'Small but Perfectly Formed' (review of Harri Pritchard Jones, *Corner People*), *Planet*, 92 (April/May 1992), 94–6.

'Unbroken on the Wheel' (review of Ned Thomas, *The Welsh Extremist*), *Planet*, 93 (June/July 1992), 89–91.

'Sex, Lies and Scandinavian Philately' (review of Alun Jones, *Simdde in [sic] y Gwyll*), *Planet*, 99 (June/July 1993), 100.

'Taxi in the Dark' (review of Jane Edwards, *Pant yn y Gwely*), *Planet*, 103 (February/March 1994), 96–7.

'FS+LI=N *or* How to be a Novelist', *Planet*, 104 (April/May 1994), 46–9.

'From a German Journal', *Planet*, 105 (June/July 1994), 66–9.

'Up the Mountain', *Planet*, 106 (August/September 1994), 36–9.

'The window facing the sea: the short stories of Dorothy Edwards', *Planet*, 107 (October/November 1994), 64–7.

'Do Redwoids dream of electric sheep?', *Planet*, 108 (December/January 1994–5), 54–7.

'Secret Rooms', *Planet*, 109 (February/March 1995), 51–4.

'Robert Crawford, *Masculinity*', *Poetry Wales*, 32/1 (July 1996), 62–3.

'Don Paterson, *God's Gift to Women*', *Poetry Wales*, 33/3 (winter 1997/8), 64–5.

Cefn Golau: Shooting a Novelist, illus. Sara Philpott (Newtown: Gwasg Gregynog, 1997).

'Do we really want to be Welsh?', *New Statesman*, 3 May 1999, 33–4.

'Telling and the Time', in Maura Dooley (ed.), *How Novelists Work* (Bridgend: Seren, 2000), pp. 56–70.

'Joan Abse, ed., *Letters from Wales*', *Times Literary Supplement*, 22 December 2000, 29.

'The Dance of Misunderstanding' (interview with Richard John Evans), *New Welsh Review*, 52 (spring 2001), 7–10.

'June Knox-Mawer, *A Ram in the Well*', *Times Literary Supplement*, 1 June 2001, 33.

Co-edited with Tony Curtis, *The Literary Review: Re-imagining Wales* (a special number on contemporary Welsh literature in English and translation), 44/2 (2001), Fairleigh Dickinson University.

'The Tension in the Line', in Tony Curtis and Christopher Meredith (eds), *The Literary Review: Re-imagining Wales*, 44/2 (2001), 210–13.

'Nigel Jenkins, *Footsore on the Frontier*', *Times Literary Supplement*, 7 September 2002, 31.

'Mario Petruccio, *Heavy Water*', *Poetry Wales*, 40/2 (autumn 2004), 69–71.

With Katja Krebs (eds), *Five Essays on Translation* (Pontypridd: University of Glamorgan, 2005).

'Introduction', in Katja Krebs and Christopher Meredith (eds), *Five Essays on Translation* (Pontypridd: University of Glamorgan, 2005), pp. 7–9.

'Double Acts and Distorting Mirrors: *Melog*', *New Welsh Review*, 73 (autumn 2006), 7–12.

(ed.), *Moment of Earth: Poems and Essays in Honour of Jeremy Hooker* (Aberystwyth: Celtic Studies Publications, 2007).

'Foreword', in Christopher Meredith (ed.), *Moment of Earth: Poems and Essays in Honour of Jeremy Hooker* (Aberystwyth: Celtic Studies Publications, 2007), pp. xiii–xv.

'Foreword', Dorothy Edwards, *Rhapsody*, ed. and intro. Christopher Meredith (1927; Cardigan: Parthian, 2007).

'*Rhapsody*'s Lost Story', in Christopher Meredith (ed.), *Moment of Earth: Poems and Essays in Honour of Jeremy Hooker* (Aberystwyth: Celtic Studies Publications, 2007), pp. 159–70.

'Getting Brecon's Autograph', *Cambria: The National Magazine for Wales*, February/March 2008, 42–3.

'Knowing the Unknowable' (Review of Sam Adams, *Prichard's Nose*), *PN Review*, 195, 37/1 (September–October 2010), 65–6.

'Miller's Answer: Making, Saying, and the Impulse to Write', *New Writing: The International Journal for the Practice and Theory of Creative Writing*, 8/1 (2011), 71–89.

'Christopher Meredith reveals how his latest novel got its name', *Wales Online*, 18 August 2012, *www.walesonline.co.uk/lifestyle/christopher-meredith-reveals-how-latest-2057* (accessed 25 November 2013).

'Cronin and the Chronotope: Place, time and pessimistic individualism in *The Citadel*', *North American Journal of Welsh Studies*, 8 (2013), 50–65.

'Scintilla Poets in Conversation', contribution, *Scintilla: The Journal of the Vaughan Association*, Blogspot, 2014, *http://vaughanassocation.blogspot.co.uk/p/scintilla-poets-in.html* (accessed 20 February 2014).

'Christopher Meredith wins international scholarship', *Wales Literature Exchange*, 2012, *http://waleslitexchange.org/en/news/view/christopher-meredith-wins-international-scholarship* (accessed 20 April 2016).

'Chris Meredith Reporting from Slovenia' ('Dispatch# 1 A Bend in the River', 'Dispatch# 2 Dogs and Toddlers', 'Dispatch# 3 I am not an elf'), *Wales Literature Exchange*, *http://waleslitexchange.org/en/news/view/christopher-meredith-reporting-from-slovenia* (accessed 20 April 2016).

'Chris Meredith (Wales→Finland)', ('Dispatch # 1 The Man on the Plane', 'Dispatch # 2 Wasteland', 'Dispatch # 3 Aalititude', 'Dispatch # 4 Finns are Very Polite People', 'Dispatch # 5 How to pronounce Jyväskylä', 'Dispatch # 6 Pictures, Tongues, Cities', 'Dispatch # 7 Stopping to drink, stopping drinking', 'Dispatch # 8 Forests, rocks, lakes'), *Wales Literature Exchange*, *http://waleslitexchange.org/en/translator's-house-wales/blog/christopher-meredit-* (accessed 20 April 2016).

Secondary texts

Reviews and interviews

Atkinson, Tiffany, '*Durer's Hare*, Anna Wigley, *The Meaning of Flight*, Christopher Meredith', *New Welsh Review*, 71 (spring 2006), 76–9.

Barnie, John, 'Christopher Meredith, *This*', *Poetry Wales*, 20/4 (1984), 98–100.

Burrows, Wayne, '*Snaring Heaven*, Christopher Meredith; *The Black Goddess*, Norman Schwenck', *New Welsh Review*, 13 (IV/1) (summer 1991), 57–8.

Clare, Horatio, 'Sound Walk', BBC Radio 3, Monday, 29 May 2017, *www.bbc.co.uk/mediacentre/proginfo/2017/22/sound-walk*.

Crown, Sarah, 'Taking Wing: *The Meaning of Flight*, Christopher
    Meredith', *The Guardian*, 4 February 2006, *www.the guardian.com.
    books/2006/feb/04/features.guardianreview26* (accessed 20 April 2016).

Cummins, Walter, '*The Book of Idiots* by Christopher Meredith', *Serving
    House: A Journal of Literary Arts*, 7 (spring 2013), *www.
    servinghousejournal.com/CumminsReviewsMeredith.aspx* (accessed
    5 September 2013).

Davies, Gwen, 'The Insider', 'Chris Meredith's last novel for adults . . .',
    Wales Online, *www.walesonline.co.uk/lifestyle/the-insider-gwen-
    davies-2041665* (accessed 5 September 2013).

Davies, Gwen, 'Interview: Chris Meredith', *New Welsh Review*, 95
    (2013), online, *www.newwelshreview.com/article.php?id=136* (accessed
    4 September 2013).

Davies, Gwen, 'Chris Meredith's new masterpiece *The Book of Idiots*',
    New Welsh Review, Blog, 13 February 2013, *www.newwelshreview.com/
    article.php?id=136* (accessed 20 April 2016).

Farringdon, Jill, 'Christopher Meredith: *Snaring Heaven*', *Poetry Wales*,
    26/2 (September 1990), 60–1.

George, Dai, 'Interview: Christopher Meredith', *Poetry Wales*, Blog
    Archive: Interviews, 28 July 2015, *http://poetrywales.co.uk/wp/2531/
    interview-christopher-meredith/* (accessed 20 April 2016).

Goodwin, Jo-Ann, 'Bonds of Steel' (*Shifts*), *Times Literary Supplement*,
    11 November 1988, 1260.

Groves, Paul, 'Profile: Christopher Meredith', *Cambria: The National
    Magazine for Wales*, 11/1 (May/June 2009), 42.

Hahn, Daniel, '*Best European Fiction 2015*, edited by West Camel –
    review', *The Guardian*, 23 December 2014, *https://the guardian.com/
    books2014/dec/23/best-european-fiction-2015-edited-west-camel-review*
    (accessed 24 October 2017).

Hitchins, Steven, 'Christopher Meredith, *Air Histories*, Mike Jenkins,
    Barkin!', *Poetry Wales*, 49/3 (winter 2013), 58–9.

Hooker, Jeremy, '*Air Histories:* Christopher Meredith', *Planet*, 212
    (winter 2013/14), 157–8.

Howe, Roger, 'Welshness and the human condition: interview with
    Christopher Meredith', *Zeitgeist Diagram*, *http://zeitgeist-diagram.com/
    index.php/interviews/8-welshness-and-the-human-condition* (accessed
    21 October 2017).

Jarvis, Matthew, 'Christopher Meredith, *The Meaning of Flight* and
    Sheenagh Pugh, *The Movement of Bodies*', *Poetry Wales*, 41/1
    (summer 2005), 57–60.

Murray, Nicholas, 'Looking to the World: Sheenagh Pugh, *The Movement of Bodies*, Christopher Meredith, *The Meaning of Flight*, Jeremy Hooker, *Arnolds Wood*', *Planet*, 174 (December 2005/January 2006), 97–9.

O'Brien, Sean, 'More Negation' (*This*), *Times Literary Supplement*, 5 June 1986, 540.

O'Reilly, Aiden, '*Best European Fiction 2015*: Review', *The Short Review*, https://thenewshortreview.wordpress.com/2016/06/06/15/best-european-fiction/ (accessed 24 October 2017).

Pedder, Cato, '*Air Histories*: Christopher Meredith', *Write Out Loud*, 13 November 2013, *www.writeoutloud.net/public/blogentry. php?blogentryid=39687* (accessed 19 February 2014).

Penn-Thomas, Liza, '*Air Histories* by Christopher Meredith', *New Welsh Review*, 100 (summer 2013), online, *www.newwelshreview.com/article. php?id=558* (accessed 20 April 2016).

Pugh, Sheenagh, 'Interview with Christopher Meredith', 22 June 2011, 'Good God! There's writing on both sides of that paper!', *Live Journal, http://sheenaghpugh.livejournal.com/68450.html* (accessed 5 September 2013).

Wallace, Diana, 'Interview: Christopher Meredith talks about *Air Histories*', University of South Wales, *https://soundcloud.com/ universityofsouthwales/professor-christopher-meredith.*

Other works

Aaron, Jane and M. Wynn Thomas, '"Pulling You Through Changes": Welsh writing in English before and after two referenda', in M. Wynn Thomas (ed.), *Welsh Writing in English, A Guide to Welsh Literature, Vol. VII* (Cardiff: University of Wales Press, 2003), pp. 278–326.

Aaron, Jane, 'Literature', in Chris Williams and Andy Croll (eds), *The Gwent County History, Volume 5: The Twentieth Century* (Cardiff: University of Wales Press on behalf of The Gwent County History Association, 2013), pp. 283–300.

Adams, Sam, 'Letter from Wales', *PN Review*, 144, 28/4 (March–April 2002), www.pnreview.co.uk/cgi-binscribe?item_id=1153 (accessed 22 October 2017).

Babbs, Helen, 'The Woollen Line', *The Guardian*, Wednesday 17 April 2013, *www.theguardian.com/lifeandstyle/gardening-blog/2013/apr/17/ woollen-line-pip-woolf* (accessed 28 July 2017).

Bohata, Kirsti, 'A Place without Boundaries: The Fiction of Christopher Meredith', *Planet*, 145 (2001), 77–82.

Bohata, Kirsti, *Postcolonialism Revisited* (Cardiff: University of Wales Press, 2004).

Bourdieu, Pierre, *Distinction: A Social Critique of the Judgement of Taste* (1979; Abingdon: Routledge, 2010).

Brut y Tywysogyon or The Chronicle of the Princes, Red Book of Hergest Version, ed. and trans. Thomas Jones (Cardiff: University of Wales Press, 1955).

Bullough, Tom, *Addlands* (2016; London: Granta, 2017).

Conran, Tony, *Welsh Verse* (1967; Bridgend: Seren, 1992).

Curtis, Tony, 'Centenary Essay: From Barry to Treforest via Vermont', *http://centenary.southwales.ac.uk/essays/tony-curtis/* (accessed 16 October 2017).

Darwin, Emma, *The Mathematics of Love* (2006; London: Headline, 2007).

Davies, Grahame, 'Sleeping with the Enemy: The tensions of literary translation', in Krebs and Meredith (eds), *Five Essays on Translation*, pp. 10–21.

Edwards, Dorothy, *Rhapsody*, ed. and intro. Christopher Meredith (1927; Cardigan: Parthian, 2007).

Elliott, John, 'The Iron and Steel Industry', in Chris Williams and Sian Rhiannon Williams (eds), *The Gwent County History, Volume 4: Industrial Monmouthshire, 1780–1914* (Cardiff: University of Wales Press on behalf of The Gwent County History Association, 2011), pp. 73–86.

Elliott, John, and Colin Deneen, 'Iron, Steel and Aluminium', in Chris Williams and Andy Croll (eds), *The Gwent County History, Volume 5: The Twentieth Century* (Cardiff: University of Wales Press on behalf of The Gwent County History Association, 2013), pp. 59–74.

Ellis, Peter Berresford, *The Celtic Revolution: A Study in Anti-Imperialism* (Talybont: Y Lolfa, 1985).

Evans, Richard John, *Entertainment* (Bridgend: Seren, 2000).

Fleishman, Avrom, *The English Historical Novel: From Walter Scott to Virginia Woolf* (Baltimore and London: Johns Hopkins Press, 1971).

George, Dai, 'Poet-Novelists', *Poetry Wales*, 51/1 (summer 2015), 68–72.

Gerald of Wales, *The Journey Through Wales and The Description of Wales*, trans. Lewis Thorpe (1978; London: Penguin, 2004).

Glaser, Eliane, 'Beyond bullshit jobs', *Soundings: A Journal of Politics and Culture*, 57 (summer 2014), 82–94, *www.lwbooks.co.uk/sites/default/files/s57_08glaser.pdf* (accessed 17 July 2017).

Graeber, David, 'On the phenomenon of bullshit jobs', *Strike! Magazine* (summer 2013). Reprinted *https://libcom.org/library/phenomenon-bullshit-jobs-david-graeber* (accessed 17 July 2017).

Graeber, David, *The Utopia of Rules: On Technology, Stupidity, and the Secret Joys of Bureaucracy* (2015; Brooklyn and London: Melville, 2016).

Heaney, Seamus, *Death of a Naturalist* (1966; London: Faber, 1969).

Heaney, Seamus, *Preoccupations: Selected Prose, 1968–1978* (New York: Farrar, Strauss and Giroux, 1981).

Hooker, Jeremy, '"Heartlands": on some poems by Ruth Bidgood and Christopher Meredith', *Scintilla: The Journal of the Vaughan Association*, 17 (18 December 2013), 186–200.

Hoyle, Fred, *Nicolaus Copernicus* (London: Heinemann, 1973).

Hubbard, Phil, and Rob Kitchen (eds), *Key Thinkers on Space and Place*, 2nd edn (2004; London: Sage, 2011).

Humphreys, Emyr, *The Taliesin Tradition: A Quest for the Welsh Identity* (1983; Bridgend: Seren, 1989).

Hutcheon, Linda, *A Poetics of Postmodernism: History, Theory, Fiction* (New York and London: Routledge, 1988).

Jarvis, Matthew, *Ruth Bidgood* (Cardiff: University of Wales Press, 2012).

Johnston, Dafydd, *The Literature of Wales* (1994; Cardiff: University of Wales Press, 1999).

Johnston, Dafydd, 'Making History in Two Languages; Wiliam Owen Roberts's *Y Pla* and Christopher Meredith's *Griffri*', *Welsh Writing in English: A Yearbook of Critical Essays*, 3 (1997), 118–33.

Jones, Glyn, *The Dream of Jake Hopkins* (London: Fortune, 1954).

Jones, Glyn, *The Island of Apples* (1965; Cardiff; University of Wales Press, 1992).

Jones, Glyn, *The Dragon Has Two Tongues*, ed. Tony Brown (rev. edn, Cardiff: University of Wales Press, 2001).

Joyce, James, *Dubliners* (1914; Harmondsworth: Penguin, 1992).

Joyce, James, *Ulysses* (1922; Harmondsworth: Penguin, 1971).

Knight, Stephen, *A Hundred Years of Fiction* (Cardiff: University of Wales Press, 2004).

Lewis, Lisa, 'Between Word and Worlds: The performance of translation', in Krebs and Meredith (eds), *Five Essays on Translation*, pp. 33–41.

Lewis, Robert, *Wenglish: The Dialect of the South Wales Valleys* (2008; Talybont: Y Lolfa, 2016).

Llewellyn, Richard, *How Green Was My Valley* (1939; London: Penguin, 2001).

Lukács, Georg, *The Historical Novel*, trans. Hannah and Stanley Mitchell (1936/7; Lincoln and London: University of Nebraska Press, 1983).

The Mabinogion, trans. Gwyn Jones and Thomas Jones (1949; London: Dent, 1978).

Marx, Karl, *The Eighteenth Brumaire of Louis Bonaparte* (1852; New York: International Publishers, 1998).

Marx, Karl, *Capital: A Critical Analysis of Capitalist Production, Vol. 1*, trans. Samuel Moore and Edward Aveling and ed. Frederick Engels (1887; Moscow: Progress, n.d.).

Massey, Doreen, *Space, Place and Gender* (Cambridge: Polity, 1994).

Mitchell, Kate, *History and Cultural Memory in Neo-Victorian Fiction: Victorian Afterimages* (Basingstoke: Palgrave, 2010).

Orwell, George, *The Road to Wigan Pier* (1937; Harmondsworth: Penguin, 1962).

Osmond, John, *Police Conspiracy* (Talybont: Y Lolfa, 1984).

Pettit, Ann, *Walking to Greenham* (Dinas Powys: Honno, 2006).

Poole, Richard, 'Eggmen and Zeroes: Christopher Meredith's *Shifts*', *New Welsh Review*, 36 (IX/IV spring 1997), 60–6.

Price, Derrick, '*How Green Was My Valley*: a romance of Wales', in Jean Radford (ed.), *The Progress of Romance: The Politics of Popular Fiction* (London: Routledge, 1986), pp. 73–94.

Protheroe-Jones, R., *Welsh Steel* (Cardiff: National Museum of Wales Press, 1995).

Sheppard, Lisa, 'Pulling Pints Not Punches: Linguistic Tensions in the Literary Pubs of Wales', *International Journal of Welsh Writing in English*, 3 (2015), 75–101.

Southgate, Beverley, *History Meets Fiction* (Harlow: Longman, 2009).

Stephens, Meic, 'The Second Flowering', *Poetry Wales*, 3/3 (winter 1967), 2–9.

Stevenson, Robert Louis, *The Black Arrow* (1888; London: Bloomsbury, 1994).

Thomas, Gwyn, *All Things Betray Thee* (1949; London: Lawrence and Wishart, 1986).

Thomas, W. Jenkyn, *The Welsh Fairy Book* (1907; Cardiff: University of Wales Press, 1952).

Tourniaire, Claudine, 'Translating Welsh Historical Fiction into French: Politics of War and Peace', in Krebs and Meredith (eds), *Five Essays on Translation*, pp. 53–71.

White, Hayden, *Tropics of Discourse: Essays in Cultural Criticism* (1978; Baltimore and London: Johns Hopkins Press, 1985).

Williams, Gwyn (ed.), *The Burning Tree* (London: Faber, 1956).

Williams, Gwyn (ed. and trans.), *Welsh Poems: Sixth Century to 1600* (London: Faber, 1973).

Williams, Raymond, 'Introduction', in Gwyn Thomas, *All Things Betray Thee* (1949; London: Lawrence and Wishart, 1986).

Williams, Raymond, *People of the Black Mountains: Vol. 1: The Beginnings* (1989; London: Paladin, 1990).

Williams, Raymond, *People of the Black Mountains: Vol. II: The Eggs of the Eagle* ([1990]; London: Paladin, 1992).

Williams, Raymond, *Who Speaks for Wales? Nation, Culture, Identity*, ed. Daniel Williams (Cardiff: University of Wales Press, 2003).

INDEX